Interdisciplinary Studies in Human Rights

Volume 14

Human rights are one of the normative cornerstones of contemporary international law and global governance. Due to the complexities of actual or potential violations of human rights and in light of current crises, new and interdisciplinary research is urgently needed. The series Interdisciplinary Studies in Human Rights recognizes the growing importance and necessity of interdisciplinary research in human rights. The series consists of monographs and collected volumes addressing human rights research from different disciplinary and interdisciplinary perspectives, including but not limited to philosophy, law, political science, education, and medical ethics. Its goal is to explore new and contested questions such as the extraterritorial application of human rights and their relevance for non-state actors, as well as the philosophical and theoretical foundations of human rights. The series also addresses policy questions of current interest including the human rights of migrants and refugees, LGBTI rights, and bioethics, as well as business and human rights.

The series editors are Members of the Centre for Human Rights Erlangen-Nürnberg (CHREN), an interdisciplinary research center at Friedrich-Alexander-University Erlangen-Nürnberg. The Advisory Board brings together human rights scholars from a wide range of academic disciplines and regional backgrounds. The series welcomes suggestions for publications of academic research falling into the series subject matter.

Otgontuya Davaanyam · Markus Krajewski
Editors

Exploring Corporate Human Rights Responsibilities in OECD Case Law

Springer

Editors
Otgontuya Davaanyam
Faculty of Law
University of Erlangen-Nuremberg
Erlangen, Bayern, Germany

Markus Krajewski
Faculty of Law
University of Erlangen-Nuremberg
Erlangen, Bayern, Germany

ISSN 2509-2960 ISSN 2509-2979 (electronic)
Interdisciplinary Studies in Human Rights
ISBN 978-3-031-75716-7 ISBN 978-3-031-75717-4 (eBook)
https://doi.org/10.1007/978-3-031-75717-4

This work was supported by Deutsche Forschungsgemeinschaft.

This Springer imprint is published by the registered company Springer Nature Switzerland AG
The registered company address is: Gewerbestrasse 11, 6330 Cham, Switzerland

Acknowledgments

This book stems from the workshop titled "Corporate Human Rights Responsibility in OECD Case Law: Actors, Issues, Responsibilities, and Remedy," held in May 2023 at Friedrich-Alexander-University Erlangen-Nürnberg. The event was organized by the German Research Foundation (DFG) funded project "Corporate Human Rights Responsibility in the OECD NCP Case Law." The primary aim of this book is to compile the diverse scholarly contributions presented at the workshop, which analyzed the roles, responsibilities, and effectiveness of NCPs in enforcing corporate human rights responsibilities. We would like to extend our heartfelt gratitude to all the contributors and participants of the workshop, whose invaluable insights and efforts made this significant contribution possible.

Contents

Introduction: Exploring Corporate Human Rights Responsibilities in OECD Case Law

Otgontuya Davaanyam and Markus Krajewski

1 Background and Objectives

Corporate human rights responsibility has increasingly become a focal point in the governance and operational practices of multinational enterprises (MNEs). The OECD Guidelines for Multinational Enterprises and Responsible Business Conduct last revised in 2023, alongside the UN Guiding Principles on Business and Human Rights (UNGPs), serve as pivotal frameworks guiding MNEs in addressing and mitigating human rights impacts. The National Contact Points (NCPs), established under the OECD Guidelines, play a crucial role in promoting these standards and providing platforms for addressing grievances related to corporate misconduct.

NCPs play a critical role not only in holding MNEs accountable but also in defining and expanding corporate human rights responsibilities. Since the early 2000s, the specific instances managed by various NCPs across the globe have significantly clarified the scope of responsibilities for MNEs across different sectors and in relation to diverse human rights abuses. These cases provide detailed insights into how NCPs delineate the roles and responsibilities of various actors, including financial institutions, investors, parent companies, and non-profit organizations, in mitigating human rights risks within their operations. Moreover, these instances highlight the potential for reforming human rights due diligence processes to effectively address the negative impacts in complex situations such as conflict-affected areas, global supply chains, and issues related to climate change. Through this detailed analysis, NCPs contribute to a deeper understanding of corporate human rights responsibilities and set precedents for future actions and policies.

The present book aims to delve deeply into the complexities and practical applications of corporate human rights responsibilities as delineated in the case law of the

O. Davaanyam (✉) · M. Krajewski
Faculty of Law, University of Erlangen-Nuremberg, Erlangen, Bayern, Germany
e-mail: Otgontuya.davaanyam@fau.de

O. Davaanyam and M. Krajewski (eds.), *Exploring Corporate Human Rights Responsibilities in OECD Case Law*, Interdisciplinary Studies in Human Rights 14,
https://doi.org/10.1007/978-3-031-75717-4_1

OECD NCPs. It explores the evolving scope of corporate accountability, addressing emerging issues such as climate change, conflicts, and the effectiveness of remedies provided by NCPs. The book strives to offer a comprehensive understanding of how NCPs contribute to the broader landscape of business and human rights, highlighting both the successes and challenges encountered by this non-judicial mechanism.

This book is organised into three main parts, each addressing critical aspects of corporate human rights responsibilities and the role of NCPs in enforcing these responsibilities.

Part I: Unpacking Substantive Elements of Corporate Human Rights Responsibilities Through OECD National Contact Point Specific Instances

This section delves into the substantive elements of corporate responsibilities as interpreted through specific cases handled by NCPs. The chapters in this part explore various dimensions of corporate responsibility, such as climate change, the financial sector, and heightened responsibilities in conflict-affected areas.

Francesca Mussi examines the contributions of NCPs in shaping the 2023 OECD Guidelines regarding climate change. Her chapter discusses the amendments to the OECD Guidelines in relation to climate change and evaluates the extent to which NCP practices have influenced these updates. By analysing climate change-related NCP complaints and their determinations, Mussi demonstrates how NCPs have integrated climate considerations into the OECD Guidelines, providing a precedent for addressing environmental impacts in future cases.

Kateryna Buriakovska and Otgontuya Davaanyam analyse the increased responsibilities of MNEs in high-risk zones. Their chapter explores over 15 cases from OECD NCPs involving corporate activities in conflict zones such as Myanmar, the Occupied Palestinian Territory, and the Democratic Republic of Congo. The authors highlight the need for MNEs to adopt heightened human rights due diligence and a conflict-sensitive approach in these areas. They argue for clearer guidance and best practices to help companies navigate the complex human rights challenges in conflict-affected regions.

Otgontuya Davaanyam provides insights into the responsibilities of financial institutions in mitigating human rights and environmental impacts. Her chapter examines the role of financial institutions within the international business and human rights framework, particularly their responsibility to address adverse impacts resulting from their investments. By scrutinising OECD cases managed by NCPs, Davaanyam discusses how financial institutions can fulfil their obligations towards sustainability, human rights, and environmental preservation, advocating for proactive measures and consistent international legal standards.

Part II: Measuring the Effectiveness of OECD National Contact Points: A Critical Review

This part critically assesses the effectiveness of NCPs in providing remedies and their overall impact on corporate practices. It addresses the challenges and limitations of NCPs and suggests improvements to enhance their effectiveness.

This section begins with a chapter by Jernej Letnar Černič evaluating the current state of supervision mechanisms under the OECD Guidelines. His chapter discusses the origins and background of the OECD Guidelines for Responsible Business Conduct and analyses the role of specific instance procedures before NCPs. Černič argues that strengthening enforcement mechanisms and increasing the capacity of NCPs to provide effective remedies are essential steps in improving the overall effectiveness of these non-judicial mechanisms.

Following this, Kari Otteburn analyses the outcomes of NCP cases to understand their effectiveness in providing remedies. Her chapter presents a new dataset of remedy outcomes for transnational business-related human rights abuses at NCPs. Otteburn's findings demonstrate that while NCPs are effective at providing access to minor forms of remedy, they often fall short in providing appropriate remedies for severe violations. She suggests that the evolving remedial landscape, alongside new mandatory rules for corporate conduct, can help situate non-judicial mechanisms within the broader remedial architecture.

Laura Íñigo Álvarez discusses the issues of legitimacy and accessibility in the context of NCPs. Her chapter assesses the requirements of legitimacy and accessibility as key entry-level points to the system of NCPs, particularly focusing on Southern European NCPs such as those in Spain and Portugal. She emphasises the importance of transparent, legitimate, and accessible mechanisms in improving the effectiveness of non-judicial remedies for business-related human rights abuses.

Finally, Tamar Meshel presents a study on the dispute resolution mechanisms offered by NCPs. Her chapter provides a qualitative and quantitative analysis of 225 specific instances concluded by NCPs between 2001 and 2022. Meshel's study uncovers trends and inconsistencies in the dispute resolution practices of different NCPs, identifying mechanisms or combinations of mechanisms that have proven effective in resolving grievances. She highlights the importance of good office, mediation, and conciliation in achieving satisfactory outcomes for the parties involved.

Part III: The Broader Impact of the OECD Guidelines for Multinational Enterprises

The final part explores the broader implications of the OECD Guidelines and NCP jurisprudence on legislative processes and corporate practices beyond individual cases.

Here, Monika Feigerlová examines the influence of OECD Guidelines on the legislative process of the EU Directive on Corporate Sustainability Due Diligence (CS3D). Her chapter analyses the extent to which the OECD Guidelines played a role in shaping the CS3D, which establishes a legal obligation for large companies to conduct due diligence in their operations and value chains to prevent and address adverse impacts on human rights and the environment. Feigerlová highlights the interactions between these two instruments and their relevance to the interpretation and implementation of the CS3D, particularly in EU Member States that adhere to the OECD Guidelines.

2 Key Themes and Insights

Several key themes emerge from the contributions in this book, offering a comprehensive analysis of the role and effectiveness of NCPs in promoting and enforcing corporate human rights responsibilities. One of the primary themes is the expanding nature of corporate responsibilities. The book underscores how NCPs have addressed emerging issues such as climate change, investment practices, and corporate conduct in conflict-affected areas, thereby setting significant precedents for future cases. The case studies illustrate how NCPs have adapted to new challenges, showcasing the dynamic nature of corporate human rights responsibilities. Through detailed analysis and interpretation of corporate responsibilities in various complex scenarios, the book emphasises the role of OECD cases as a valuable source of law in developing corporate accountability towards human rights and environmental protection.

Another critical theme is the effectiveness of non-judicial mechanisms, particularly the NCPs' case handling procedures. The chapters critically evaluate the strengths and weaknesses of NCPs in providing remedies and influencing corporate behaviour. The effectiveness of NCPs as non-judicial mechanisms is assessed based on several criteria, including legitimacy, accessibility, and their ability to provide appropriate remedies for severe violations. The findings reveal both the successes and limitations of NCPs, offering valuable insights into how these mechanisms can be improved to better serve affected parties.

The broader impact of NCP jurisprudence on policy-making and legislative processes is another significant theme. The book explores how the outcomes of NCP cases influence corporate practices and contribute to the development of legislative frameworks, such as the EU Directive on Corporate Sustainability Due Diligence. This theme highlights the importance of aligning the OECD Guidelines with other international frameworks to ensure coherent and robust standards for corporate human rights responsibilities. By examining the interaction between NCP jurisprudence and legislative developments, the book demonstrates the potential of NCPs to shape and strengthen global human rights and environmental standards.

3 Future Directions

The book offers several sophisticated recommendations to enhance the effectiveness and legitimacy of NCPs. A primary suggestion is the necessity for a more cohesive alignment of the OECD Guidelines and the UNGPs with other relevant international regulations. This strategic alignment aims to create a coherent framework that can adeptly address the evolving nature of corporate responsibilities, especially in rapidly developing areas such as climate change and sustainable investment. By integrating these frameworks, the book envisions a more unified and comprehensive approach to corporate human rights responsibilities, ensuring that businesses are held to consistent and rigorous standards globally.

Moreover, the book emphasises the urgent need to strengthen the supervision mechanisms embedded within the OECD Guidelines. Enhancing these enforcement mechanisms and bolstering the capacity of NCPs to provide effective remedies are identified as critical steps towards improving the overall efficacy of these non-judicial mechanisms. Such enhancements would ensure that NCPs are not only able to address grievances more effectively but also capable of providing meaningful remedies to affected right-holders, thereby reinforcing their legitimacy and accessibility.

Unpacking Substantive Elements of Corporate Human Rights Responsibilities Through OECD National Contact Point Specific Instances

A Climate Change Outlook on the 2023 OECD Guidelines for Multinational Enterprises on Responsible Business Conduct: Which Contribution from the Practice of the NCPs?

F. Mussi

This chapter has been researched for and written within the project: "Le nuove frontiere della responsabilità sociale d'impresa: verso una crescita verde, sostenibile ed inclusiva", funded by the European Union—FSE-REACT-EU, PON Research and Innovation 2014–2020.

Abstract The present contribution discusses the most relevant amendments to the OECD Guidelines for Multinational Enterprises in respect of climate change, as included in the 2023 OECD Guidelines for Multinational Enterprises on Responsible Business Conduct. Starting from the fact that, even though the 2011 edition of the OECD Guidelines did not specifically address climate change, NCPs have however often confronted with climate issues related to this phenomenon, the analysis is undertaken considering the climate change-related NCP complaints brought to date and the NCPs' determinations. The ultimate goal is to verify whether and, if so, to what extent the practice of the NCPs has influenced and is reflected in the relevant 2023 OECD Guidelines. To do so, after analysing the recommendations about climate change included in the recently updated version of the OECD Guidelines, the present contribution will undertake a thorough analysis of the relevant complaints, paying particular attention to those which best reflect the trend to use the 2011 OECD Guidelines also with regard to climate change-related issues.

F. Mussi (✉)
School of International Studies, University of Trento, Trento, Italy
e-mail: francesca.mussi@unitn.it

O. Davaanyam and M. Krajewski (eds.), *Exploring Corporate Human Rights Responsibilities in OECD Case Law*, Interdisciplinary Studies in Human Rights 14,
https://doi.org/10.1007/978-3-031-75717-4_2

1 Introduction

On 8 June 2023, the Organisation for Economic Co-operation and Development (OECD) launched an updated version of its Guidelines for Multinational Enterprises (the OECD Guidelines), the OECD Guidelines for Multinational Enterprises on Responsible Business Conduct (the 2023 OECD Guidelines). Since their adoption in 1976,[1] the OECD Guidelines have been revised on several occasions to address emerging issues and challenges.[2] In this sense, the recent update reflects "a decade of experience since [the OECD Guidelines'] last review in 2011 and responds to urgent social, environmental, and technological priorities facing societies and businesses".[3]

Reflecting expectations from governments to businesses on what constitutes responsible business conduct, the 2023 OECD Guidelines provide updated recommendations across key areas, such as climate change, biodiversity, technology, business integrity and supply chain due diligence. For the purposes of the present analysis, particularly relevant are the recommendations for enterprises to align with internationally agreed goals on climate change, the latter being clearly identified as a leading environmental impact that companies should address in their due diligence. This can be regarded as a significant improvement with respect to the 2011 version of the OECD Guidelines (the 2011 OECD Guidelines). Indeed, as is well known, the 2011 OECD Guidelines did not specifically consider climate change, even though they encouraged reporting on greenhouse gas (GHG) reductions at paragraphs 6(b) and (c) of Chapter VI (Environment). The lack of provisions specifically addressing and responding to climate change has been flagged by non-governmental organisations (NGOs),[4] National Contact Points (NCPs)[5] and the OECD[6] as an omission, also

---

[1] For an overview on the OECD Guidelines, see among others Letnar Černič (2008), pp. 71–100.

[2] On the last review in 2011, see Liberti (2011), pp. 35–50.

[3] OECD (2023), *OECD Guidelines for Multinational Enterprises on Responsible Business Conduct*, adopted 8 June 2023, https://www.oecd-ilibrary.org/docserver/81f92357-en.pdf?expires=1695482162&id=id&accname=guest&checksum=B1AF50BE886B795ED0A27C8C7FC5C9D5 (last accessed April 2024), p. 3.

[4] See, among others, OECD Watch (2021), State of Remedy Report, 27 June 2022, www.oecdwatch.org/state-of-remedy2021/#:~:text=The%20year%202021%20marked%20another,(NCPs)%20reached%20full%20agreement (last accessed April 2024). With regard to climate, the Report notes that the OECD Guidelines need updating such that enterprises should, under the Guidelines, be expected to set and achieve GHG emission targets to avoid adverse environment impacts (p. 5).

[5] In this sense, see OECD Database for Specific Instances, Friends of the Earth and Individuals &. ANZ Banking Group, https://mneguidelines.oecd.org/database/instances/au0016.htm (last accessed April 2024).

[6] In the 2022 Stocktaking Report on the OECD Guidelines for Multinational Enterprises, https://mneguidelines.oecd.org/stocktaking-report-on-the-oecd-guidelines-for-multinational-enterprises.pdf (last accessed April 2024), the OECD Working Party on Responsible Business Conduct (the OECD Working Party) highlights that the OECD Guidelines do not contain clear expectations on climate change mitigation, adaptation or just transition principles (p. 7), and the effectiveness of the Guidelines would be enhanced through alignment with the Paris Agreement (p. 8). The OECD Working Party flags the need for greater clarity and effectiveness in relation to environmental impacts, including climate change and biodiversity (p. 17).

considering a recent trend to use the 2011 OECD Guidelines for climate change-related complaints.[7] In light of this, one could reasonably ask oneself whether, and if so, to what extent, the climate change-related NCPs complaints brought to date under the 2011 OECD Guidelines and the NCPs' determinations have somehow influenced and are now reflected in the 2023 OECD Guidelines concerning climate change.

After analysing the updated recommendations about climate change included in the 2023 OECD Guidelines, the present contribution aims at verifying whether the indications provided so far by NCPs with regard to climate change-related complaints have been acknowledged in the latest version of the OECD Guidelines. To do so, the paper will undertake a thorough analysis of the relevant complaints, paying particular attention to those which best reflect the trend to use the 2011 OECD Guidelines with regard to climate change-related issues.

2 Climate Change in the 2023 OECD Guidelines

The 2023 OECD Guidelines lay out the expectation that business contributes to sustainable development, while avoiding and addressing adverse impacts of their activities on people and the planet. They provide an international standard on responsible business conduct that is comprehensive in nature, covering all areas of business responsibility and including a dedicated Chapter—Chapter VI—on the Environment, amongst others. The recalled Chapter provides a set of recommendations for enterprises to play a key role in advancing sustainable economies and contribute to delivering an effective and progressive response to global, regional and local environmental challenges, including the urgent threat of climate change.

The amendments in relation to Chapter VI are potentially the most far-reaching and consequential of any of the updates to the 2023 OECD Guidelines. The revised text sets out the expectations of companies in relation to a greatly expanded concept of environmental due diligence. The Guidelines note that companies should consider the following in the course of their environmental due diligence: "(a) climate change; (b) biodiversity loss; (c) degradation of land, marine and freshwater ecosystems; d) deforestation; (e) air, water and soil pollution; (f) mismanagement of waste, including hazardous substances".[8] According to the commentary to Chapter VI, this is a non-exhaustive list and companies should understand environmental impacts to be: "significant changes in the environment or biota which have harmful effects on the

[7] According to the OECD Database for Specific Instances, since 2017, almost 40% of the complaints that refer to the environmental provisions of the OECD Guidelines also reference climate change. See https://mneguidelines.oecd.org/database/?hf=10&b=0&r=%2Bf%2Fmne_mne_theme%2Fenvironment&s=desc(mne_datereceived) (last accessed April 2024).

[8] OECD (2023), *OECD Guidelines for Multinational Enterprises on Responsible Business Conduct*, adopted 8 June 2023, https://www.oecd-ilibrary.org/docserver/81f92357-en.pdf?expires=1695482162&id=id&accname=guest&checksum=B1AF50BE886B795ED0A27C8C7FC5C9D5 (last accessed April 2024), p. 33.

composition, resilience, productivity or carrying capacity of natural and managed ecosystems, or on the operation of socio-economic systems or on people".[9]

As with other changes to the 2023 OECD Guidelines, environmental due diligence will include due diligence in companies' operations and within their business relationships, including relationships with business partners, sub-contractors, franchisees, investee companies, clients, and joint venture partners, entities in the supply chain which supply products or services that contribute to the enterprise's own operations, products or services or which receive, license, buy or use products or services from the enterprise, and any other non-State or State entities directly linked to its operations, products or services.[10] Importantly, the Guidelines concede that given that some environmental impacts are not well understood or evolving, it will not always be possible to assess environmental impacts based on available "science and information".[11] In such circumstances, companies should therefore consider the extent to which the activity or proposed activity is in line with existing standards or benchmarks.[12] The baseline for companies should thus be to ensure that any activity is in line with existing standards or benchmarks, including by reference to international agreements, regulatory frameworks and existing processes and safeguards. In this regard, the commentary to the Environment Chapter provides that the text of the Chapter "broadly reflects the principles and objectives contained in the Rio Declaration on Environment and Development, in Agenda 21 (within the Rio Declaration) and the United Nations 2030 Agenda for Sustainable Development. It is also consistent with the UN Framework Convention on Climate Change (UNFCCC), the Paris Agreement, the Convention on Biological Diversity, the Kunming-Montreal Global Biodiversity Framework, relevant regional conventions on access to information, public participation, and justice in environmental matters, the UN Convention to Combat Desertification, relevant regional environmental agreements, and reflects standards contained in such instruments as the ISO Standard on Environmental Management Systems, the International Finance Corporation's Environmental and

[9] OECD (2023), *OECD Guidelines for Multinational Enterprises on Responsible Business Conduct*, adopted 8 June 2023, https://www.oecd-ilibrary.org/docserver/81f92357-en.pdf?expires=1695482162&id=id&accname=guest&checksum=B1AF50BE886B795ED0A27C8C7FC5C9D5 (last accessed April 2024), p. 35, para. 68.

[10] OECD (2023), *OECD Guidelines for Multinational Enterprises on Responsible Business Conduct*, adopted 8 June 2023, https://www.oecd-ilibrary.org/docserver/81f92357-en.pdf?expires=1695482162&id=id&accname=guest&checksum=B1AF50BE886B795ED0A27C8C7FC5C9D5 (last accessed April 2024), p. 18, para. 17.

[11] OECD (2023), *OECD Guidelines for Multinational Enterprises on Responsible Business Conduct*, adopted 8 June 2023, https://www.oecd-ilibrary.org/docserver/81f92357-en.pdf?expires=1695482162&id=id&accname=guest&checksum=B1AF50BE886B795ED0A27C8C7FC5C9D5 (last accessed April 2024), p. 36, para. 69.

[12] OECD (2023), *OECD Guidelines for Multinational Enterprises on Responsible Business Conduct*, adopted 8 June 2023, https://www.oecd-ilibrary.org/docserver/81f92357-en.pdf?expires=1695482162&id=id&accname=guest&checksum=B1AF50BE886B795ED0A27C8C7FC5C9D5 (last accessed April 2024), p. 36, para 69.

Social Performance Standards, and Strategic Approach to International Chemicals Management (SAICM)".[13]

The commentary to Chapter VI also notes that environmental impacts are interlinked with other factors covered by the 2023 OECD Guidelines, such as health and safety and worker rights, and acknowledges that environmental due diligence will necessarily involve taking into account competing environmental or social priorities.[14] The Guidelines also place a greater emphasis on the "just transition",[15] noting that companies should address social impacts in their transition away from environmentally harmful practices and towards greener energy. To this purpose, companies are encouraged to reduce emissions, instead of implementing other measures to offset, compensate, or neutralise them. Carbon credits are specifically referred to and the Guidelines require that they should be of "high environmental integrity" in order not to draw attention away from the need to reduce emissions.[16] Similarly, the Guidelines reflect the latest scientific assessment on emissions and include text in relation to adopting, implementing, monitoring, and reporting short, medium and long term GHG emission reduction targets on scope 1, 2, and, to the extent possible based on best available information, scope 3 GHG emissions (the latter referring to emissions not produced by enterprises themselves, but by entities in their value chain).[17] In addition, they highlight that companies should continually assess their emissions based on the latest internationally agreed global temperature goals.[18]

The innovative character of the amendments included in Chapter VI of the 2023 OECD Guidelines is even more evident if one considers the text of the corresponding

[13] OECD (2023), *OECD Guidelines for Multinational Enterprises on Responsible Business Conduct*, adopted 8 June 2023, https://www.oecd-ilibrary.org/docserver/81f92357-en.pdf?expires=1695482162&id=id&accname=guest&checksum=B1AF50BE886B795ED0A27C8C7FC5C9D5 (last accessed April 2024), p. 35, para. 66.

[14] OECD (2023), *OECD Guidelines for Multinational Enterprises on Responsible Business Conduct*, adopted 8 June 2023, https://www.oecd-ilibrary.org/docserver/81f92357-en.pdf?expires=1695482162&id=id&accname=guest&checksum=B1AF50BE886B795ED0A27C8C7FC5C9D5 (last accessed April 2024), p. 36, para. 70.

[15] OECD (2023), *OECD Guidelines for Multinational Enterprises on Responsible Business Conduct*, adopted 8 June 2023, https://www.oecd-ilibrary.org/docserver/81f92357-en.pdf?expires=1695482162&id=id&accname=guest&checksum=B1AF50BE886B795ED0A27C8C7FC5C9D5 (last accessed April 2024), p. 36, para. 70.

[16] OECD (2023), *OECD Guidelines for Multinational Enterprises on Responsible Business Conduct*, adopted 8 June 2023, https://www.oecd-ilibrary.org/docserver/81f92357-en.pdf?expires=1695482162&id=id&accname=guest&checksum=B1AF50BE886B795ED0A27C8C7FC5C9D5 (last accessed April 2024), p. 37, para. 77.

[17] OECD (2023), *OECD Guidelines for Multinational Enterprises on Responsible Business Conduct*, adopted 8 June 2023, https://www.oecd-ilibrary.org/docserver/81f92357-en.pdf?expires=1695482162&id=id&accname=guest&checksum=B1AF50BE886B795ED0A27C8C7FC5C9D5 (last accessed April 2024), p. 37, para. 77.

[18] OECD (2023), *OECD Guidelines for Multinational Enterprises on Responsible Business Conduct*, adopted 8 June 2023, https://www.oecd-ilibrary.org/docserver/81f92357-en.pdf?expires=1695482162&id=id&accname=guest&checksum=B1AF50BE886B795ED0A27C8C7FC5C9D5 (last accessed April 2024), p. 37, para. 76.

Chapter of the 2011 OECD Guidelines. In the previous version of the OECD Guidelines, climate change was not even mentioned. This notwithstanding, several provisions across the Chapter intersected with climate-related mitigation and adaptation considerations for business. For example, paragraph 1(b) provided that enterprises should have an environmental management system in place, which included establishing "measurable objectives and, where appropriate, targets for improved environmental performance and resource utilisation". This expectation also included periodically reviewing the continuing relevance of these objectives and that, where appropriate, "targets should be consistent with relevant national policies and international environmental commitments" (paragraph 1(b)). The Environment Chapter also provided that businesses should "continually seek to improve corporate environmental performance, at the level of the enterprise and, where appropriate, of its supply chain" (paragraph 6) and referenced a number of activities including: the "development and provision of products or services that [...] reduce greenhouse gas emissions" (paragraph 6(b)); the promotion of "higher levels of awareness among customers of the environmental implications of using the products and services of the enterprise, including, by providing accurate information on their products (for example, on greenhouse gas emissions [...]" (paragraph 6(c)); and the exploration and assessment of ways of "improving the environmental performance of the enterprise over the longer term, for instance by developing strategies for emission reduction" (paragraph 6(d)).

A number of the expectations related to climate change considerations by business extended beyond the Environment Chapter of the 2011 OECD Guidelines and were addressed in Chapters on General Policies, Disclosure, Science and Technology, Human Rights, Competition and Consumer Interests.

3 The Climate Change-Related Complaints and the Determinations of the NCPs

NCPs play a key role in not only resolving cases and promoting the OECD Guidelines but also in facilitating dialogue and progressing the understanding among all stakeholders of the intersections between responsible business conduct and evolving areas of risk and responsibility.[19] This is particularly the case with regard to global environmental and climate change challenges. The number of NCP cases referencing the Environment Chapter of the 2011 OECD Guidelines indicates the significance of environment-related recommendations on responsible business conduct. At the time of writing (April 2024), 23,5% of all specific instances submitted to NCPs make reference to provisions of the Environment Chapter, with the latter being the 4th most cited Chapter of the OECD Guidelines following the General Policies (62%),

[19] In this sense, see Ochoa Sanchez (2015), pp. 89–90; Schliemann (2019), pp. 51–52; Bhatt and Erdem Türkelli (2021), p. 426.

Employment and Industrial Relations (54%), Human Rights (45%) Chapters.[20] This signals an important trend in enterprises being held to account on matters relating to responsible business conduct and the environment (where impacts have occurred within both adherent and non-adherent countries), as well as the critical role of NCPs in providing guidance on how the OECD Guidelines are to be interpreted and applied in such circumstances.

With respect to climate change-related cases specifically, the number of case submissions has increased in recent years. Since 2011, a total of seventeen specific instances concerning climate change were filed, of which fourteen were filed between 2017 and March 2024.[21] As it will be shown in the following sections, the relevant complaints deal with three key issues: the alleged misinformation to consumers about the impact on climate change of financial institutions' activities; the issue of (in)accurate provision of climate-relevant information in the context of growing global concern over the phenomenon of "greenwashing"; finally, with regard to some early complaints filed before the finalisation of the Paris Agreement in 2015, the specific, substantive emission-reduction obligations.

3.1 Alleged Misinformation to Consumers about the Impact on Climate-Change of Financial Institutions' Activities

Recent assessments by NCPs have often highlighted the need for credit and finance agencies to address their due diligence and disclosure obligations in the climate context. In the broader environmental scenario, NCPs have been clear that financial institutions are required to actively engage with the potential impacts of the projects and organisations to which they provide services. For example, the Dutch NCP, deliberating on the submission against Rabobank by Friends of the Earth Europe and Netherlands,[22] noted that the disengagement of financial institutions (like the Rabobank, as in the case at hand) is not favourable to the goal of sustainability. In its final statement issued on 15 January 2016, the Dutch NCP further emphasised that financial institutions have a responsibility of their own to exercise individual leverage to seek to prevent or mitigate the impact of their business conduct, to increase their leverage on their own clients if necessary, and respond identified adverse impacts

[20] Data available at OECD Database for Specific Instances, https://mneguidelines.oecd.org/database/ (last accessed April 2024).

[21] Data available at OECD Database for Specific Instances, https://mneguidelines.oecd.org/database/?hf=10&b=0&r=%2Bf%2Fmne_mne_theme%2Fenvironment&s=desc(mne_datereceived) (last accessed April 2024).

[22] OECD Database for Specific Instances, *Rabobank, Bumitama Agri Group (BGA) and the NGOs Friends of the Earth Europe and Friends of the Earth Netherlands/Milieudefensie* (2014), https://mneguidelines.oecd.org/database/instances/nl0024.htm (last accessed April 2024).

through engagement or, as last resort, divestment.[23] The Duch NCP also encouraged financial institutions in general to actively take part in due diligence initiatives in the financial sector and in the industry.[24] A few months later, this found resonance also in the Dutch NCP's final statement concluding the specific instance filed by the Dutch NGO Both ENDS, in conjunction with and on behalf of Associação Fórum Suape Espaço Socioambiental, Conectas Direitos Humanos and Colônia de Pescadores do Município do Cabo de Santo Agostinho, against Atradius Dutch State Business.[25]

Disclosure by financial institutions is integral to public understanding of corporate operations and their social, economic and environmental impacts. For instance, in 2019 the Polish NCP issued a final statement about a complaint filed by an NGO called the Development Yes—Open Pit Mines No! Foundation,[26] alleging that information provided by the financial institution PZU on the environmental and climate-related impacts of its activities and services was, though legal, not sufficient to provide the majority of consumers a full picture of the nature and scope of the enterprise's activities. In its final statement, the Polish NCP expressed its commitment to strengthen responsible business conduct standards, highlighting that a responsible enterprise should, among other things, care for the natural environment, conduct a dialogue with stakeholders, participate in the economic, environmental and social development, minimize adverse impacts of its activities, as well as commit to respecting human rights and informing diligently about any actions it may take up.[27]

Other cases have moved beyond the issue of transparency and engagement and have tackled specific questions regarding substantive emission-reduction obligations for indirect GHG emissions. In 2019, the Dutch NCP led the way by recognising that, according to the 2011 OECD Guidelines, financial institutions are required to work towards setting emissions reduction targets in line with the Paris Agreement. With regard to a complaint filed by four NGOs against ING Bank,[28] the NCP's submission

---

[23] NCP Netherlands, *Friends of the Earth Europe and Netherlands versus Rabobank*, Final Statement, 15 January 2016, https://www.oecdguidelines.nl/documents/publication/2016/1/15/fs-foe-milieudefensie-rabobank (last accessed April 2024), p. 4.

[24] NCP Netherlands, *Friends of the Earth Europe and Netherlands versus Rabobank*, Final Statement, 15 January 2016, https://www.oecdguidelines.nl/documents/publication/2016/1/15/fs-foe-milieudefensie-rabobank (last accessed April 2024), p. 4.

[25] NCP Netherlands, *Both ENDS, Fórum Suape, Conectas, Colônia de Pescadores Cabo de Santo Agostinho versus Atradius Dutch State Business,* Final Statement, 30 November 2016, https://www.oecdguidelines.nl/notifications/documents/publication/2016/11/30/final-statement-notification-both-ends--forum-suape-vs-atradius-dsb (last accessed April 2024).

[26] NCP Poland, *Development Yes—Open Pit Mines No! Foundation versus Group PZU S.A*, Final Statement, 26 July 2019, https://www.gov.pl/web/fundusze-regiony/notifications (last accessed April 2024).

[27] NCP Poland, *Development Yes—Open Pit Mines No! Foundation versus Group PZU S.A.*, Final Statement, 26 July 2019, https://www.gov.pl/web/fundusze-regiony/notifications (last accessed April 2024), p. 7.

[28] NCP Netherlands, *Oxfam Novib, Greenpeace Netherlands, BankTrack and Friends of the Earth Netherlands (Milieudefensie) versus ING,* Final Statement, 19 April 2019, https://www.oecdguidelines.nl/latest/news/2019/04/19/final-statement-dutch-ncp-specific-instance-4-ngos-versus-ing-bank (last accessed April 2024).

alleged that although ING reported on its direct GHG emissions, it failed to report on the indirect emissions resulting from its investments. ING had also failed to set concrete emissions reduction targets for its indirect emissions. The final assessment by the NCP represents an excellent example of an updated understanding of international climate obligations and a purposive application of the 2011 OECD Guidelines.[29] Indeed, the Dutch NCP first clarified that companies are expected to conduct a due diligence process in respect of their environmental impact, including climate impact, which relates not only to their own negative environmental impact, but also to the impact in their value chain.[30] Second, reflecting the precautionary principle, it stated that the absence of a methodology or internationally accepted standard does not dismiss companies from seeking to measure and disclose their GHG emissions, whilst acknowledging that indirect emissions can be more difficult to measure.[31] Third, the Dutch NCP emphasised that ING, and other commercial banks, should "put effort into defining, where appropriate, concrete targets to manage its impact towards alignment with relevant national policies and international environmental commitments".[32] In addition, since such targets must be consistent with "international environmental commitments", the NCP noted that "the Paris Agreement is currently the most relevant international agreement between states, a landmark for climate change, signed by the State of the Netherlands".[33]

The Australian NCP also adopted a progressive approach in admitting the instance submitted by an NGO and four individuals against ANZ Banking Group.[34] The case concerned the alleged ANZ's failure to adhere to emission reduction commitments under the Paris Agreement and the lack of full disclosure regarding its climate change impacts, which ultimately prevented consumers from making informed decisions as to whether or not to engage with the bank. In concluding that ANZ actions, conduct, and commitment towards making better alignments gradually were consistent with

---

[29] In this sense, see Svoboda (2020), pp. 33–34.

[30] NCP Netherlands, *Oxfam Novib, Greenpeace Netherlands, BankTrack and Friends of the Earth Netherlands (Milieudefensie) versus ING Bank*, Final Statement, 19 April 2019, https://www.oecdguidelines.nl/notifications/documents/publication/2019/04/19/ncp-final-statement-4-ngos-vs-ing (last accessed April 2024), p. 3.

[31] NCP Netherlands, *Oxfam Novib, Greenpeace Netherlands, BankTrack and Friends of the Earth Netherlands (Milieudefensie) versus ING Bank*, Final Statement, 19 April 2019, https://www.oecdguidelines.nl/notifications/documents/publication/2019/04/19/ncp-final-statement-4-ngos-vs-ing (last accessed April 2024), p. 5.

[32] NCP Netherlands, *Oxfam Novib, Greenpeace Netherlands, BankTrack and Friends of the Earth Netherlands (Milieudefensie) versus ING Bank*, Final Statement, 19 April 2019, https://www.oecdguidelines.nl/notifications/documents/publication/2019/04/19/ncp-final-statement-4-ngos-vs-ing (last accessed April 2024), p. 5.

[33] NCP Netherlands, *Oxfam Novib, Greenpeace Netherlands, BankTrack and Friends of the Earth Netherlands (Milieudefensie) versus ING Bank*, Final Statement, 19 April 2019, https://www.oecdguidelines.nl/notifications/documents/publication/2019/04/19/ncp-final-statement-4-ngos-vs-ing (last accessed April 2024), p.5.

[34] NCP Australia, *Friends of the Earth, Egan Dodds and Simons versus ANZ Group*, Final Statement, 15 December 2021, https://ausncp.gov.au/sites/default/files/2021-12/AusNCP_Final_Statement_Friends_of_Earth_0.pdf (last accessed April 2024).

the 2011 OECD Guidelines, the Australian NCP preliminary noted the increasing awareness that the Guidelines' text around climate change and environmental expectations of companies was behind current practise.[35] Then, it highlighted that, even though Guidelines' expectations specifically addressing climate change are limited and ambiguous,[36] there are international standards including the Paris Agreement (agreed by governments) and related measures and tools guiding companies,[37] such as the Paris Agreement Capital Transition Assessment and Taskforce on Climate-related Financial Disclosures framework.

A different approach was taken by the Japanese NCP. In 2018, it confronted with a specific instance against Mitsubishi UFJ Financial Group and Mizuho Financial Group,[38] concerning the alleged lack of influence on environmental information disclosure in relation to the planned construction of a coal-fired power plant in Vietnam, given the intent of the said financial enterprises to finance the project. This case represented a missed opportunity, as the Japanese NCP published the final statement on 15 January 2021, without however issuing recommendations.

3.2 "Greenwashing" and Misinformation

The issue of (in)accurate provision of climate-relevant information by enterprises has arisen also in the context of growing global concern over the phenomenon of "greenwashing".

A specific instance was filed against BP before the UK NCP by ClientEarth in 2019,[39] questioning the accuracy of statements made by the company in advertising campaigns focused on its renewable energy operations. It alleged, for example, that the advertising campaigns were misleading in the way that BP's low-carbon energy activities were presented, thus obscuring the company's broader contributions to climate and environmental impacts. The case was initially accepted on the basis that the issues were material and substantiated. However, it was ultimately discontinued by the UK NCP after BP withdrew the advertisements and undertook not to replace

---

[35] NCP Australia, *Friends of the Earth, Egan, Dodds and Simons versus ANZ Group*, Final Statement, 15 December 2021, https://ausncp.gov.au/sites/default/files/2021-12/AusNCP_Final_Statement_Friends_of_Earth_0.pdf (last accessed April 2024), p. 27, para. 75.

[36] NCP Australia, *Friends of the Earth, Egan, Dodds and Simons versus ANZ Group*, Final Statement, 15 December 2021, https://ausncp.gov.au/sites/default/files/2021-12/AusNCP_Final_Statement_Friends_of_Earth_0.pdf (last accessed April 2024), p. 4, paras. 3.2 and 3.5.

[37] NCP Australia, *Friends of the Earth, Egan, Dodds and Simons versus ANZ Group*, Final Statement, 15 December 2021, https://ausncp.gov.au/sites/default/files/2021-12/AusNCP_Final_Statement_Friends_of_Earth_0.pdf (last accessed April 2024), p. 4, para. 3.3.

[38] NCP Japan, *Market Forces versus Mizuho Financial Group, Inc., Sumitomo Mitsui Banking Corporation and Mitsubishi UFJ*, Final Statement, 15 January 2021, https://www.mofa.go.jp/files/100138168.pdf (last accessed April 2024).

[39] NCP UK, *ClientEarth versus BP*, Initial Assessment, 16 June 2020, https://www.gov.uk/government/publications/client-earth-complaint-to-the-uk-ncp-about-bp/initial-assessment-clientearth-complaint-to-the-uk-ncp-about-bp (last accessed April 2024).

them and to stop corporate reputation advertising campaigns. The discontinuation of this case means that the UK NCP did not determine whether, in the case at hand, the company has or has not acted consistently with the OECD Guidelines.

A second relevant complaint against Drax Group was brought to the UK NCP by a group of NGOs in 2021,[40] concerning alleged inaccurate and misleading statements issued by the company regarding the climate and wider environmental impacts of the energy it produces by burning woody biomass at its UK power plant, in breach of paragraphs 2(a) and 6(c) of Chapter VI of the 2011 OECD Guidelines. On 27 July 2022, the UK NCP published its initial assessment accepting the complaint for further consideration. It accepted four out of five of Drax's allegedly misleading statements identified by the complainants. One of Drax's statements, concerning its target to become carbon negative by 2030, was rejected on the basis that the evidence provided by the complainants did not substantiate the allegation, and that Drax's statement in this regard was consequently misleading.

Finally, in 2022, a specific instance against ENI s.p.a. was filed before the Italian NCP by a group of Italian NGOs and environmental movements,[41] alleging the inadequacy of the business plan of ENI, related to the extraction and marketing of fossil fuels. More precisely, the complaint highlights that ENI has committed to "net zero" emissions by 2050, but its actions run contrary to this goal. At the time of writing (April 2024), the complainants are seeking mediation from the NCP.

Even though there has not yet been a final assessment concerning greenwashing, the complaints against BP, Drax and ENI reflect a broader trend in climate change litigation against private sector actors,[42] much of which is centred on the provision of information—or indeed disinformation—to shareholders and consumers. Such disinformation is often highly damaging to climate action, with impacts on both political consensus and behavioural change at the individual level. Current litigation of this nature includes both challenges by shareholders centred on misrepresentation of climate risks[43] and challenges by sub-national governments and others centred on misleading advertising under consumer protection laws.[44]

---

[40] OECD Watch Complaints Database, *The Lifescape Project* et al. *versus Drax Group plc* (2021), https://www.oecdwatch.org/complaint/lifescape-et-al-vs-drax/ (last accessed April 2024).

[41] OECD Watch Complaints Database, *Legalità per il clima on behalf of 10 CSOs versus ENI S.p.A* (2022), https://www.oecdwatch.org/complaint/legalita-per-il-clima-on-behalf-of-10-csos-vs-eni-s-p-a/ (last accessed April 2024).

[42] On climate change litigation against private sector actors, see Weller and Tran (2022), pp. 1–14; Luporini (2023), pp. 202–236.

[43] US District Court for the Northern District of Texas, *Saratoga Advantage Trust Energy & Basic Materials Portfolio against Woods*, case number 3:2020cv02995, filing date 29 September 2020.

[44] On 15 September 2023, the California Attorney General sued five big oil companies (BP, Chevron, ConocoPhillips, Exxon Mobil, and Shell) along with the American Petroleum Institute, a trade organization that represents them, alleging a decadelong disinformation campaign to hide the correlation between fossil fuel production and climate change. A copy of the lawsuit available at https://oag.ca.gov/system/files/attachments/press-docs/FINAL%209-15%20COMPLAINT.pdf (last accessed April 2024). It is the latest in a slew of climate litigation against oil companies in cities nationwide: in recent years, seven US States (Connecticut, Delaware, Maryland, Massachusetts, Minnesota,

Disinformation-centred complaints are likely to increase in the coming years, particularly in light of growing concerns about greenwashing among companies making "net zero" commitments that may not be backed up by robust, credible emissions reduction plans. This was seen in the first-of-its-kind case of Australian Centre for Corporate Responsibility against Santos Ltd,[45] filed in 2021 and currently pending, which represents the first court case in the world to challenge the veracity of a company's net zero emissions plan.

3.3 *Obligations to Reduce Emissions*

The early climate-related NCP complaints, filed before the adoption of the Paris Agreement in 2015, dealt with specific, substantive emission-reduction obligations. A specific complaint[46] was filed by Norwegian Climate Network and Concerned Scientists Norway against Statoil ASA,[47] concerning the incompatibility of oil sands operations with the provisions of the 2011 OECD Guidelines as set out in Chapter VI, first paragraph.[48] The complaint was rejected by the Norwegian NCP on the grounds that the issues raised were outside the scope of the recalled OECD Guidelines. In doing so, the NCP observed that the complaint concerned the State conduct and that it lacked particularised allegations against the enterprise; the complainant did not

New York, Rhode Island) have sued fossil fuel companies: for an overview, see https://stateimpactcenter.org/issues/climate-action/suits-against-oil-companies (last accessed April 2024).

[45] Federal Court of Australia, *Australasian Centre for Corporate Responsibility against Santos*, case number: NSD858/2021, filing date 25 August 2021.

[46] There are two other relevant cases which deserve to be mentioned. The first one is a complaint submitted in 2007 by NGO Germanwatch against Volkswagen, alleging violation of various climate obligations because of the enterprise's climate damaging product range and business strategy. The second case is a complaint submitted in 2009 by NGO Greenpeace against Vattenfall Europe AG, Vattenfall Europe Generation AG & Co. KG and Kernkraftwerk Krümmel GmbH & Co.HG, alleging that the construction of the company coal-fired power plant was in violation of the OECD Guidelines on national environmental policies and consumer protection. However, both cases are beyond the scope of the present contribution, as at the filing dates, the 2000 version of the OECD Guidelines applied. Further information on the cases available at https://climatecasechart.com/non-us-case/germanwatch-vs-volkswagen/ (last accessed April 2024) and https://www.bmwk.de/Redaktion/EN/Beschwerdefaelle-NKS/Erklaerung/greenpeace-vattenfall.pdf?__blob=publicationFile&v=1 (last accessed April 2024).

[47] OECD Database of Specific Instances, *Oil sands extraction in Canada* (2011), https://mneguidelines.oecd.org/database/instances/no0008.htm (last accessed April 2024).

[48] The Norwegian Climate Network and Concerned Scientists Norway claimed that Statoil did not consider relevant international agreements such as the Kyoto Protocol when the company began its involvement in the oil sands industry in Canada. The complainants claimed that Statoil's investments had contributed to the violation by Canada of international agreements between 2008 and 2012 by increasing rather than reducing undisclosed climate gas emissions. They asserted that this, in turn, undermined international efforts to limit global warming to a 2 °C increase above pre-industrial levels, see NCP Norway, *Climate Network and Concerned Scientists Norway versus Statoil*, Initial and Concluding Statement, 13 March 2012, https://mneguidelines.oecd.org/database/instances/no0008.htm (last accessed April 2024), p. 2.

remedy this when it was suggested by the NCP. However, the NCP highlighted the risk posed by oil sands operation to the climate and the environment.

Since this complaint was filed, there has been a significant shift in global understanding of the responsibility to reduce GHG emissions arising from an enterprise's operations. Many enterprises now recognise they have an urgent responsibility to develop central emissions reduction policies. This is evidenced by the more than 8,000 companies that have joined the UNFCCC's Race to Zero initiative, aiming at achieving net zero carbon emissions by 2050 at the latest.[49]

While litigation concerning companies' contributions to emissions has initially focused on a small group of major emitters from the energy sector, more recently this has expanded to include companies in other high-emitting industries, such as meat and dairy.[50] Reflecting the changes in the international context since the early complaints to NCPs on emissions reductions were decided, more recent related complaints filed before NCPs have been treated differently, as highlighted in the previous sections.

4 The Impact of the Climate Change-Related Practice of the NCPs on Chapter VI of the 2023 OECD Guidelines

The analysis undertaken in the previous sections has shown that, also before the update of the OECD Guidelines for Multinational Enterprises in 2023, which explicitly identify climate change as a leading environmental impact that enterprises should address in their due diligence for the first time, NCPs have often confronted with climate change-related complaints. This notwithstanding, as is well known, the 2011 version of the OECD Guidelines applicable at the time the complaints were filed lacked recommendations specifically addressing the entire range of climate change consequences. In so doing, NCPs have frequently offered important insights as to corporate due diligence expectations related to climate change risks, which—at least to a certain extent—seem to have been acknowledged in Chapter VI of the 2023 OECD Guidelines.

The relevance of the contribution provided by NCPs immediately appears from the revised text of the recalled Chapter, as it explicitly mentions climate change in the first lines and identifies the phenomenon in question not only as an "urgent threat" but also as one of the adverse environmental impacts in which enterprises can be

[49] See UNFCCC, Race to Zero Campaign https://unfccc.int/climate-action/race-to-zero-campaign (last accessed April 2024).

[50] See, for instance, the climate change proceeding before the New Zealand courts in the case Smith against Fonterra Co-operative Group Limited [2022] NZSC 35. On 7 February 2024, the Supreme Court unanimously allowed the appeal and reinstated all causes of action to proceed to trial. Further information available at https://www.courtsofnz.govt.nz/cases/michael-john-smith-v-fonterra-co-operative-group-limited (last accessed April 2024).

involved.[51] In so doing, the 2023 OECD Guidelines seem to reflect the indications (as well as the instances) of the NCPs, which—as seen above with regard to the complaint against ANZ Banking Group submitted to the Australian NCP—on several occasions highlighted the need to reference climate change explicitly.[52]

From a more substantial point of view, Chapter VI—in conjunction with Chapter II (General Policies)—sets out significant changes to the scope of due diligence expected of companies. In particular, risk-based due diligence is now expected for all business relationships, both upstream and downstream of the company in question beyond contractual or immediate (i.e., direct) relationships. The 2023 OECD Guidelines make now clear that this includes "entities in the supply chain, which supply products or services that contribute to the enterprise's own operations, products or services or which receive, license, buy or use products or services from the enterprise".[53] This seems to reflect the final statement in the above discussed case filed by four NGOs against ING bank, in which—as said—the Dutch NCP recognised that the duty to perform climate due diligence extends to the entire value chain. In addition, Chapter VI also specifically underscores the importance of conducting meaningful engagement with relevant stakeholders affected by adverse environmental impacts associated with an enterprise's operations, products or services, which—as seen in the previous sections—was highlighted already in 2019 by the Polish NCP in the final statement about a complaint against the financial institution PZU.

However, the amendments in relation to Chapter VI of the 2023 OECD Guidelines which best reflect the feedback from NCPs dealing with climate change-related complaints are those concerning the update of references to relevant international environmental frameworks and agreements and the target setting for climate change. Starting from the assumption that the OECD Guidelines are a living instrument and should be interpreted in light of broader trends in international law, since 2011—year of the last review—the environmental agenda has evolved significantly. Key international legal instruments have been adopted, including the Paris Agreement on climate change, the 2030 Agenda for Sustainable Development, and the Aichi Biodiversity Targets 2011–2020 under the Convention for Biological Diversity. In addition, there has been considerable momentum by States and enterprises to align with the goals of the Paris Agreement. Relevant developments there have been also in measurement and reporting of business impacts on the environment including metrics, benchmarks, science-based targets and advancements in quantifying the costs of environmental

---

[51] OECD (2023), *OECD Guidelines for Multinational Enterprises on Responsible Business Conduct,* 8 June 2023, https://www.oecd-ilibrary.org/docserver/81f92357-en.pdf?expires=1695482162&id=id&accname=guest&checksum=B1AF50BE886B795ED0A27C8C7FC5C9D5 (last accessed April 2024), p. 33.

[52] See also OECD (2022), *Stocktaking Report on the OECD Guidelines for Multinational Enterprises*, https://mneguidelines.oecd.org/stocktaking-report-on-the-oecd-guidelines-for-multinational-enterprises.pdf (last accessed April 2024), p. 54.

[53] OECD (2023), *OECD Guidelines for Multinational Enterprises on Responsible Business Conduct*, 8 June 2023, https://www.oecd-ilibrary.org/docserver/81f92357-en.pdf?expires=1695482162&id=id&accname=guest&checksum=B1AF50BE886B795ED0A27C8C7FC5C9D5 (last accessed April 2024), p. 18, para. 17.

externalities. This includes internationally adopted disclosure frameworks as well as standardising "green" activities. In this regard, high profile cases such as the Dutch NCP's case "ING Bank and NGOs concerning climate policy" and the Australian NCP's case "ANZ Banking Group" have greatly contributed by highlighting the need to explicitly reference the Paris Agreement and the other existing relevant international standards and offering detailed guidance on the interpretation of climate action expectations for business,[54] such as the adoption of short and long term emission reduction targets and public disclosure of Paris aligned climate action.

The above considerations show that the 2023 OECD Guidelines have the potential to play a significant role in the governance of corporate conduct in the climate context. The pre-Paris view that the OECD Guidelines had limited relevance to climate change has shifted thanks to the NCPs purposive and progressive approach in climate change-related cases. In light of this, it is therefore surprising that the 2023 OECD Guidelines do not have fully taken into account the need to provide further safeguards to prevent the promotion of false or misleading climate information in its Chapter VI. However, it is only at first glance that this looks like a lacuna. Indeed, Chapter III (Disclosure) of the recently amended OECD Guidelines, which aims at building transparency around the operations of multinational enterprises, provides relevant recommendations—not included in the 2011 version—on the disclosure of information relating to topics of interest to a wider category of stakeholders, now referred to as "responsible business conduct (RBC) information". According to the commentary to the Chapter in question, such information shall include also the enterprise's actual or potential adverse impacts on people, the environment and society, and related due diligence processes, which may be relevant for local communities and civil society, among others.[55] These requirements seem to be in line with the fact that a growing number of enterprises have issued voluntary codes of corporate conduct, which are expressions of commitments to international standards or ethical values in such areas as environment, including climate change and biodiversity, and specialised management systems have been or are being developed and continue to evolve with the aim of helping them respect these commitments.

5 Conclusions

The present contribution has assessed the most relevant amendments to the OECD Guidelines for Multinational Enterprises in respect of climate change, as included in the recently adopted OECD Guidelines for Multinational Enterprises on Responsible Business Conduct.

---

[54] In this sense, see Achtouk-Spivak and Garden (2022), p. 610.

[55] OECD (2023), *OECD Guidelines for Multinational Enterprises on Responsible Business Conduct*, 8 June 2023, https://www.oecd-ilibrary.org/docserver/81f92357-en.pdf?expires=1695482162&id=id&accname=guest&checksum=B1AF50BE886B795ED0A27C8C7FC5C9D5 (last accessed April 2024), p. 23, para. 32.

Through the analysis of the climate change-related NCP complaints brought to date under the 2011 edition of the OECD Guidelines and the NCPs' determinations, the chapter has highlighted how the practice developed so far by the NCPs has influenced and is overall reflected in the relevant 2023 OECD Guidelines. In this regard, suffice it to mention the explicit reference to climate change in Chapter VI, which was highlighted as necessary by the Australian NCP already in 2020. The same can be said with regard to the extended scope of environmental due diligence expected of companies. Indeed, according to the recently amended OECD Guidelines, it is now expected for all the entities in their supply chain, thus reflecting the content of the final statement of the Dutch NCP in the case filed by four NGOs against ING bank. In the same vein, Chapter VI also acknowledges the importance of conducting meaningful engagement with relevant stakeholders affected by adverse environmental impacts associated with an enterprise's operations, products or services, in line with the indications provided in 2019 by the Polish NCP. However, the analysis undertaken has clearly shown that the amendments in relation to Chapter VI of the 2023 OECD Guidelines which best reflect the insights offered by the NCPs dealing with climate change-related complaints are those concerning the update of references to relevant international environmental frameworks and agreements and the target setting for climate change, in conformity with the indications provided with regard to the cases ING Bank and ANZ Banking Group.

In light of the above, it is undeniable that the approach of the NCPs confronting with climate change-related cases has proven to be crucial in making the 2023 OECD Guidelines a significant instrument in the governance of corporate conduct in the climate context. The hope is that the NCPs currently dealing with cases concerning greenwashing and the promotion of false or misleading climate information will soon provide specific indications also on these matters, which are at the heart of the recent start of a conversation about transparency, disclosure, emissions reduction targets and value chain emissions.

References

Achtouk-Spivak L, Garden R (2022) OECD national contact point specific instances: when 'soft law' bites? J Int Dispute Settl 13(4):608–642

Bhatt K, Erdem Türkelli G (2021) OECD national contact points as sites of effective remedy: new expressions of the role and rule of law within market globalization? Bus Human Rights J 6(3):423–448

Letnar Černič J (2008) Corporate responsibility for human rights: a critical analysis of the OECD guidelines for multinational enterprises. Hanse Law Rev 4(1):71–100

Liberti L (2012) OECD 50th anniversary: the updated OECD guidelines for multinational enterprises and the new OECD recommendation on due diligence guidance for conflict-free mineral supply chains. Bus Law Intern 13(1):35–50

Luporini R (2023) Strategic litigation at the domestic and international levels as a tool to advance climate change adaptation? challenges and prospects. Yearbook Intern Dis Law 4(1):202–236

Ochoa Sanchez JC (2015) The roles and powers of the OECD national contact points regarding complaints on an alleged breach of the OECD guidelines for multinational enterprises by a transnational corporation. Nordic J Intern Law 84(1):89–126

Schliemann C (2019) Procedural rules for the implementation of the OECD guidelines for multinational enterprises—a public international law perspective. German Law J 13(1):51–85

Svoboda O (2020) Coming of age: the system of OECD national contact points for responsible business conduct in its 20 years. In: Bungenberg M, Krajewski M, Tams CJ, Terhechte JP, Ziegler AR (eds) European yearbook of international economic law, vol 11 Springer, Heidelberg, pp 31–54

Weller MP, Tran ML (2022) Climate litigation against companies. Climate Action 1(1):1–14

Analysing Heightened Corporate Human Rights Responsibilities in the Context of OECD Case Law

Kateryna Buriakovska and Otgontuya Davaanyam

Abstract Operating in conflict-affected and high-risk areas poses complex challenges for multinational enterprises (MNEs) concerning human rights abuses and modern slavery within global supply chains. The presence of MNEs in such environments often worsens human rights violations, necessitating a shift from neutrality to proactive engagement. This shift entails increased responsibility for MNEs operating in conflict-affected, high-risk zones, including the implementation of rigorous human rights due diligence and the adoption of a conflict-sensitive approach in decision-making processes. While the international framework offers guidance on responsible conduct in such challenging situations, the practical implementation of heightened human rights due diligence and responsible disengagement processes presents significant obstacles for MNEs, underscoring the need for clearer guidance and best practices.

This chapter explores over 15 cases from OECD National Contact Points (NCPs) involving corporate activities in conflict zones like Myanmar, the Occupied Palestinian Territory, and the Democratic Republic of Congo. By analysing these cases, the chapter aims to illuminate how companies can fulfil their human rights responsibilities in conflict environments. It underscores the expanded role of companies in upholding human rights through enhanced due diligence, stakeholder engagement, and responsible exit strategies. The critical analysis of case law provides insights into effectively meeting human rights obligations amidst the complexities of conflict situations.

K. Buriakovska (✉) · O. Davaanyam
Friedrich-Alexander-Universität Erlangen-Nürnberg, Erlangen, Germany
e-mail: kburiakovska@gmail.com

O. Davaanyam
e-mail: Otgontuya.davaanyam@fau.de

O. Davaanyam and M. Krajewski (eds.), *Exploring Corporate Human Rights Responsibilities in OECD Case Law*, Interdisciplinary Studies in Human Rights 14,
https://doi.org/10.1007/978-3-031-75717-4_3

1 Introduction

Multinational enterprises (MNEs) operating in developing countries face a variety of challenges, the most serious being human rights abuses and instances of modern slavery within their extensive global supply chains. This dilemma is particularly acute in conflict regions, where pervasive violence sets the scene. A key realisation is that businesses operating in conflict zones can no longer maintain neutrality. Rather, their presence increases the duration, severity and likelihood of human rights violations and other breaches of international law.[1]

In light of these challenges, MNEs operating in conflict-affected and high-risk areas have an increased responsibility. They are obliged to exercise heightened human rights due diligence and to adopt a conflict-sensitive approach in all decision-making processes that have an impact on the affected population.[2] The UN Working Group on Business and Human Rights (UN Working Group) underlines the paramount importance of victim-centred reparation programmes and advocates for the implementation of the UN Guiding Principles on Business and Human Rights (UNGPs) in post-conflict and transitional justice scenarios.[3] The heightened human rights due diligence process delineated in the UNGPs and outlined by the UN Working Group stands out as a pivotal responsibility for MNEs operating in conflict-affected areas.[4] Nevertheless, practical implementation often grapples with confusions and challenges.[5]

Crucially, the international framework on business and human rights does not advocate a complete withdrawal of MNEs from difficult contexts. Rather, they advocate for thoughtful decision-making, support for those who have been left behind, and the creation of accessible avenues to remedy.[6] However, the UNGPs recognise that withdrawal may be an unavoidable and critical decision for MNEs in certain situations, particularly when they are unable to positively influence the situation affected by a conflict.[7] In such instances, responsible disengagement becomes an obligation. Despite this, MNEs frequently find themselves in a struggle to navigate their human rights responsibilities, encompassing both heightened human rights due diligence

---

[1] Azarova (2018) pp. 187–209.

[2] [57] UN Human Rights Council (HRC) (2011), *UN Guiding Principles on Business and Human Rights: Implementing the United Nation's "Protect, Respect and Remedy" Framework* (New York and Geneva 2011).

[3] UN Working Group on Business and Human Rights (WGBHR) (2020), "*Business, Human Rights and Conflict-Affected Regions: Towards Heightened Action*" 21 July 2020 UN Doc A/75/212', UN Doc A/75/212.

[4] WGBHR (2020), *"Business, Human Rights and Conflict-Affected Regions: Towards Heightened Action"* 21 July 2020 UN Doc A/75/212', UN Doc A/75/212, para 13.

[5] Aguirre and Pietropaoli (2023), pp. 541–558; Tripathi (2023) Chapter 30.

[6] OECD (2017), Session Note – Responsible disengagement, Global Forum on Responsible Business Conduct, https://mneguidelines.oecd.org/global-forum/2017-GFRBC-Session-Note-Responsible-Disengagement.pdf (last accessed 1 February 2024).

[7] HRC (2011), *UN Guiding Principles on Business and Human Rights: Implementing the United Nation's "Protect, Respect and Remedy" Framework*, Commentary to the Principle 19.

and responsible disengagement processes.[8] This underscores the pressing need for clearer guidance and best practices to effectively handle the intricacies of these situations.

The primary objective of this chapter is to delve into the practical manifestations of increased corporate responsibility for human rights within the context of conflict and to unravel the specific challenges and opportunities they pose for businesses. In pursuit of this objective, the chapter analyses more than 15 cases from OECD National Contact Points (NCPs) dealing with corporate activities in conflict zones. These cases concern various regions, including Myanmar, the Occupied Palestinian Territory (OPT) and the Democratic Republic of Congo (DRC). Through the examination of these cases, the chapter aims to shed light on how companies can fulfil their human rights responsibilities in a difficult environment. It emphasises the expanded role of companies in upholding human rights, particularly in the area of heightened human rights due diligence, stakeholder engagement and responsible exit in conflict-affected areas. This critical analysis of case law is intended to provide essential insights into the practical aspects of implementing heightened human rights due diligence and responsible engagement. The focus is on effectively meeting human rights obligations within the complex landscape of conflict situations.

2 Examining Multinational Enterprises' Heightened Responsibilities in Conflict-Affected Regions Under International Business and Human Rights Framework

In navigating the complex terrain of international business, the question of specific legal duties for MNEs undertaking heightened human rights responsibilities in conflict-affected and high-risks areas becomes a focal point of scrutiny. As MNEs operate in regions marked by conflict, the need for a comprehensive understanding of their legal obligations is paramount, especially concerning adherence to global standards like the UNGPs and the OECD Guidelines for Multinational Enterprises on Responsibility Business Conduct (OECD Guidelines).[9] This section of the chapter seeks to unravel the intricacies of human rights responsibilities incumbent upon corporations engaged in heightened HRDD within conflict zones, shedding light on the nuanced intersection of business operations, human rights, and international legal frameworks.

---

[8] Aguirre and Pietropaoli (2023), pp. 541–558.

[9] Organisation for Economic Cooperation and Development (OECD) (2023), *OECD Guidelines for Multinational Enterprises on Responsible Business Conduct* (2023 edition), 8 June 2023, available at: https://www.oecd-ilibrary.org/finance-and-investment/oecd-guidelines-for-multinational-enterprises-on-responsible-business-conduct_81f92357-en (last accessed 1 February 2024).

2.1 Unpacking the Meaning of Conflict-Affected and High-Risks Environments

At the core of the business and human rights framework lies human rights due diligence. In practical terms, human rights due diligence is an ongoing management process that mandates businesses to: identify human rights risks, prevent them where feasible, mitigate them if they arise, and be accountable for how they address the impacts on human rights. This process involves actively engaging with affected individuals and communities throughout.[10] Companies can be held accountable not only for directly causing human rights impacts or harm but also for contributing to such harm through their actions or relationships with other actors. Both the UNGPs and OECD Guidelines emphasise that MNEs have a responsibility to prevent or mitigate impacts on human rights that are directly linked to their operations, products, or services, even if they are not the primary cause. This may involve using their influence to encourage entities causing harm to change their practices. Regardless of the nature of the linkage to human rights impacts or risks, MNEs should consistently conduct human rights due diligence to fulfill their responsibilities.

Human rights due diligence is guided by the principle of proportionality, meaning that the complexity and comprehensiveness of the due diligence process should correspond to the level of risk present in a business's operational environment. Principle 17 of the UNGPs highlights that the depth and intricacy of human rights due diligence should be tailored to factors such as the scale of the business, the potential for severe human rights impacts, and the specific nature and context of its operations. The commentary accompanying this Principle advises businesses to prioritize addressing specific risks based on their unique operational circumstances.[11]

Hence, in various operational environments, certain contexts necessitate a heightened level of human rights due diligence. One such scenario where this is particularly crucial is in conflict-affected areas. These regions present unique challenges and risks that underscore the importance of robust and thorough human rights assessments and monitoring to ensure compliance and accountability.[12]

The UNGPs address armed conflicts in Principle 7, outlining the responsibilities of states to assist businesses in upholding human rights in conflict-affected regions. The commentary accompanying this principle elaborates on how conflicts typically arise from disputes over territory, resources, or government control, often occurring in states with weak rule of law where the risk of human rights abuses is significantly elevated. In such instances, businesses are obligated to adhere to international humanitarian law and must refrain from involvement in activities that could lead

[10] UN OHCHR (2012), The Corporate Responsibility to Respect Human Rights: An Interpretative Guide, 33.

[11] HRC (2011), *UN Guiding Principles on Business and Human Rights: Implementing the United Nation's "Protect, Respect and Remedy" Framework*, Commentary to the Principle 17.

[12] HRC (2011), *UN Guiding Principles on Business and Human Rights: Implementing the United Nation's "Protect, Respect and Remedy" Framework*, Commentary to the Principle 17 section (b).

to complicity in crimes under international criminal law.[13] In addition to armed conflicts, the UNGPs identify other complex operating environments, such as escalating social tensions, that pose challenges requiring proactive measures from businesses. The OECD Guidelines highlight armed conflicts as specific settings where enterprises must adhere to the principles of international humanitarian law and carry out thorough due diligence tailored to the risks of potential breaches of international humanitarian law.[14]

Other OECD instruments, such as the OECD Due Diligence Guidance for Responsible Supply Chains of Minerals from Conflict-Affected and High-Risk Areas, do not offer a definitive or all-encompassing definition of a "conflict-affected area". Instead, they define it as regions where armed conflicts are ongoing, international humanitarian law applies, and there is a high likelihood of international crimes and severe human rights violations.[15]

In recent efforts taken by the UN Working Group and other stakeholders, the scope of triggers for increased responsibilities has broadened. In addition to armed conflicts, factors such as the fragility or absence of state institutions, a history of previous violence, and environments with a high potential for future violence are now recognized as high-risk areas.[16] The 2022 United Nations Development Programme (UNDP) Guide on heightened human rights due diligence, building upon the aforementioned report, defines "conflict-affected areas" as geographic locations, regions, or nations that: (a) are impacted by varying degrees of armed conflict, (b) exhibit widespread violence such as interstate or civil wars, armed uprisings, extremist activities, or other organized forms of violence, and (c) represent post-conflict environments where the risks of a resurgence of violence are significant.[17] Therefore, according to the interpretations of the UNDP and the UN Working Group, the factors prompting heightened human rights due diligence extend beyond just armed conflicts to encompass various forms of violence, environments at risk, and post-conflict scenarios that may not be governed by international humanitarian law. This implies that guidance should be sought not only from the laws of armed conflicts but also from other sources such as state policies, peace agreements, and so on. This article examines instances from OECD NCPs that pertain to both situations involving armed

[13] HRC (2011), *UN Guiding Principles on Business and Human Rights: Implementing the United Nation's "Protect, Respect and Remedy" Framework*, Commentary to the Principle 23.

[14] Organisation for Economic Cooperation and Development (OECD) (2023), *OECD Guidelines for Multinational Enterprises on Responsible Business Conduct,* 8 June 2023, available at: https://www.oecd-ilibrary.org/finance-and-investment/oecd-guidelines-for-multinational-enterprises-on-responsible-business-conduct_81f92357-en (last accessed 1 February 2024), Chapter IV: Human Rights, para 45.

[15] OECD (2016), *OECD Due Diligence Guidance for Responsible Supply Chains of Minerals from Conflict-Affected and High-Risk Areas*, Third Edition, OECD Publishing, Paris. http://dx.doi.org/10.1787/9789264252479-en (last accessed 25 April 2024).

[16] WGBHR (2020), *"Business, Human Rights and Conflict-Affected Regions: Towards Heightened Action"*, UN Doc A/75/212, 21 July 2020, sec.14–21.

[17] United Nations Development Programme (UNDP) and WGBHR (2022), *Heightened Human Rights Due Diligence for Business in Conflict-Affected Contexts: A Guide.*

conflicts under international humanitarian law and other intricate settings where human rights violations take place.

2.2 Heightened Responsibilities of MNEs Operating in Conflict-Affected Areas and High-Risks Environments

As per UNGP Principles 12, 17, and 23, MNEs are mandated to recognize the increased risks present in conflict zones and assume a specific and heightened duty to uphold human rights norms and abide by international humanitarian law.[18] This is essential not only to prevent exacerbating the ongoing conflict but also to mitigate the risk of multinational enterprises (MNEs) becoming complicit in human rights abuses and international crimes.

However, the UNGPs do not explain how the norms of international humanitarian law can be translated into specific rules for companies when exercising human rights due diligence. Instead, the commentary to Principle 17 is more explanatory regarding international criminal law and warns that gross human rights violations to which MNEs may contribute can lead to legal complicity under international criminal law.[19] Appropriate human rights due diligence is described as an instrument to prevent potential legal actions against company directors or companies as legal entities. However, the UNGPs lack more specific guidelines, particularly on the concrete steps and processes of heightened due diligence.

Conversely, OECD Guidelines, Chapter IV, Human Rights, commentary paragraph 45, asserts that in situations of armed conflict, enterprises should adhere to international humanitarian law standards.[20] In contexts of armed conflict or elevated risk of severe abuses, enterprises are advised to conduct heightened due diligence regarding adverse impacts, including violations of international humanitarian law. While the OECD Guidelines also lack guidance on specific steps, the OECD Due Diligence Guidance for Responsible Supply Chains of Minerals from Conflict-Affected and High-Risk Areas outlines some steps and processes for heightened due diligence, particularly for extractive businesses.[21] The Guidance outlines customized steps and approaches for businesses in the mineral sector that source from or operate in conflict-affected areas. It includes recommendations to map out key actors and provides

[18] HRC (2011), *UN Guiding Principles on Business and Human Rights: Implementing the United Nation's "Protect, Respect and Remedy" Framework*, Principle 7.

[19] HRC (2011), *UN Guiding Principles on Business and Human Rights: Implementing the United Nation's "Protect, Respect and Remedy" Framework*, Principle 17, Commentary.

[20] OECD (2023), *OECD Guidelines for Multinational Enterprises on Responsible Business Conduct*, 8 June 2023, available at: https://www.oecd-ilibrary.org/finance-and-investment/oecd-guidelines-for-multinational-enterprises-on-responsible-business-conduct_81f92357-en (last accessed 1 February 2024), Chapter IV: Human Rights: Commentary, para 45.

[21] OECD (2016), *OECD Due Diligence Guidance for Responsible Supply Chains of Minerals from Conflict-Affected and High-Risk Areas*, Third Edition, OECD Publishing, Paris. http://dx.doi.org/10.1787/9789264252479-en (last accessed 25 April 2024).

guidance on identifying both armed and non-armed groups. Additionally, the Guidance emphasises robust human rights management and transparency in supply chain reporting.[22] However, it notably falls short in offering guidance on mitigating risks for individuals in conflict-affected situations, lacking strategies for their protection and overall well-being. Furthermore, it lacks specific insights into addressing practical challenges concerning the identification of potential escalation of heightened risks, effective communication with stakeholders, and making informed decisions on disengagement, excluding disengagement solely with suppliers. Therefore, the Guidance appears to be more tailored for businesses operating outside conflict-affected areas but sourcing from such regions by engaging with various suppliers.

In response to this critical gap, the UN Working Group has crafted a comprehensive guidance document explicitly designed for MNEs operating in conflict-affected areas.[23] This document articulates their specific heightened responsibilities, particularly emphasising the need for heightened human rights due diligence. Within this guidance, four pivotal components are outlined, demanding an elevated level of corporate human rights due diligence.[24] Firstly, MNEs discern the underlying causes of tensions and potential triggers, considering contextual factors such as the characteristics of a country or region that can influence conflict, as well as real and perceived grievances driving conflict. Subsequently, this assessment intricately identifies key actors, encompassing both those engaged in violence and those contributing to peaceful conflict resolution mechanisms. Thirdly, MNEs are expected to anticipate how their activities might impact or exacerbate armed conflicts. Lastly, personnel within these enterprises should be well-equipped to operate in delicate environments, possessing comprehensive knowledge about the causes and actors involved in armed conflicts.

Furthermore, MNEs are encouraged to adopt a conflict-sensitive approach that prioritizes assessing the likelihood and consequences of conflicts and their impact on people.[25] The document also emphasises the significance of establishing robust stakeholder engagement, encompassing a broad range of stakeholders.[26] Adding to this, the document covers guidance on responsible disengagement, stressing the importance of exit strategies that do not harm local communities or exacerbate

---

[22] OECD Annex I: Five-Step Framework for Risk-Based Due Diligence in the Mineral Supply Chain.

[23] WGBHR (2020), *"Business, Human Rights and Conflict-Affected Regions: Towards Heightened Action"*, UN Doc A/75/212, 21 July 2020.

[24] WGBHR (2020), *"Business, Human Rights and Conflict-Affected Regions: Towards Heightened Action"*, UN Doc A/75/212, 21 July 2020, para 46–49.

[25] WGBHR (2020), *"Business, Human Rights and Conflict-Affected Regions: Towards Heightened Action"*, UN Doc A/75/212, 21 July 2020, para 50–51.

[26] WGBHR (2020), *"Business, Human Rights and Conflict-Affected Regions: Towards Heightened Action"*, UN Doc A/75/212, 21 July 2020, para 52–53.

existing vulnerabilities.[27] Rather than advocating for a mere withdrawal from challenging contexts, the UNGPs encourages companies to make well-considered decisions and provide support for those left behind.[28] Thus, companies operating in conflict-affected areas are called upon to integrate human rights considerations into their decision-making processes, engage with affected communities, and actively contribute to peace and stability.

The document touches also upon post-conflict settings, i.e. how to ensure respect human rights by "captive" businesses which for different reasons might be dependent upon a conflict zone with little chance of relocating. Pointing out on that the problem of business conduct of such businesses is underexamined, the Report provides only recommendations on how to approach to 'captive businesses' during transitional period. It is worth noting that post-conflict settings also fall within the Report; it concentrates on responsible reconstruction investment and access to remedy and justice by bringing businesses complicit to war crimes and uncovering the truth about the past atrocities.

However, these recommendations pose a challenge for businesses, as they are the entities responsible for actual implementation in real-life scenarios.[29] Therefore, it is crucial to closely observe practical applications to understand how easily these recommendations can be implemented. In practical terms, businesses often grapple with the intricate process of translating these recommendations into actionable strategies that align with their operations. It necessitates a careful examination of existing frameworks and a tailored approach to ensure seamless integration into day-to-day practices. Additionally, assessing case studies of successful implementation can offer valuable insights into overcoming challenges and refining the feasibility of these recommendations in diverse business contexts.

3 Analysis of Heightened Corporate Responsibilities Through OECD Case Law

The OECD framework serves as a valuable tool for observing and comprehending the dynamic landscape of corporate behaviour and accountability. This segment of the chapter seeks to untangle the intricate layers of heightened corporate responsibilities ingrained in OECD case law. It endeavours to provide a thorough examination

[27] WGBHR (2020), *"Business, Human Rights and Conflict-Affected Regions: Towards Heightened Action"*, UN Doc A/75/212, 21 July 2020., para 64–65.

[28] HRC (2011), *UN Guiding Principles on Business and Human Rights: Implementing the United Nation's "Protect, Respect and Remedy" Framework*, Principle 19, Commentary.

[29] For example, in the UNDP Report (2023), Responsible Business Conduct During War in Ukraine: Context Assessment Study, it is resumed, that 'the war in Ukraine significantly changes the scope of corporate responsibility for human rights'. The Report showcases how developed guidelines in the sphere of business and human rights do not cover all the challenges businesses in Ukraine are faced with. See full text here: https://www.undp.org/ukraine/publications/responsible-business-conduct-during-war-ukraine-context-assessment-study (last accessed 25 April 2024).

that transcends mere theoretical frameworks. Specifically, this section addresses the research question: What insights does OECD case law offer regarding the application and effectiveness of heightened corporate human rights responsibilities in real-world business scenarios?

Through an analysis of over 15 specific cases falling within the OECD's jurisdiction, this exploration aims to illuminate the practical implications of heightened corporate responsibilities, particularly in conflict-affected areas. It delves into the multifaceted dimensions of these obligations, assessing their impact on human rights, ethical business practices, and the broader societal implications. This focused inquiry seeks to contribute nuanced perspectives on the application and efficacy of heightened HRDD, offering valuable insights for businesses navigating real-world complexities. By scrutinizing real-world instances, this analysis not only enhances our understanding of the responsibilities borne by corporations but also contributes to the ongoing discourse on corporate governance, ethical conduct, and the pursuit of a socially responsible business landscape.

This part of the chapter is segmented into three sections, each dedicated to essential aspects of corporate heightened responsibility in conflict-affected areas. Firstly, it will examine conflict-sensitive analysis and heightened human rights due diligence. Following this, the focus will shift to stakeholder engagement. Lastly, the chapter assesses the concept of responsible disengagement. Furthermore, it examines different cases that underscore adverse human rights impacts in conflict-affected areas. Specifically, it will analyse cases with unsuccessful outcomes where both the NCP and the parties involved failed to consider the critical aspect of conflict-affected areas and the heightened due diligence responsibilities of the company. This oversight signifies a missed opportunity, especially considering the prevalence of adverse impacts in conflict-affected regions.

3.1 Heightened Human Rights Due Diligence Responsibilities

Several OECD cases thoroughly analyse the essential requirement for MNEs operating in conflict-affected areas to conduct heightened human rights due diligence, emphasising distinctions from the general human rights due diligence outlined in the UNGPs, Principles 17–21. It is noteworthy that even before the adoption of revised version of the OECD Guidelines in 2011, which provided more specific guidance on corporate human rights due diligence, cases from 2005 to 2009 had already addressed corporate responsibility in conflict-affected areas. For example, the case against Chemie Pharmacie Holland BV (CPH), brought forward by the Netherlands Institute for Southern Africa (NIZA) in 2003, alleges that CPH violated the requirements outlined in the OECD Guidelines (2000) through its involvement in ore mining in the DRC.[30] Upon examining the case, the Dutch NCP emphasises the crucial need for robust due diligence and assessment for companies operating in conflict zones. The NCP also acknowledges the absence of clear policy guidance provided by itself and the Dutch Government for businesses in conflict zones. Consequently, the NCP calls for international and governmental organizations to provide clear and consistent advice to companies engaging in business within conflict zones. Similarly, in 2005, the NGO Rights and Accountability in Development (RAID) lodged a complaint with the UK NCP against DAS Air. The complaint asserts that DAS Air transported coltan from the DRC, including flights between the DRC and Uganda from 1998 to 2001, when airspace was closed due to conflict.[31] DAS Air argued unawareness of the minerals' conflict-zone origin. The UK NCP found it implausible, given DAS Air's significant African presence. Concluding that DAS Air violated OECD Guidelines, the UK NCP highlighted failures in contributing to sustainable development, respecting human rights, and encouraging ethical corporate conduct among business partners. These two cases underscore those discussions about businesses' specific responsibility towards human rights in conflict-affected zones predated the adoption of the UNGPs and concept of human rights due diligence.

Following the adoption of the UNGPs and an increased awareness of businesses' heightened responsibility in conflict-affected areas, numerous cases within the OECD case handling system now specifically address heightened human rights due diligence in these contexts. Initially, several instances from NCPs indicate that, due to the high-risk human rights environment in conflict-affected areas, businesses are obligated to establish explicit policies addressing these elevated risks. One notable instance is the case against JCB brought to the UK NCP by Lawyers for Palestinian Human Rights (LPHR).[32] The complaint asserts that JCB's products and machinery were utilized in the demolition of Palestinian properties and structures linked to settlements. In response, the UK NCP emphasizes that when operating in complex environments, especially in human rights high-risk or conflict zones, businesses must explicitly commit to protecting human rights. A clear commitment to respecting and safeguarding human rights by businesses provides clarity to employees, suppliers, stakeholders, and customers about their position. Likewise, in the case against Sjøvik AS filed with the Norwegian NCP by the Norwegian Support Committee, the NCP

---

[30] NCP Netherlands, *NIZA* et al. *against CHP*, Final Statement, 01 May 2004, https://www.oecdguidelines.nl/notifications/documents/publication/2015/1/6/ncp-statement-on-specific-instance-cfh---niza (last accessed 29 May 2024).

[31] NCP United Kingdom, *RAID against DAS Air*, Final Statement, 17 July 2008, https://webarchive.nationalarchives.gov.uk/ukgwa/20121204133419/http://www.bis.gov.uk/policies/business-sectors/green-economy/sustainable-development/corporate-responsibility/uk-ncp-oecd-guidelines/cases/final-statements (last accessed 29 May 2024).

[32] NCP United Kingdom, *LPHR against JCB*, Final Statement, 12 November 2021, https://www.gov.uk/government/publications/lawyers-for-palestinian-human-rights-complaint-to-uk-ncp-about-jcb (last accessed 29 May 2024).

recommended that the company implement a human rights policy and conduct a risk assessment, with particular attention to the status and vulnerability of the territory.[33]

Additional cases underscore the necessity for heightened due diligence to surpass the standard requirements outlined in the UNGPs and OECD Guidelines for human rights due diligence. These instances emphasise the critical importance of adopting conflict-sensitive approaches during the process of conducting risk assessments. For example, in the case against Mallee Resources Limited presented to the Australian NCP, the Australian NCP emphasised that the effectiveness of heightened due diligence is reliant on the company already having a robust foundation in human rights due diligence performance. In this specific instance, Publish What You Pay Australia accused the company of insufficient due diligence and irresponsible disengagement in Myanmar.[34] The Australian NCP emphasized the crucial role of human rights due diligence before investing in a local company. If the company had conducted HRDD before and throughout its engagement with BJV, it would have been better prepared to respond in accordance with the OECD Guidelines after the military coup. This highlights the essential requirement for companies in conflict-affected areas to embed comprehensive human rights practices into their organizational structure and then it will help them to conduct heightened due diligence during the conflict areas.

In a case brought before the Danish NCP against Bestseller, the complainant alleges that Bestseller is maintaining connections with local suppliers linked to the Myanmar military, thereby contributing to conflict financing.[35] In alignment with the Australian NCP's methodology, the Danish NCP meticulously assessed Bestseller's initial risk evaluation prior to its investment in Myanmar. Additionally, the Danish NCP thoroughly reviewed Bestseller's risk assessments at three distinct periods: before the investment in 2014, during the operational phase from 2014 to 2019, and following the military coups in 2019. The Danish NCP expressed satisfaction with Bestseller's due diligence processes. They acknowledged that Bestseller has given priority to the risks associated with the conflict and consistently enhanced and tailored its due diligence approaches in response to these risks. Furthermore, Bestseller had documented a comprehensive due diligence process, continuously adjusting to the changing risk landscape and acquiring new information about the situation in Myanmar. Bestseller had consistently investigated to minimize any contribution to or association with negative impacts while concurrently fostering income generation and promoting positive industry development in Myanmar. This case serves as an example of effectively conducting heightened due diligence, demonstrating how human rights due diligence must be consistently customized to align with the

---

[33] NCP Norway, *Norwegian Support Committee for Western Sahara versus Sjøvik* AS, Final Statement, 3 July 2013, https://files.nettsteder.regjeringen.no/wpuploads01/blogs.dir/263/files/2013/12/130702-NCP-Norway-Final-Statement-MEDIATION-NSCWS.pdf (last accessed 29 May 2024).

[34] NCP Australia, *Publish What You Pay versus t Mallee Resources Limited*, Final Statement, 2 August 2023, https://ausncp.gov.au/sites/default/files/2023-08/27-ausncp-final-statement.pdf (last accessed 29 May 2024).

[35] NCP Denmark, *Christian Juhl versus Bestseller*, Final Statement, 30 September 2022, https://ncp-danmark.dk/sites/default/files/2022-12/Decison-Bestseller-30092022_WA.pdf (last accessed 29 May 2024).

ever-changing risks associated with conflicts. Moreover, in this case, the Danish NCP determined that due to the conflict situation, Bestseller's risk assessments draw from a diverse array of sources. These include the company's own investigations, third-party audits, self-assessment forms, engagement with suppliers and various stakeholders (such as multi-stakeholder initiatives and external experts), and information gathered from key local and international stakeholders. The Danish NCP also underscores the importance of embedding responsible business behaviour in management. For instance, decisions such as entering the Myanmar market and subsequently halting the onboarding of new suppliers were made and communicated internally at the Bestseller's highest management level.

In contrast, the case brought before the Korean National Contact Point (NCP) concerning Myanmar highlights a misunderstanding of responsible business conduct in armed conflict and the assessment methodologies associated with it.[36] The case filed with the Korean National Contact Point involved six companies accused of contributing to human rights violations against the Rohingya minority in Myanmar. Specifically, three of the companies were involved in joint ventures with MEHL (Myanmar Economic Holdings Limited), a military conglomerate established by the Ministry of Defence that operates in various sectors from banking to beverages. The fourth company participated in a project to build a hotel on military-owned land in Yangon with an 18.49% stake, while the last two companies were accused of supplying equipment that enhanced the military's combat capabilities, in violation of the Arms Trade Treaty and the human rights provisions of the OECD Guidelines.

One of the first three companies argued that the allegations were vague and lacked specific evidence, asserting that the UN Guiding Principles on Business and Human Rights (UNGPs) are voluntary and not legally binding on enterprises. They contended that general awareness of the human rights situation in Myanmar did not automatically imply complicity based on their transactions or tax payments. The other two companies claimed that their business relationships with a company controlled by the military dictatorship actually contributed to improving the welfare of workers by creating job opportunities. In relation to their delivery of civilian ships to Myanmar, they stated that they could not foresee or control any potential exploitation of the equipment after it was supplied to the country.

The Korean NCP adopted the main arguments put forth by the respondent companies. It referenced the OECD Guidelines Commentary's interpretation of "contribution" and determined that for an action to constitute a contribution, it should involve activities that might encourage or incentivize other businesses to have a negative impact. The Korean NCP expressed uncertainty about whether the conflict between the military government of Myanmar and the Rohingya people would have taken place if the respondent companies had not engaged in business activities. This set a very high threshold for proving "contribution," which may not be necessary at the

[36] NCP Korea, *Korean Civil Society in Solidarity with Rohingya, Korean Transnational Corporation Watch and Justice for Myanmar versus POSCO*, Initial Assessment, 14 July 2021, http://www.ncp.or.kr/servlet/kncp/eng/4001 (last accessed 29 May 2024).

initial assessment stage.[37] Furthermore, the Korean NCP deemed it inappropriate for them to pass judgment on the policies of the military regime, even though they were not specifically asked to do so. The NCP did not delve into what measures companies should have taken before entering into relationships with MEHL or the military dictatorship, such as conducting heightened human rights due diligence. Nor did it assess whether the companies provided assurances that they had implemented robust human rights due diligence in line with the Guidelines. Ultimately, the Korean NCP concluded that the case did not warrant further investigation and was unlikely to contribute to the objectives and advantages of the Guidelines.

The discussion within the NCP case handling system not only addresses the heightened responsibility of MNEs in conflict-affected areas but also looks into the responsibility of investors in these regions. A notable case illustrating this is the one brought forward by KTNC Watch and others against ABP/ABG and NBIM, discussed before the Norwegian NCP, which particularly elaborates on the investor's role in conflict-affected areas.[38] In this instance, the Norwegian NCP recommends that portfolio investors develop an approach that integrates Environmental, Social, and Governance (ESG) factors into their analysis. This integration aims to provide a better understanding of investments with the potential for significant human rights harm, allowing investors to focus their assessments on these specific areas. The suggested focus areas include (i) the operating context, considering high-risk regions like conflict zones; (ii) the particular operations, products, or services involved, especially those typically associated with human rights risks; and (iii) other relevant considerations, such as a company's poor track record on human rights performance.

3.2 Stakeholder Engagement

The importance of establishing such engagement was also highlighted in the WGBHR's document, as discussed in the preceding section of this chapter. This aspect is particularly crucial in conflict-affected areas where strong connections exist between local communities and armed groups.[39] Several compelling examples

---

[37] See the analysis here: OECD Watch, *Korean Civil Society in Solidarity with Rohingya, Korean Transnational Corporation Watch and Justice for Myanmar versus POSCO International*, 26 February 2021, https://www.oecdwatch.org/complaint/ktnc-watch-et-al-vs-posco-2/ (last accessed 25 April 2024).

[38] NCP Norway, *Lok Shakti Abhiyan, Korean transnational corporations watch, fair green and global alliance and forum for environment and development versus POSCO (South Korea), ABP/ APG (Netherlands) and NBIM (Norway)*, Final Statement, 27 May 2013, https://files.nettsteder.regjeringen.no/wpuploads01/blogs.dir/263/files/2013/12/nbim_final.pdf (last accessed 29 May 2024).

[39] WGBHR (2020), *"Business, Human Rights and Conflict-Affected Regions: Towards Heightened Action"*, UN Doc A/75/212, 21 July 2020, paras 53–54.

demonstrate that local communities can assist businesses in addressing challenges, including those arising from the activities of local armed groups.[40]

Cases brought before the OECD NCP mechanisms, emphasizing heightened corporate responsibility in conflict-affected areas, highlight the crucial role of fostering robust stakeholder engagement. In the case against Bestseller at the Danish NCP, it was found that Bestseller conducted extensive stakeholder engagement to map out and gather information on the conflict-related risks.[41] This effort led to the acquisition of information on the local legal and governance framework, socio-economic and political context. The engagement involved collaboration with various stakeholders, including international organizations, civil society groups, government agencies, trade unions, employers, and industry, providing relevant insights as part of the mapping process. The Danish NCP also emphasises the vital role of extensive and meaningful stakeholder engagement in conflict-affected areas. Involving local communities in companies' decisions regarding business activities in the country is especially crucial in a conflict-affected context. It is recommended that companies with operations in Myanmar closely monitor the situation to swiftly respond to new developments and information that might impact their presence in the country, aligning with the expectations outlined in the OECD Guidelines and the UNGPs.

In several other cases, NCPs have highlighted the significant risks and consequences for companies that lack robust stakeholder engagement when operating in conflict-affected areas. For instance, the case against Telenor brought before the Norwegian NCP primarily revolves around the argument of whether Telenor should have been aware of the risk of its ICT towers being misused by military for conducting genocide against minorities.[42] While the Norwegian NCP acknowledged that the risk was unforeseeable for Telenor to prevent such misuse, it stated that if Telenor had conducted sufficient stakeholder engagement before and during the escalation of the conflict, the risk could have been identified prior to the misuse.

Moreover, certain OECD cases underscore the significance of clear communication with specific stakeholders, particularly employees, for businesses operating in conflict-affected areas. In the case against Philips Lighting presented to the Dutch NCP, an individual from Ukraine alleged that the company's negligent transfer to Russian management resulted in discrimination and harassment due to the Ukrainian/Russian conflict (Eastern Ukraine/Crimea).[43] The Dutch NCP advised the company to be vigilant regarding the risks associated with the conflict situation. It underscored the significance of establishing transparent communication channels with relevant

---

[40] WGBHR (2020), *"Business, Human Rights and Conflict-Affected Regions: Towards Heightened Action"*, UN Doc A/75/212, 21 July 2020, paras 53–54.

[41] NCP Denmark, *Christian Juhl versus Bestseller*, Final Statement, 30 September 2022, https://ausncp.gov.au/sites/default/files/2023-08/27-ausncp-final-statement.pdf (last accessed 29 May 2024).

[42] NCP Norway, *Committee Seeking Justice for Alethankyaw versus Telenor ASA*, Final Statement, 29 August 2022, https://www.responsiblebusiness.no/committee-seeking-justice-for-alethankyaw-csja-vs-telenor/ (last accessed 29 May 2024).

[43] NCP Netherlands, *Former employee against Philips Lighting*, Final Statement, 25 October 2017. https://www.oecdguidelines.nl/documents/publication/2017/10/25/ia-former-employee-of-philips-lighting-vs.-philips-lighting (last accessed 29 May 2024).

stakeholders, particularly employees operating in this area. The Dutch NCP specifically highlighted that enterprises should offer clear and transparent information to employees about their actions and any changes that could significantly impact their livelihoods. This approach allows enterprises to articulate their position effectively in discussions about their actions or decisions.

The most recent case brought before the Norwegian NCP serves as a prime example of the complexities associated with regions marked by a history of past human rights violations. It underscores the importance for businesses to genuinely consider and factor in this challenging context when operating in such areas.[44] This case brought by Civil Society Organizations (CSOs) against companies Aker ASA and Aker BP ASA, they are accused of failing to adhere to the OECD Guidelines when they decided to merge with Lundin Energy Norway AS (formerly known as Lundin Oil). Lundin Energy Norway AS is alleged to have been involved in gross and systematic human rights violations in Sudan during a military campaign that took place between 1997 and 2003. The military campaign was aimed at securing and gaining control of the oil fields in the region. In 1997, Lundin Oil signed a contract with the Government of Sudan to exploit the oil in that area. The conflict over the oil fields led to the violent displacement of 160,000 people and resulted in 12,000 casualties. This information was extensively documented by NGOs[45] and further supported by ongoing criminal proceedings initiated by Swedish authorities against executives of Lundin Energy for their alleged complicity in violations of international law. These legal actions include claims for compensation on behalf of the victims affected by the conflict.

The complainants are arguing before the Norwegian NCP that the merger of Aker ASA and Aker BP ASA with Lundin Energy Norway would greatly diminish Lundin's net assets. This reduction in resources would prevent adequate redress for human rights violations linked to Lundin's actions, leaving victims without the necessary remediation. In simpler terms, after the merger, there may not be enough funds available to compensate victims of Lundin's involvement in atrocities. This case highlights the importance of responsible merger and acquisition practices in regions affected by conflict. It also underscores the need for a victim-centered approach and engagement with stakeholders in complex environments. The complainants allege that the merger was not disclosed to the affected communities in Sudan before its announcement on December 21, 2021. Additionally, there was a lack of meaningful dialogue with NGOs representing victims and the victims themselves. This failure to engage with victims and stakeholders meant that their voices were not heard, and the harm they experienced was disregarded by the companies involved.

The NCP emphasises that "the right to effective remedy is a fundamental human right," and highlights that a company's merger or acquisition can potentially impede

---

[44] NCP Norway, *Eight civil society organisations from South Sudan, Norway, Sweden, and the Netherlands versus Aker BP ASA and Aker ASA*, Initial Statement, 27 February 2023, https://www.responsiblebusiness.no/pax-and-others-vs-aker-bp-asa-and-aker-asa/ (last accessed 29 May 2024).

[45] "Unpaid Debt", The Legacy of Lundin, Petronas and OMV in Block 5A, Sudan 1997 – 2003. https://www.ecosonline.org/reports/2010/UNPAID_DEBT_fullreportweb.pdf (last accessed 20 April 2024).

this right for affected individuals. The NCP believes that the complaint raises issues relevant to the OECD Guidelines. Given that the connection between due diligence and the right to an effective remedy for victims has not been extensively clarified through NCP practices, the NCP will proceed to address this specific case.

3.3 Responsible Disengagement

Responsible disengagement, a crucial aspect of heightened corporate responsibility toward human rights and the environment in conflict-affected areas, is a recurring theme in OECD case law. A noteworthy example illustrating responsible disengagement under the NCP mechanism is the case against Mallee Resources in the Australian NCP.[46] In this instance, the complainant argued that Mallee Resources irresponsibly disengaged from its business in Myanmar and failed to conduct any human rights due diligence to address the impacts resulting from its disengagement. The Australian NCP observed that the company did not adequately address or mitigate potential adverse human rights impacts stemming from its disengagement, regardless of whether it caused, contributed to, or was directly connected to these impacts. In reviewing the case, the Australian NCP emphasized the significance of companies prioritizing thorough human rights due diligence when ending their engagement with a local business due to conflicts.[47] The process should include a thorough assessment of potential risks associated with the disengagement. Furthermore, the Australian NCP referenced the OECD Guidelines, highlighting that disengagement is considered a last resort—an effort by an enterprise to leverage influence over a third-party entity to respect human rights. The Australian NCP noted that Mallee Resources' divestment was not viewed as an exercise of leverage; rather, it appeared to be a reaction to a radical change in the governance and security of the country.[48] Nonetheless, the Australian NCP emphasized that in both scenarios outlined in the OECD Guidelines—disengagement as an exercise of leverage and the context of a business decision to extract a company from a venture in challenging circumstances—the expectation is that some level of due diligence should

[46] NCP Australia, *Publish What You Pay versus Mallee Resources Limited*, Final Statement, 2 August 2023 https://ausncp.gov.au/sites/default/files/2023-08/27-ausncp-final-statement.pdf (last accessed 29 May 2024).

[47] NCP Australia, *Publish What You Pay versus Mallee Resources Limited*, Final Statement, 2 August 2023https://ausncp.gov.au/sites/default/files/2023-08/27-ausncp-final-statement.pdf (last accessed 29 May 2024).

[48] NCP Australia, *Publish What You Pay versus Mallee Resources Limited*, Final Statement, 2 August 2023 https://ausncp.gov.au/sites/default/files/2023-08/27-ausncp-final-statement.pdf (last accessed 29 May 2024).

be conducted to "take into account potential social and economic adverse impacts related to the decision to disengage."[49]

In another pertinent case against Bestseller before the Danish NCP, the company was similarly advised to conduct a comprehensive risk assessment if it chose to disengage from the country.[50] The Danish NCP specified that any withdrawal must be executed responsibly and based on an enhanced risk assessment. Such a thorough assessment should always be evidence-based and guided by an up-to-date evaluation of social and economic consequences.

Several other OECD NCP cases have underscored the importance of responsible disengagement and the necessity of consulting and communicating the decision to disengage with relevant stakeholders. In the case against DNO ASA brought before the Norwegian NCP by Trade Union Industry Energi, it was stated that DNO ASA did not notify or consult with the workers or their representatives before making dismissals and suspending production in Yemen.[51] DNO explained that the company deemed it impractical to conduct individual or collective consultations due to the risk the workers faced in the war-like situation prevailing in the country. Additionally, DNO asserted that it had not received subsequent input or indications that consultations would have been genuinely impactful.

The Norwegian NCP expressed that a company like DNO, operating in high-risk and demanding areas globally, should have explored alternative ways to provide reasonable notice of collective dismissals to employee representatives and their organizations.[52] It would have been reasonable for DNO to engage in advance consultations with employee representatives on alternative notification procedures, particularly if the security situation suggested a temporary suspension of production and potential layoffs.

Similarly, the case against Heineken before the Dutch NCP highlights a situation where Heineken conducted mass dismissals of employees in its subsidiary Bralima in the DRC due to the conflict, without consulting or reasonably compensating the employees.[53] In this instance, the Dutch NCP examined the company Bralima, Heineken's subsidiary in the DRC, emphasizing its significant economic and social impact on employees. The Dutch NCP specifically highlighted that Bralima is one

---

[49] NCP Australia, *Publish What You Pay versus Mallee Resources Limited*, Final Statement, 2 August 2023 https://ausncp.gov.au/sites/default/files/2023-08/27-ausncp-final-statement.pdf (last accessed 29 May 2024).

[50] NCP Denmark, *Christian Juhl versus Bestseller*, Final Statement, 30 September 2022, https://ncp-danmark.dk/sites/default/files/2022-12/Decison-Bestseller-30092022_WA.pdf (last accessed 29 May 2024).

[51] NCP Norway, *Indusri Energi versus DNO ASA*, Final Statement, 9 April 2018, https://files.nettsteder.regjeringen.no/wpuploads01/blogs.dir/263/files/2018/04/Final-statement-DNO-Industri-Energi_EN.pdf (last accessed 29 May 2024).

[52] NCP Norway, *Indusri Energi versus DNO ASA*, Final Statement, 9 April 2018, 11, https://files.nettsteder.regjeringen.no/wpuploads01/blogs.dir/263/files/2018/04/Final-statement-DNO-Industri-Energi_EN.pdf (last accessed).

[53] NCP Netherlands, *Former employees versus Bralima, Heineken*, Final Statement, 18 August 2017, https://www.oecdguidelines.nl/latest/news/2017/08/18/final-statement-notification-former-employees-bralima-vs.-bralima-heineken.

of the largest producers of beer and soft drinks in the DRC, contributing significantly to the economic and social landscape. Notably, Bralima has operated clinics in the DRC from its early stages, including in Bukavu, providing medical care for current employees, retired employees, and their dependents (children and spouses). Furthermore, Bralima supports the education of the children of its employees and retirees.[54] Considering these economic and social impacts, the Dutch NCP recommended that companies establish transparent and clear communication with employees as part of their policies for dealing with conflict settings.[55]

In other cases, like the one involving G4S before the UK NCP, where G4S faced accusations of providing services and facilities to Israeli state agencies in the Palestinian Occupied Territory, the focus of the discussion was on prioritization and leveraging influence in conflict-affected areas before considering withdrawal.[56] The UK NCP advised G4S to conduct comprehensive human rights due diligence, stressing the importance of prioritizing the most serious abuses or those requiring urgent action to prevent the potential loss of remedial opportunities.[57]

Addressing the complainants' request for G4S to withdraw from Israeli activities, the UK NCP clarified that international frameworks do not simply endorse withdrawal; instead, G4S has a responsibility to initially address negative impacts and must exercise its leverage. Furthermore, regarding G4S's capacity to exert influence, the UK NCP highlighted that G4S, with its 8,000 employees serving 50,000 customers, including 35,000 private individuals, has successfully influenced the Israeli government on changes to employment law and government tendering. Consequently, the UK NCP concluded that there is evidence of G4S possessing leverage and suggested potential actions, including lobbying immediate business partners and/or government and legal representatives, sharing best practices within the business community and wider sector, and committing to new practices in future contracts.[58]

The analysed OECD cases above offer practical guidance and insights into implementing heightened responsibilities in conflict-affected areas. While some cases yielded successful outcomes with tangible remedies, the forthcoming analysis will uncover instances where certain NCPs missed the opportunity to thoroughly examine cases regarding potential connections with human rights risks in conflict-affected

---

[54] NCP Netherlands, *Former employees versus Bralima, Heineken*, Final Statement, 18 August 2017, 5, https://www.oecdguidelines.nl/latest/news/2017/08/18/final-statement-notification-former-employees-bralima-vs.-bralima-heineken (last accessed 29 May 2024).

[55] NCP Netherlands, *Former employees versus Bralima, Heineken*, Final Statement, 18 August 2017, 6, https://www.oecdguidelines.nl/latest/news/2017/08/18/final-statement-notification-former-employees-bralima-vs.-bralima-heineken (last accessed 29 May 2024).

[56] NCP United Kingdom, *LPHR versus G4S*, Final Statement, March 2015, https://www.gov.uk/government/publications/lawyers-for-palestinian-human-rights-complaint-to-uk-ncp-about-g4s (last accessed 29 May 2024).

[57] NCP United Kingdom, *LPHR versus G4S*, Final Statement, March 2015, https://www.gov.uk/government/publications/lawyers-for-palestinian-human-rights-complaint-to-uk-ncp-about-g4s (last accessed 29 May 2024), 13.

[58] NCP United Kingdom, *LPHR versus G4S*, Final Statement, March 2015, https://www.gov.uk/government/publications/lawyers-for-palestinian-human-rights-complaint-to-uk-ncp-about-g4s (last accessed 29 May 2024),18.

areas. Notably, most unsuccessful cases in this regard involve the Canadian NCP and the US NCP. In these cases, all of which unfolded in conflict-affected areas, the respective NCPs either overlooked the impact or vehemently rejected the cases. In the Canadian NCP, the cases against ChinaGold operating in the China-Occupied Tibetan region and GoldCorp in Guatemala failed to address the heightened responsibility of both mining companies in conflict-prone areas.[59] Notably, the globally renowned conflict between GoldCorp and the indigenous people, marked by its violent and cruel nature, received mere recommendations from the Canadian NCP.[60] The NCP suggested the company conduct due diligence without explicitly addressing its responsibility in the conflict situation.

Equally disheartening are the two cases brought to the US NCP regarding human rights risks in conflict-affected areas against Coca Cola and Boeing Company.[61] The US NCP vehemently rejected both cases without considering resolution. In the first case against Coca Cola, involving the alleged unfair dismissal of four employees in the DRC branch, the US NCP expressed sympathy for the challenging circumstances faced by the submitters.[62] However, it stated that the U.S. NCP is not the appropriate venue to address what essentially amounts to employment disputes against a DRC company raised by four former employees, even considering the challenging context of their location. In the second case against Boeing Company, accused of transporting products for use by Saudi Arabia that would adversely impact people in Yemen, the US NCP rejected the case.[63] The rejection was based on the argument that intervening inappropriately in the domestic affairs of another country through the Specific Instance procedure would be highly detrimental to the effectiveness of the Guidelines.

---

[59] NCP Canada, *Canada Tibetan Committee versus ChinaGold*, Final Statement, 13 May 2021, https://www.international.gc.ca/trade-agreements-accords-commerciaux/ncp-pcn/statement-gyama-valley.aspx?lang=eng (last accessed 29 May 2024); NCP Canada, *Centre for International Environmental Law (CIEL),* et al. *versus GoldCorp*, Final Statement, 3 May 2011, https://www.international.gc.ca/trade-agreements-accords-commerciaux/ncp-pcn/final_stat-marlin-decl_finale.aspx?lang=eng.

[60] Hill D, Welcome to Guatemala: Goldmine Protestor beaten and burnt alive, Guardian, 12 August 2014, https://www.theguardian.com/environment/andes-to-the-amazon/2014/aug/12/guatemala-gold-mine-protester-beaten-burnt-alive (last accessed 5 March 2024).

[61] NCP United States, *Formed employees versus Coca Cola*, Final Statement, 21 December 2022, https://www.state.gov/specific-instance-between-leonce-safari-kajangu-anicet-tambwe-byadunia-and-francois-zabene-zagabe-and-the-coca-cola-company-regarding-events-in-the-democratic-republic-of-the-congo/ (last accessed 29 May 2024).

[62] NCP United States, *Formed employees versus Coca Cola*, Final Statement, 21 December 2022, https://www.state.gov/specific-instance-between-leonce-safari-kajangu-anicet-tambwe-byadunia-and-francois-zabene-zagabe-and-the-coca-cola-company-regarding-events-in-the-democratic-republic-of-the-congo/ (last accessed 29 May 2024).

[63] NCP United States, *European Centre for Democracy and Human Rights* et al. *versus the Boeing Company and Lockheed Martin Corporation*, Final Statement, 18 November 2016 https://2009-2017.state.gov/e/eb/oecd/usncp/specificinstance/finalstatements/264328.htm (last accessed 29 May 2024).

4 Conclusion

In conclusion, the examined cases within the OECD NCP mechanisms shed light on the complex landscape of heightened corporate responsibilities in conflict-affected areas. The analysis provided practical insights into implementing heightened human rights due diligence, robust stakeholder engagement and responsible disengagement, showcasing instances of success and missed opportunities.

The review underscores the significance of tailoring corporate responsibilities to the specific challenges posed by conflict situations. It is evident that MNEs operating in such regions must go beyond general human rights due diligence and adopt conflict-sensitive approaches. Understanding the root causes of tensions, identifying key actors, and anticipating the impact of activities on armed conflicts are crucial steps in navigating these intricate environments.

Stakeholder engagement emerges as a pivotal element, with cases emphasizing the need for robust and meaningful interactions. The importance of transparent communication channels, both internal and external, is paramount. MNEs are urged to consider the broader implications of their operations on local communities, armed groups, and the overall socio-economic fabric.

The chapter also explored the responsibilities regarding responsible disengagement, acknowledging it as a critical facet of heightened corporate responsibility. However, cases reveal that disengagement decisions should be underpinned by thorough human rights due diligence to mitigate potential adverse impacts. The OECD Guidelines stress that disengagement should be a last resort, and even in challenging circumstances, a measure of due diligence should be carried out to address social and economic adverse impacts.

The analysis notably points out instances where certain NCPs missed opportunities to investigate cases related to human rights risks in conflict-affected areas. Cases brought before the Canadian and US NCPs underscore the importance of these mechanisms taking a proactive approach to addressing human rights abuses, especially in conflict zones. The rejection of cases against Coca-Cola and Boeing by the US NCP raises concerns about the efficacy of the Specific Instance procedure and its potential impact on global guidelines. Another case rejected by the Korean NCP highlighted a misinterpretation of the importance and focus on heightened due diligence. The NCP opted out of investigating the role of the military dictatorship, which should have been a key factor in requiring enhanced corporate responsibility.

In summary, the journey through these OECD cases underscores the evolving landscape of corporate responsibility in conflict-affected areas. The challenges are substantial, but the opportunities for positive impact remain. Implementing heightened responsibilities requires a nuanced and context-specific approach, with continuous stakeholder engagement and robust due diligence at its core. The cases serve as a valuable repository of lessons for both businesses and NCPs, offering a roadmap for navigating the intricate intersection of corporate activities, human rights, and conflict dynamics.

See Table 1.

Table 1 OECD cases that cover the heightened corporate human rights responsibility in conflict-affected areas

No	NCP (in alphabetical order)	OECD case	Completed date	Outcome
1	NCP Australia	Publish What you Pay Australia against Mallee Resources Limited	2 August 2023	Concluded
2	NCP Canada	Gold International Resources Corp. Ltd., at the Copper Polymetallic Mine at the Gyama Valley, Tibet Autonomous Region	13 May 2021	Concluded
3	NCP Canada	Centre for International Environmental Law (CIEL) et al. against GoldCorp	3 May 2011	Concluded
4	NCP Denmark	Christian Juhl versus Best seller AS	30 September 2022	Concluded
5	NCP Korea	Korean Civil Society in Solidarity with Rohingya, Korean Transnational Corporation Watch and Justice for Myanmar versus POSCO	14 July 2021	Rejected
6	NCP Netherlands	Employees of Philip Lighting versus Philips Lighting	25 October 2017	Concluded
7	NCP Netherlands	Niza et al. v CPH		Concluded
8	NCP Netherlands	Former employees versus Bralima and Heineken	18 August 2017	Concluded
9	NCP Norway	SOMO versus Telenor	29 August 2022	Concluded
10	NCP Norway	The Norwegian Support Committee for Western Sahara and Sjøvik AS	3 July 2013	Concluded
11	NCP Norway	Industri Energy and DNO ASA	9 April 2018	Concluded
12	NCP Norway	Lok Shakti Abhiyan, Korean transnational corporations watch, fair green and global alliance and forum for environment and development versus POSCO (South Korea), ABP/APG (Netherlands) and NBIM (Norway)	27 May 2013	Concluded
13	NCP Norway	Eight civil society organisations from South Sudan, Norway, Sweden, and the Netherlands versus Aker BP ASA and Aker ASA	Initial assessment 27 February 2023	Under review
14	NCP United Kingdom	Lawyers for Palestinian Human Rights versus JCB	12 November 2021	Concluded
15	NCP United Kingdom	Lawyers for Palestinian Human Rights versus G4S	March 2015	Concluded
16	NCP United Kingdom	RAID against DAS Air	17 July 2008	Concluded

(continued)

Table 1 (continued)

No	NCP (in alphabetical order)	OECD case	Completed date	Outcome
17	NCP United States	ECDHR et al. against Boeing Company and Lockheed Martin Corporation	18 November 2016	Rejected
18	NCP United States	4 individuals against Coca Cola	21 December 2022	Rejected

References

International documents:

Organisation for Economic Cooperation and Development (OECD) (2023) OECD guidelines for multinational enterprises on responsible business conduct, 8 June 2023, https://www.oecd-ilibrary.org/finance-and-investment/oecd-guidelines-for-multinational-enterprises-on-responsible-business-conduct_81f92357-en (last accessed 1 February 2024)

OECD (2016) OECD due diligence guidance for responsible supply chains of minerals from conflict-affected and high-risk areas. Third Edition, OECD Publishing, Paris. https://doi.org/10.1787/9789264252479-en (last accessed 25 April 2024)

OECD (2017) Session note—responsible disengagement. Global Forum on Responsible Business Conduct. https://mneguidelines.oecd.org/global-forum/2017-GFRBC-Session-Note-Responsible-Disengagement.pdf (last accessed 1 February 2024)

United Nations Development Programme (UNDP) and WGBHR (2022) Heightened Human Rights Due Diligence for Business in Conflict-Affected Contexts: A Guide

UNDP Report (2023) Responsible business conduct during war in Ukraine: context assessment study. https://www.undp.org/ukraine/publications/responsible-business-conduct-during-war-ukraine-context-assessment-study (last accessed 25 April 2024)

UN Human Rights Council (2011) UN guiding principles on business and human rights: implementing the united nation's "Protect, Respect and Remedy" Framework

UN OHCHR (2012) The Corporate Responsibility to Respect Human Rights: An Interpretative Guide, 33

UN Working Group on Business and Human Rights (WGBHR) (2020) Business, Human Rights and Conflict-Affected Regions: Towards Heightened Action, UN Doc A/75/212

Journal articles:

Aguirre D, Pietropaoli I (2023) Heightened human rights due diligence in practice: prohibiting or facilitating investment in conflict affected areas? J Human Rights Pract 2(15):541–558. https://doi.org/10.1093/jhuman/huad011(lastaccessed1February2024)

Azarova V (2018) Business and human rights in occupied territory: The UN database of business active in Israel's settlements. Cambridge University Press. pp 187–209

Tripathi S (2023) Business in conflict in anthony ewing teaching business and human rights. Elgar Guides to Teaching Chapter 30

Other sources:

Hill D (2014) Welcome to Guatemala: Goldmine Protestor beaten and burnt alive. Guardian. https://www.theguardian.com/environment/andes-to-the-amazon/2014/aug/12/guatemala-gold-mine-protester-beaten-burnt-alive (last accessed 5 March 2024)
OECD Watch (2021) Korean civil society in solidarity with Rohingya, Korean Transnational Corporation Watch and Justice for Myanmar versus POSCO International. https://www.oecdwatch.org/complaint/ktnc-watch-et-al-vs-posco-2/ (last accessed 25 April 2024)

Articulating Responsibility for Human Rights and the Environment in the Financial Sector: Outlook on the Concrete Cases of the OECD National Contact Points

Otgontuya Davaanyam

Abstract The chapter explores the responsibility of financial institutions (FIs) within the international business and human rights framework, specifically examining their role in addressing adverse human rights and environmental impacts stemming from their investments and their corresponding responsibility to mitigate and rectify such harm. FIs acting as pivotal facilitators and intermediaries, play a critical role in allocating funds that contribute to societal well-being. Despite the growing global emphasis on sustainability, there remains a notable absence of consistent international legal standards that hold FIs answerable for their impacts on human rights and the environment. This chapter advocates for FIs to take proactive measures to address both direct and indirect negative effects on human rights and the environment throughout their investment processes. By scrutinising OECD cases managed by National Contact Points (NCPs), the chapter seeks to explore how FIs can fulfill their obligations towards sustainability, human rights, and environmental preservation. Through an in-depth analysis of these cases, the chapter aims to illuminate the evolving landscape of corporate responsibility, potential regulatory advancements, and industry-wide norms that will shape the future of ethical business practices within the financial sector.

1 Introduction

With the challenges brought on by the global health crisis receding, the world now confronts a diverse array of urgent and interconnected global issues. These include emerging conflicts, persistent extreme poverty, economic slowdowns, rising inflation rates, the energy crisis, and the pressing climate emergency. At the 2023 Annual Meeting of the World Economic Forum in Davos, the UN Conference on Trade and

O. Davaanyam (✉)
Friedrich-Alexander-Universität Erlangen-Nürnberg, Erlangen, Germany
e-mail: Otgontuya.davaanyam@fau.de

O. Davaanyam and M. Krajewski (eds.), *Exploring Corporate Human Rights Responsibilities in OECD Case Law*, Interdisciplinary Studies in Human Rights 14,
https://doi.org/10.1007/978-3-031-75717-4_4

Development (UNCTAD) Chief emphasised the role of financial institutions (FIs) in providing more investment to get the Sustainable Development Goals (SDGs) back on track.[1] There is no doubt that FIs, as facilitators and intermediaries, play a crucial role in promoting, mobilising and distributing funds that bring the greatest benefits to society.[2] As a result of public pressure and the gradual shift in global perceptions of sustainability, global actors in the financial markets have been actively engaged in the development of various initiatives that address environmental and social risks and the potential opportunities to accelerate progress on the SDGs.[3] Although a growing number of governmental, voluntary and corporate-led efforts have been developed, there is still a lack of an international law-based approach to the responsibility of FIs regarding their direct and indirect impacts on human rights and the environment.[4] Despite progress in promoting human rights in the context of investment activities, the legal basis for investment decisions is largely inconsistent with the concept of corporate human rights responsibility under the UN Guiding Principles on Business and Human Rights (UNGPs) and the Organisation for Economic Co-operation and Development (OECD) Guidelines for Multinational Enterprises on Responsible Business Conduct (OECD Guidelines or Guidelines), and is rarely enforced.[5] Although the Office of the United Nations High Commissioner for Human Rights (OHCHR) and the OECD have produced guidance documents that explain the responsibilities of FIs when they cause, contribute to or have a direct link to human rights and environmental impacts, there are still specific circumstances in which it can be difficult to determine what responsibilities and actions they are expected to take when addressing, preventing and remedying direct and indirect

[1] UN Conference on Trade and Development (UNCTAD) (2023), More investment needed to get global goals back on track, says UNCTAD chief, https://unctad.org/news/more-investment-needed-get-global-goals-back-track-says-unctad-chief-0 (last accessed 14 April 2023).

[2] Business for Society (BSR) (2022), *Human Rights Roadmap for Transforming Finance, Priorities for Progress in the Next Decade for the Implementation of the UN Guiding Principles on Business and Human Rights, Report 2022*, https://www.bsr.org/en/reports/human-rights-roadmap-for-transforming-finance (last accessed 27 May 2024), p. 4.

[3] For example, the UN Principles for Responsible Investment (PRI) (2023), *The Principles for Responsible Investment Reporting Framework* (23 January 2023) https://www.unpri.org/about-us/what-are-the-principles-for-responsible-investment (last accessed 26 April 2023); Investor Alliance for Human Rights (2020), *Investor Toolkit on Human Rights,* New York, May 2020, https://investorsforhumanrights.org/publications/investor-toolkit-human-rights (last accessed 27 May 2024); Task force on Climate-related Financial Disclosure (TCFD) (2017), *Recommendations of Task Force on Climate-related Disclosure*, Final Report, June 2017, https://www.fsb-tcfd.org/recommendations/ (last accessed 27 May 2024); Glasgow Financial Alliance for Net Zero (GFANZ) (2022), *Towards a Global Baseline for Net-zero Transition Planning*, updated 1 November 2022, https://assets.bbhub.io/company/sites/63/2022/10/GFANZ_Towards-a-Global-Baseline-for-Net-Zero-Transition-Planning_November2022.pdf (last accessed 27 May 2024).

[4] Macchi and Bernaz (2021), p. 8391.

[5] UN Working Group on Business and Human Rights (WGBHR) (2021), *Taking stock of investor implementation of the UN Guiding Principles on Business and Human Rights.* Addendum report of the Working Group on the issue of human rights and transnational corporations and other business enterprises corporations A/HRC/47/39/Add.2, II, Geneva, June 2021.

impacts.[6] Moreover, the most significant impacts that FIs have on human rights and the environment are indirect.[7] Given the indirect impacts caused and contributed to by the companies in which they invest, it is unclear how FIs can be held accountable for mitigating these impacts. Moreover, FIs' vague understanding of their obligations may lead them to ignore sustainability and human rights, and even foster a culture where human rights abuses are tolerated.[8]

In this chapter, I argue that FIs (including asset owners, asset managers, development finance institutions, banks and insurers) not only have a duty to use all possible means (in their case, leverage) to address their direct and especially indirect negative impacts on human rights and the environment in their investment chain but also to contribute to an enabling environment that promotes economic equality, the SDGs and environmental sustainability. In doing so, their responsibility should not only be to develop sustainable policies and conduct human rights due diligence on their investment portfolio, but also to actively influence companies and provide leadership on human rights and the environment. For this reason, this chapter seeks to explicitly conceptualise the responsibilities of FIs in relation to sustainability to outline the key elements they should consider in order to fulfil their role concerning human rights and the environment. This chapter focuses on specific cases addressed by National Contact Points (NCPs) dealing with the responsibility of FIs for human rights and the environment. Like UNGPs, OECD Guidelines are essential for promoting responsible business conduct globally. The National Contact Points (NCPs) handle non-compliance cases, offering redress for human rights abuses. NCP decisions set standards for corporate responsibility and best practices, despite criticisms of limited redress. Since the update of the OECD Guidelines in 2011, more than 20 cases dealing with the responsibility of financial actors have been examined under the NCP case handling system (OECD Cases).[9] In short, the paper will answer the following research question: How can the responsibility of FIs to address human rights and environmental impacts in their activities be conceptualised by analysing the OECD cases?

First, this chapter will provide an overview of current international instruments and some widely accepted guidelines based on multi-stakeholder initiatives that define the human rights obligations of FIs in relation to their direct and indirect links to corporate human rights abuses. The second part of our discussion will focus on practice by examining the OECD cases filed with the NCP against several financial organisations for their alleged links to negative environmental and human rights impacts. The focus will be on the activities of the FIs, their stance on their impacts and accountability,

---

[6] OHCHR (2017), *Response to Request from BankTrack for Advice Regarding the Application of the UN Guiding Principles on Business and Human Rights in the context of the Banking Sector*, adopted 12 june 2017, p. 5; OECD (2017), *OECD Responsible business conduct for institutional investors: Key considerations for due diligence under the OECD Guidelines for Multinational Enterprises*; Van Ho (2021), pp. 625, 629.

[7] UNEP (2021) Principles for Responsible Banking Guidance Document, https://wedocs.unep.org/handle/20.500.11822/32227 (last accessed 27 May 2024), p. 21.

[8] Evans (2016), p. 327.

[9] See the Table in Annex.

and the actual outcomes of the cases. Third, the chapter discusses what these OECD cases mean for the future regulatory developments on FIs' responsibility towards human rights and the environment, new litigation and proceedings against FIs, as well as the industry-wide standards.

2 Current Challenges in the International Framework Governing the Responsibilities of FIs for Human Rights and the Environment

This section outlines the existing responsibilities of FIs for human rights and the environment as well as to highlight the gaps in international soft law relating to FIs' responsibilities by assessing the effectiveness of current legal instruments and examining their suitability for effective implementation. This requires drawing on relevant soft law instruments, such as the UNGPs, the OECD Guidelines, the UN Environment Programme Principles for Responsible Banking Guidance Document (UNEP Guidance document), and the series of guidance documents produced by the OECD and the OHCHR.[10] In addition, other widely recognised instruments International Finance Corporation's Performance Standard on Environmental and Social Sustainability (IFC Performance Standard), and multi-stakeholder-based instruments such as the Thun Group Discussion Paper and the Equator Principles were analysed.[11] Furthermore, this section will expand on prior academic and practitioner studies in addition to primary sources, with particular attention on FIs, human rights, and the environment.[12]

The UNGPs and the OECD Guidelines are the instruments that detail corporate responsibility for human rights and the environment and have the greatest degree

---

[10] HRC (2011), *United Nations Guiding Principles on Business and Human Rights* (UNGPs), A/HRC/17/31, adopted 16 June 2011; OECD (2023), *OECD Guidelines on Multinational Enterprises on Responsible Business Conduct,* adopted 8 June 2023, Commentary; UNEP (2021), *Principles for Responsible Banking' Guidance Document*, p. 21; OHCHR (2017), *Response to Request from BankTrack for Advice Regarding the Application of the UN Guiding Principles on Business and Human Rights in the context of the Banking Sector,* p. 5; OECD (2017), *OECD Responsible business conduct for institutional investors: Key considerations for due diligence under the OECD Guidelines for Multinational Enterprises*; OHCHR (2013a, b), *The application of the Guiding Principles on Business and Human Rights to minority shareholdings of institutional investors*, adopted 26 April 2013; OHCHR (2013a, b), *Advise regarding the UNGPs and the Finance Sector' Response to the request from the Chair of the OECD Working Party on Responsible Business Conduct*; OECD (2019), *Due Diligence for Responsible Corporate Lending and Securities Underwriting: Key considerations for banks implementing the OECD Guidelines for Multinational Enterprises* OECD Publishing, Paris; OECD (2022), *Responsible business conduct due diligence for project and asset finance transactions*, OECD Publishing, Paris, p. 14.

[11] IFC (2012), *Performance standard on Social and Environmental Sustainability*, https://www.ifc.org/en/insights-reports/2012/ifc-performance-standards (last accessed 27 May 2024).

[12] For example, Macchi and Bernaz (2021), p. 8391; Van Ho (2021), pp. 625, 629; Bordignon (2022), p. 381; Van Ho and Alshaleel (2018), p. 1, 2; Bohoslavsky (2020), pp. 203, 208.

of accreditation and international recognition. The UNGPs and the OECD Guidelines require all businesses, including FIs, to respect human rights in their operations by identifying, preventing and mitigating actual and potential adverse human rights impacts.[13] In addition, they set out what is expected of companies when they are directly linked to or contribute to adverse impacts through their economic interactions. However, in both cases, the role of FIs in relation to human rights and the environment is not adequately conceptualised. The current stipulation on corporate responsibility for due diligence and remedial action under the UNGPs and the OECD remain broad and limited in their ability to clearly define the involvement of FIs in human rights abuses and the associated responsibilities that must be charged as a result of such involvement. Moreover, as Van Ho pointed out, neither instrument fully captured the concepts of corporate responsibility as they only vaguely defined their involvement in harm.[14]

Furthermore, within the realm of multinational enterprises (MNEs), FIs worldwide are increasingly expected not only avoid causing harm but also actively contribute to the SDGs by aligning their investment decisions with principles of human rights and environmental sustainability. According to a recent publication by the UN Working Group on Business and Human Rights (WGBHR), institutional investors should link their policies, which encompass all their investment activities, to the SDGs and focus on achieving sustainable economic development.[15] In contrast to the UNGPs, the OECD Guidelines set explicit expectations for MNEs to contribute to the SDGs, and this regulation could be further developed to create a more explicit responsibility of FIs to contribute to the SDGs.[16] Building on the previous academic literature of corporate involvement in human rights abuses, this chapter argues that FIs, given their strong power or influence over corporations, should be responsible for redressing harm even if they have passively participated in human rights abuses.[17] In addition, the chapter contends that the responsibility of FIs for human rights and environmental impacts has both substantive and procedural aspects and needs to be conceptualised in distinct ways for effective implementation. To this end, this section is divided into three parts to clarify the analysis of the definition of FIs' involvement in human rights violations, their associated responsibility for remedial action arising from such involvement, and their responsibility towards the SDGs.

---

[13] OHCHR (2013a, b), *The application of the Guiding Principles on Business and Human Rights to minority shareholdings of institutional investors*, 26 April 2013.

[14] Van Ho (2021), pp. 625, 629.

[15] WGBHR (2021), *Taking stock of investor implementation of the UN Guiding Principles on Business and Human Rights*. Addendum report of the Working Group on the issue of human rights and transnational corporations and other business enterprises corporations A/HRC/47/39/Add.2, III, Geneva, June 2021.

[16] OECD (2017), *OECD Responsible business conduct for institutional investors: Key considerations for due diligence under the OECD Guidelines for Multinational Enterprises* Chapter II (1) states that Enterprises should contribute to economic, environmental and social progress with a view to achieving sustainable development.

[17] Macchi and Bernaz (2021), p. 8391; Van Ho (2021), pp. 625, 629. Bordignon (2022), p. 381.

2.1 The Analysis of the Involvement of FIs in Adverse Impacts

To identify which actions are required from FIs to mitigate and remediate adverse human rights impacts, it is necessary to determine how FIs are involved in these impacts. Sadly, the complexity of their relationship with companies makes it difficult to draw the line as to whether FI is directly linked to or has contributed to human rights abuses.[18] Furthermore, the recently adopted EU Corporate Sustainability Due Diligence Directive (EU CSDDD) recognizes the adverse impacts on human rights by financial institutions and is planning to adopt tailored due diligence requirements aligned with the directive for financial institutions.[19] Also, the OECD and the OHCHR have produced guidance documents that strive to reconcile investment practices with the concept of UNGPs.[20] OHCHR stated that although FIs are often directly involved in human rights abuses, it can be argued that they contribute to perpetuating the problem if they do not mitigate human rights impacts and continue to do business with the company.[21] In their response to BankTrack,[22] drawing on the UNGPs' commentary on the contribution, they attempt to conceptualise the different types of contributions a bank makes to human rights violations by elaborating on the 'act of facilitation' and the 'act of incentivisation'.[23] Specifically, a bank may facilitate when it knows or should have known that there are human rights risks associated with the company in which it invests, but fails to request, encourage or assist the client to avoid or mitigate these risks.[24] The term 'incentive' is somewhat complicated as it relates to the bank's action or inaction concerning the conduct of

---

[18] OECD (2014), *Due diligence in the financial sector: adverse impacts directly linked to financial sector operations, products or services by a business relationship' Global Forum on Responsible Business Conduct*, p. 9.

[19] WGBHR (2023), *Statement by the United Nations Working Group on Business and Human Rights: "Financial Sector and the European Union Corporate Sustainability Due Diligence Directive"*, adopted 12 July 2023.

[20] OHCHR (2017), *Response to Request from BankTrack for Advice Regarding the Application of the UN Guiding Principles on Business and Human Rights in the context of the Banking Sector*, p. 5; OECD (2017), *Responsible business conduct for institutional investors: Key considerations for due diligence under the OECD Guidelines for Multinational Enterprises.*

[21] OHCHR (2017), *Response to Request from BankTrack for Advice Regarding the Application of the UN Guiding Principles on Business and Human Rights in the context of the Banking Sector,* p. 5.

[22] BankTrack is an international organization dedicated to tracking, campaigning, and supporting NGOs focused on private sector commercial banks and the activities they finance.

[23] OHCHR (2017), *Response to Request from BankTrack for Advice Regarding the Application of the UN Guiding Principles on Business and Human Rights in the context of the Banking Sector,* p. 8.

[24] OHCHR (2017), *Response to Request from BankTrack for Advice Regarding the Application of the UN Guiding Principles on Business and Human Rights in the context of the Banking Sector,* p. 8.

human rights abuse.[25] In reviewing OHCHR's response to BankTrack, Van Ho noted that the examples of incentives do not make clear sense because the meaning of the act of incentivising could be the cause and not the contribution.[26] Yet, other UN and the OECD guidance documents, as well as other multi-stakeholder instruments, followed this interpretation and emphasised the act of facilitating and incentivising under the context of contributing to adverse impacts.[27] This approach, however, still lacks an explanation for the apparent distinction between contribution and linkage. The distinction between linkage and contribution is highly significant because if FIs are seen as contributors, they would be responsible for remediating the negative impact.[28] As Ruggie noted, linkage and contribution are on a continuum, and considering his explanation, it appears that this depends to a significant extent on the inaction and continued negligence of FIs towards the associated negative impacts.[29]

Therefore, there is a need to further develop the conceptualisation of potential factors that could help determine whether FIs incentivise or facilitate corporate human rights abuses. Perhaps the solution could be to look at the involvement of financial intermediaries from a different perspective.[30] Van Ho held that the company's responsibility for the remedy should be defined by its power and independence to facilitate or prevent harm.[31] In light of the above, the current concept of FIs in terms of human rights and accountability could be reconceptualised by taking into account their power and their actual and potential ability to influence companies (leverage) to mitigate and remedy human rights violations. Otherwise, FIs benefit from being caught between this blurred line, and without a clearer understanding of their role in negative impacts, they are unlikely to actively contribute to remedying human rights violations. The in-depth analysis of some OECD cases dealing with the responsibility of FIs for human rights and the environment could help to capture the real situations where FIs are involved in human rights abuses by ignoring the negative human rights impacts, failing to act or requiring the companies in which they invest to remedy the harms.

---

[25] OHCHR (2017), *Response to Request from BankTrack for Advice Regarding the Application of the UN Guiding Principles on Business and Human Rights in the context of the Banking Sector,* p. 8.

[26] Van Ho (2021), p. 643.

[27] For instance, OECD (2022), *OECD Responsible business conduct due diligence for project and asset finance transactions,* p. 14; UN PRI and UN Global Compact (2020), *Why and how investors should act on human rights,* https://www.unpri.org/human-rights/why-and-how-investors-should-act-on-human-rights/6636.article (last accessed 27 May 2024).

[28] Ruggie (2017), *Comments on Thun Group of Banks Discussion Paper on the Implications of UN Guiding Principles 13 & 17.* In a Corporate and Investment Banking Context. Harvard Kennedy School, 21 February 2017.

[29] Ruggie (2017), *Comments on Thun Group of Banks Discussion Paper on the Implications of UN Guiding Principles 13 & 17.* In a Corporate and Investment Banking Context. Harvard Kennedy School, 21 February 2017, p. 2.

[30] Van Ho (2021), p. 647.

[31] Van Ho (2021), p. 648.

2.2 The Analysis of FIs' Responsibilities to Address the Adverse Impacts

The existing framework for financial institutions (FIs) falls short in fully addressing their human rights and environmental responsibilities.[32] While FIs are required to conduct human rights due diligence under the UNGPs and OECD Guidelines,[33] these standards are not tailored enough to their financial activities. The concept of investors' sustainability-related responsibilities led to the development of the Environmental, Social, and Governance (ESG) framework in the financial market.[34] However, current ESG practices do not fully align with international human rights standards, as they primarily focus on risks to investors rather than broader societal impacts.[35] ESG practice is often criticized for focusing solely on risks to investors and investments, neglecting broader societal impacts.[36] In response to this, the recent EU regulation on sustainability-related disclosure introduced the concept of 'double materiality,' emphasizing the human rights and environmental risks posed by investments rather than just financial risks to investors.[37]

To address this gap, recent guidance documents from the OECD and WGBHR provide recommendations for FIs to enhance their human rights due diligence.[38] These documents provide guidance on human rights due diligence obligations for FIs.[39] For instance, the WGBHR released a report on 'rights-respected investing' tailored for institutional investors, emphasizing proactive steps like engaging with

---

[32] Macchi and Bernaz (2021), p. 8391.

[33] HRC (2011), *United Nations Guiding Principles on Business and Human Rights (UNGPs)*, A/HRC/17/31, adopted 16 June 2011, Principle 17; OECD (2023), *OECD Guidelines on Multinational Enterprises on Responsible Business Conduct*, Commentary on General Policies, para 19 and 20.

[34] Business for Society (BSR) (2022), *Human Rights Roadmap for Transforming Finance, Priorities for Progress in the Next Decade for the Implementation of the UN Guiding Principles on Business and Human Rights, Report 2022*, https://www.bsr.org/en/reports/human-rights-roadmap-for-transforming-finance (last accessed 27 May 2024), pp. 5, 6.

[35] WGBHR (2021), *Taking stock of investor implementation of the UN Guiding Principles on Business and Human Rights.* Addendum report of the Working Group on the issue of human rights and transnational corporations and other business enterprises corporations A/HRC/47/39/Add.2, II, Geneva, June 2021.

[36] Mohr, Riquelme, Muñoz Quick (2022) *Double Materiality for Financial Institutions Survey Findings and Recommendations*, BSR. https://www.bsr.org/reports/BSR_Issue_Brief_Materiality_Survey_December_2022_final.pdf (last accessed 7 April 2023).

[37] Regulation (EU) 2019/2088 on sustainability-related disclosures in the financial services sector, OJ L317/1.

[38] WGBHR (2021), *Taking stock of investor implementation of the UN Guiding Principles on Business and Human Rights.* Addendum report of the Working Group on the issue of human rights and transnational corporations and other business enterprises corporations, A/HRC/47/39/Add.2, II., Geneva, June 2021; OECD (2017), *Responsible business conduct for institutional investors: Key considerations for due diligence under the OECD Guidelines for Multinational Enterprises.*

[39] WGBHR (2021), *Taking stock of investor implementation of the UN Guiding Principles on Business and Human Rights.* Addendum report of the Working Group on the issue of human rights and transnational corporations and other business enterprises corporations, A/HRC/47/39/Add.2,

investee companies, leveraging influence, and collaborating with stakeholders to mitigate negative impacts.[40] The OECD's recent policy paper on Responsible Business Conduct Due Diligence for FIs in project and asset finance transactions suggests a risk-based due diligence approach, including scoping, screening, and operating an 'early warning system' to assess and address human rights and environmental risks early on in investments. This system involves engaging with stakeholders before projects begin to anticipate and manage potential risks.[41]

In these recent documents focusing on FI's human rights and environmental responsibilities, leverage is emphasized as a key tool to address and mitigate human rights violations. While leverage is not a legal obligation, it is considered a significant responsibility under the UNGPs and OECD Guidelines.[42] Failure to use leverage effectively could result in FIs not meeting their human rights due diligence responsibilities. The concept of leverage as a remedial responsibility is not extensively elaborated in the UNGPs or OECD Guidelines. Companies lacking leverage are encouraged to seek ways to increase it, such as through capacity building or collaboration with other entities.[43] The WGBHR report underscores the importance of leveraging influence, recommending actions like engaging in dialogue with companies and participating in multi-stakeholder initiatives to uphold human rights standards in operations.[44] Instruments like the UNEP Guidance Document also stress the need for FIs to engage with clients, which can be seen as leveraging influence in line with the UNGPs and OECD Guidelines.[45]

FIs are expected to interact with clients, potentially leveraging their influence in line with the UNGPs and OECD Guidelines.[46] For instance, UNEP Guidelines Principle 3 suggests that banks identify opportunities to support clients, engage proactively on sustainability commitments, raise awareness, and form partnerships, actions that can be viewed as leveraging their influence effectively.[47]

II, Geneva, June 2021; OECD (2017), *Responsible business conduct for institutional investors: Key considerations for due diligence under the OECD Guidelines for Multinational Enterprises.*

[40] WGBHR (2021), *Taking stock of investor implementation of the UN Guiding Principles on Business and Human Rights.* Addendum report of the Working Group on the issue of human rights and transnational corporations and other business enterprises corporations, A/HRC/47/39/Add.2, II., Geneva, June 2021, p. 14.

[41] OECD (2022), *Responsible business conduct due diligence for project and asset finance transactions*, OECD Publishing, Paris, p. 14.

[42] Bordignon (2022), p. 393.

[43] HRC (2011), *United Nations Guiding Principles on Business and Human Rights* (UNGPs), A/HRC/17/31, Principle 19, Commentary.

[44] WGBHR (2021), *Taking stock of investor implementation of the UN Guiding Principles on Business and Human Rights.* Addendum report of the Working Group on the issue of human rights and transnational corporations and other business enterprises corporations, A/HRC/47/39/Add.2, II, Geneva, June 2021, p. 6.

[45] UNEP (2021), Principles for Responsible Banking' Guidance Document, p. 21.

[46] UNEP (2021), Principles for Responsible Banking' Guidance Document, p. 21.

[47] UNEP (2021), Principles for Responsible Banking' Guidance Document, p. 21.

The Equator Principles and IFC Performance Standards demonstrate how financial institutions (FIs) can leverage their influence to fulfill due diligence obligations regarding human rights and the environment.[48] While these standards are not definitive in outlining divestment responsibilities, they serve as tools for FIs to manage risks and impacts. The Equator Principles, for example, emphasize partnering with clients to address environmental and social risks and encourage thorough impact assessments.[49] However, both frameworks lack clear guidance on divestment as a last resort when leverage fails. Divestment is crucial for mitigating negative impacts, yet current practices among FIs vary, with some choosing to continue investments despite serious human rights risks without adequate stakeholder communication. The OECD provides detailed guidance on divestment, recommending transparency and ongoing monitoring if maintaining a relationship with a problematic entity.[50]

While practical recommendations from organizations like WGBHR and the OECD are important for shaping FIs' responsibilities, they often lack normative and substantive elements to solidify these obligations. Key responsibilities like leveraging influence and divestment are sometimes presented as optional suggestions rather than essential requirements. To strengthen these responsibilities, international law should reformulate them with clear substantive and procedural aspects. Substantive rules define lawful conduct, while procedural rules govern their implementation. Breaches of procedural rules can lead to secondary obligations stemming from substantive breaches.[51] FIs' responsibilities under the UNGPs and OECD Guidelines, such as human rights due diligence and stakeholder engagement, can be seen as substantive rules, while actions like leveraging influence and publishing impact assessments have procedural aspects.. Moreover, as Morgera argued, a process-oriented approach is crucial to ensure effective implementation of these measures.[52] Binding laws and regulations should further define these responsibilities as procedural requirements to enhance corporate human rights accountability and address risks effectively. Legally binding instruments like the EU Regulation on sustainability-related disclosure can detail FIs' sustainability responsibilities in addressing human rights and environmental risks.[53]

---

[48] Equator Principles (2020), *Equator Principles: A financial industry benchmark for determining, assessing and managing environmental and social risk in project*; IFC (2012), *Performance standard on Social and Environmental Sustainability*, https://www.ifc.org/en/insights-reports/2012/ifc-performance-standards (last accessed 27 May 2024).

[49] Equator Principles (2020) *Equator Principles: A financial industry benchmark for determining, assessing and managing environmental and social risk in projects*, Principle 3.

[50] OECD (2022), *Responsible business conduct due diligence for project and asset finance transactions*, 14 OECD Publishing, Paris, p. 47.

[51] Talmon (2012), pp. 979, 981.

[52] Morgera (2020), p. 230.

[53] Regulation (EU) 2019/2088 on sustainability-related disclosures in the financial services sector, OJ L317/1.

2.3 The FIs' Responsibility Towards the SDGs and Promoting the Sustainable Economic Development

As mentioned above, FIs expect that they will contribute to the achievement of the SDGs. This expectation is formally elaborated in the OECD Guidelines. Chapter 2, Sect. 1 of the Guidelines states that MNEs should contribute to economic, environmental and social progress towards sustainable development in their activities in a host country.[54] In their commentary, the OECD Guidelines also clarify that there should be no contradiction between the activities of MNEs and sustainable development.[55] This concept of the responsibility of MNEs to contribute to the SDGs in their host country goes beyond the concept of respect for human rights under the UNGPs. It calls on MNEs, including FIs, to align their investment decisions with the SDGs. This concept of responsibility is timely and needs further clarification as recent reports and initiatives call on FIs to abandon their practice of 'short-termism' and acknowledge their impact on the economy and society.[56] Short-termism, as the WGBHR report notes, is a pressure that comes from investors, especially hedge funds, some types of activist investors and private equity firms, whose main objective is to make short-term financial gains and then move on.[57] The recent initiatives of the WBA, which has begun to rate the 400 global FIs on their commitment to achieving the SDG targets.[58] Specifically, global FIs were rated on whether they provide loans and investments in developing countries to address economic inequality.[59] According to the result of their 2022 ranking, only 2 percent of global FIs say they invest in low-income countries, SMEs and other excluded groups.[60] This initiative is a good start as it recognises the role of FIs in promoting a sustainable economy in the world, going beyond assessing their due diligence and engagement with investee companies. Following these initiatives, the current regulations on FIs, human rights and the environment need to further strengthen these concepts of responsibility towards the SDGs. Some OECD cases also shed light on whether companies are aligning their decisions and activities to promote the SDGs which are discussed in the following section.

---

[54] OECD (2023), *OECD Guidelines on Multinational Enterprises on Responsible Business Conduct, Commentary*; OECD Publishing: Paris, France, Chapter 2(1).

[55] OECD (2023), *OECD Guidelines on Multinational Enterprises on Responsible Business Conduct, Commentary*; OECD Publishing: Paris, France.

[56] WGBHR (2021), *Taking stock of investor implementation of the UN Guiding Principles on Business and Human Rights.* Addendum report of the Working Group on the issue of human rights and transnational corporations and other business enterprises corporations, A/HRC/47/39/Add.2, II, Geneva, June 2021.

[57] WGBHR (2021), *Taking stock of investor implementation of the UN Guiding Principles on Business and Human Rights* Addendum report of the Working Group on the issue of human rights and transnational corporations and other business enterprises corporations, A/HRC/47/39/Add.2, II, Geneva, June 2021.

[58] World Benchmarking Alliance (WBA) (2021) *Financial System Benchmark Methodology.*

[59] WBA (2021), *Financial System Benchmark Methodology*, p. 51.

[60] WBA (2021), *Financial System Benchmark Methodology*, p. 51.

3 The Responsibility of FIs for Human Rights and the Environment Developed in OECD Case Law

This section analyses OECD cases, relevant to the FIs and examined by NCPs between 2011 and 2022, to assess how the international standards discussed in the previous chapter can be illustrated in specific circumstances.[61] The cases listed in Appendix were handled by various NCPs, including those of Australia, Denmark, France, Japan, Korea, the Netherlands, Norway, Poland, Switzerland, the United Kingdom and the United States, and specifically target FIs accused of being linked to corporate human rights abuses and environmental damages through their financial services. In addition, these cases target different types of FIs, such as asset owners (including pension funds, development finance institutions and sovereign wealth funds), asset managers (including investment advisors), banks and insurance companies. Moreover, most FIs are headquartered in the global North, mainly in Europe and the United States of America. Although FIs have been linked to various human rights violations, most of the cases are about the involvement of FIs in climate change, environmental degradation and human rights violations against indigenous and local communities.

Some of these cases can serve as setting best examples for FIs to fulfil their human rights due diligence responsibilities and engage with stakeholders. In this context, "best examples" refers to exemplary instances where investors have demonstrated a proactive and effective approach in implementing the OECD Guidelines for Multinational Enterprises. These cases illustrate how investors can exceed the basic expectations outlined in the Guidelines by taking additional steps to address complaints and leverage their influence to promote responsible business conduct. Some cases can be seen as lessons for the future on how existing laws and regulations can be further developed so that FIs can effectively consider human rights and environmental impacts. Only four of the total cases were considered satisfactorily resolved in terms of the outcome leading to an actual remedy. In some cases, an agreement was reached, but it is not sufficient to analyse whether a successful remedy was achieved without examining the follow-up report. In contrast, these cases are significant because they help to ensure that the norms of international financial actors remain coherent, even though in some cases no agreement was reached that would have led to a solution. This is because the NCPs clarified in their final statement the application of the OECD Guidelines to FIs and explicitly expected FIs to take human rights and environmental concerns into account in their operations. In addition, several global financial actors including ANZ, ING and NBIM, have received several complaints. It may therefore be helpful to examine how these FIs have changed and evolved in relation to their human rights and environmental obligations. This chapter consists of two parts: first, an analysis of some OECD cases (some with successful outcomes) that set out expectations for FIs concerning human rights and the environment that go beyond the requirements of the UNGPs and the

[61] See the Table in Annex.

OECD Guidelines; second, some NCP decisions that illustrate current challenges to the human rights and environmental responsibilities of FIs in the international context that need to be addressed.

3.1 OECD Cases Illustrating the Responsibility of Financial Institutions for Human Rights and the Environment

In some notable cases, NCPs have clarified how the OECD Guidelines apply to the financial activities of FIs and have further elaborated on their responsibilities towards human rights and the environment by setting out clear expectations for managing the human rights risks directly associated with their financial products and services. Some of these cases, including the case against Government Pension Fund Global's Norwegian Bank Investment Management (NBIM) under the Norwegian NCP and the case against the Dutch pension fund ABP and its pension manager APG (ABP/APG) and Rabobank under the Dutch NCP from 2014 to 2017, were developed to conceptualise the responsibilities of FIs towards human rights when detailed interpretation and guidance did not yet exist.[62] Building on the analysis of these cases, the current guidance documents, including the OECD and OHCHR documents, had been developed. However, as mentioned above, these guidance documents were developed to only provide FIs with practical guidance on how to deal with human rights risks in the context of their financial activities. They lack normative content and substantive elements that do not sufficiently interpret their responsibilities from the perspective of international law. Moreover, these cases are not sufficiently analysed and discussed in the discourse on business and human rights to question the implications of these cases for the future development of the responsibilities of FIs in the context of international human rights and environmental law.

The cases against ABP/APG and NBIM in the Dutch and Norwegian NCPs were the first cases to assert that corporate human rights responsibilities under the OECD Guidelines apply to all investors, including minority shareholders, even if they own a very small stake in the company. In these cases, clear expectations have been formulated for FIs when they are directly linked to the company causing human rights violations. In particular, these cases call for FIs to perform their own human

[62] NCP Netherlands, *Lok Shakti Abhiyan, KTNC Watch, Fair Green and Global Alliance, Forum for Environment and Development vs. ABP/APG*, Final Statement, 18 November 2013, https://www.oecdguidelines.nl/latest/news/2013/9/18/publication-final-statement-posco-a.o.---lok-shakti-abhiyan-a.o (last accessed 27 May 2024); NCP Norway, *Lok Shakti Abhiyan, Korean Transnational Corporations Watch, Fair Green And Global Alliance And Forum For Environment And Development vs. Posco (South Korea), ABP/ABP (Netherlands) and NBIM (Norway)*, Final Statement, 27 May 2013, https://files.nettsteder.regjeringen.no/wpuploads01/blogs.dir/263/files/2013/12/nbim_final.pdf (last accessed 27 May 2024); NCP Netherlands, *Friends of the Earth Europe and Friends of the Earth Netherlands/Milieudefensie vs. Rabobank*, Final Statement, 15 January 2016, https://www.oecdguidelines.nl/notifications/documents/publication/2016/1/15/fs-foe-milieudefensie-rabobank (last accessed 27 May 2024).

rights due diligence on their investment portfolios and strongly emphasises the use of leverage. In the case of NBIM in particular, NBIM responded to the Norwegian NCP that the Guidelines did not apply to them as a minority shareholder (in NBIM's case, NBIM held only 0.9 per cent of POSCO's shares at the time).[63] However, the Norwegian NCP concluded that NBIM was directly linked to the alleged human rights violations by POSCO through its business relationships and was obliged under both the UNGPs and the Guidelines.[64] It is therefore required to use leverage, which is the appropriate action when the company is directly linked to human rights violations. Furthermore, in explaining the use of leverage, the NCP notes that the extent of leverage cannot automatically be defined by the percentage of ownership.[65] The NCP has attempted to assess NBIM's approaches to the use of leverage and asks the company to provide information on strategies or indicators to determine when and how it should engage with a company for its human rights impacts.[66] While the NCP recognises that it may not be possible for institutional investors to assess the negative impacts of every company in their investment portfolio, it recommends that the NBIM, alone or in collaboration with other institutions, use a variety of approaches to increase its leverage to the company.[67] Similarly, the Dutch NCP concluded that the size of the shares is not determinative of whether there is a business relationship within the meaning of the UNGPs and given that [... The (large overall) size of its fund, its prominent role in international sustainable financing and its cooperation (including coalitions) with other similar funds ...] outweighs its small shareholding in POSCO.[68] This is significant in that the Dutch NCP believed that ABP/APG must

[63] NCP Netherlands, *Lok Shakti Abhiyan, KTNC Watch, Fair Green and Global Alliance, Forum for Environment and Development vs. ABP/APG*, Final Statement, 18 November 2013, p. 5, https://www.oecdguidelines.nl/latest/news/2013/9/18/publication-final-statement-posco-a.o.---lok-shakti-abhiyan-a.o (last accessed 27 May 2024).

[64] NCP Norway, *Lok Shakti Abhiyan, Korean Transnational Corporations Watch, Fair Green And Global Alliance And Forum For Environment And Development vs. Posco (South Korea), ABP/ABP (Netherlands) and NBIM (Norway)*, Final Statement, 27 May 2013, p. 35, https://files.nettsteder.regjeringen.no/wpuploads01/blogs.dir/263/files/2013/12/nbim_final.pdf (last accessed 27 May 2024).

[65] NCP Norway, *Lok Shakti Abhiyan, Korean Transnational Corporations Watch, Fair Green And Global Alliance And Forum For Environment And Development vs. Posco (South Korea), ABP/ABP (Netherlands) and NBIM (Norway)*, Final Statement, 27 May 2013, p. 35, https://files.nettsteder.regjeringen.no/wpuploads01/blogs.dir/263/files/2013/12/nbim_final.pdf (last accessed 27 May 2024).

[66] NCP Norway, *Lok Shakti Abhiyan, Korean Transnational Corporations Watch, Fair Green And Global Alliance And Forum For Environment And Development vs. Posco (South Korea), ABP/ABP (Netherlands) and NBIM (Norway)*, Final Statement, 27 May 2013, p. 35, https://files.nettsteder.regjeringen.no/wpuploads01/blogs.dir/263/files/2013/12/nbim_final.pdf (last accessed 27 May 2024).

[67] NCP Norway, *Lok Shakti Abhiyan, Korean Transnational Corporations Watch, Fair Green And Global Alliance And Forum For Environment And Development vs. Posco (South Korea), ABP/ABP (Netherlands) and NBIM (Norway)*, Final Statement, 27 May 2013, pp. 35–36, https://files.nettsteder.regjeringen.no/wpuploads01/blogs.dir/263/files/2013/12/nbim_final.pdf (last accessed 27 May 2024).

[68] NCP Netherlands, *Lok Shakti Abhiyan, KTNC Watch, Fair Green and Global Alliance, Forum for Environment and Development vs. ABP/APG*, Final Statement, 18 November 2013, p. 5, https://www.oecdguidelines.nl/latest/news/2013/9/18/publication-final-statement-posco-a.o.---lok-shakti-abhiyan-a.o (last accessed 27 May 2024).

use leverage to influence POSCO's misconduct in its construction project, as it has superior power and ability to do so in the investment market.[69] In addition, the Dutch NCP noted that one of the factors determining the degree of leverage can be realised through the capacity and potential abilities of the FIs, given their high profile and role in the economic market.[70] This could support the analysis from the previous chapter that the responsibility of FIs can be broader when considering the power and independence they hold in the economic market.

Following on from these cases, the latter cases against Rabobank and Atradius Dutch State Business (ADSB) in the Dutch NCP also clarified the role of certain types of FIs in the area of human rights and the environment.[71] In the case of ADSB, the Dutch NCP considered that although ADSB acts on behalf of and in the name of the Dutch state, its export credits are part of the business relationship in the sense of the Guidelines, and it questioned the quality of the monitoring of ADSB's activities at the insured companies in relation to social and environmental assessments as well as its stakeholder engagement with the relevant stakeholders and recommended that they engage with stakeholders whose rights are affected by the project.[72] In the case of Rabobank, NCP noted that while the bank can exercise its responsibility for human rights by engaging in multi-stakeholder initiatives, this does not negate the fact that it should exercise its own responsibility for human rights, including the use of leverage to seek and prevent negative impacts. In this case, the concept of disengagement was highlighted by saying that this should be the last option as it will not support the goal of sustainability. Also, the Mylan case is perhaps a good example of how to exercise the responsibility to divest from companies.[73] Although the Mylan case was brought against the pharmaceutical company for supplying lethal injections to US prisons, this case shows how some of the FIs that invested in Mylan handled their

---

[69] NCP Netherlands, *Lok Shakti Abhiyan, KTNC Watch, Fair Green and Global Alliance, Forum for Environment and Development vs. ABP/APG*, Final Statement, 18 November 2013, p. 5, https://www.oecdguidelines.nl/latest/news/2013/9/18/publication-final-statement-posco-a.o.---lok-shakti-abhiyan-a.o (last accessed 27 May 2024).

[70] NCP Netherlands, *Lok Shakti Abhiyan, KTNC Watch, Fair Green and Global Alliance, Forum for Environment and Development vs. ABP/APG*, Final Statement, 18 November 2013, p. 5, https://www.oecdguidelines.nl/latest/news/2013/9/18/publication-final-statement-posco-a.o.---lok-shakti-abhiyan-a.o (last accessed 27 May 2024).

[71] NCP Netherlands, *Both ENDS, Associação Fórum Suape Espaço Socioambiental, Conectas Direitos Humanos and Colônia de Pescadores do Município do Cabo de Santo Agostinho vs. Atradius Dutch State Business*, Final Statement, 30 November 2016, https://www.oecdguidelines.nl/notifications/news/2016/11/30/final-statement-both-ends-associacao-forum-suape-vs-atradius-dutch-state-business (last accessed 27 May 2024).

[72] NCP Netherlands, *Both ENDS, Associação Fórum Suape Espaço Socioambiental, Conectas Direitos Humanos and Colônia de Pescadores do Município do Cabo de Santo Agostinho vs. Atradius Dutch State Business*, Final Statement, 30 November 2016, https://www.oecdguidelines.nl/notifications/news/2016/11/30/final-statement-both-ends-associacao-forum-suape-vs-atradius-dutch-state-business (last accessed 27 May 2024).

[73] NCP Netherlands, *Bart Stapert, attorney vs. Mylan*, Final Statement, 11 April 2016, https://www.oecdguidelines.nl/notifications/documents/publication/2016/4/11/bart-stapert-attorney-vs-mylan (last accessed 27 May 2024).

human rights responsibilities.[74] In this case, following allegations against Mylan of supplying lethal injections to US prisons for executions, the state pension fund ABP divested itself of Mylan, selling all its shares on the grounds that it had spoken to Mylan about the distributions but had not received adequate answers.[75] However, other investors, including ROBECO, PGGM-Pensioenfonds Zorg & Welzijn and NNGroup N.V., decided to remain in business with Mylan, stating that they will continue to use their influence on Mylan to ensure that the distribution of medicines complies with international human rights standards.[76] In this case, the NCP found that the divestment of ABP had in some way influenced Mylan's actions to respond seriously to the allegations and cease all sales to the US prison.[77] However, NCP could have advised other investors who decided to continue their relationship with Mylan on how to progressively engage with Mylan in relation to its distribution in the US.

Some OECD cases can serve as best examples among others, showing how investors can go beyond the general requirements of the Guidelines to exercise their leverage and handle the complaints. These are the cases against the Danish FI[78] in the Danish NCP, the case against Natixis in the French NCP and the case against ANZ in the Australian NCP.[79] In the case of the Danish FI, the Danish NCP considered that the company had carried out due diligence adequately and had exercised its influence over the companies. In this case, the Danish FI provided a financial guarantee to finance the Danish pension fund's loan to a Russian bank, and the bank financed a loan to Company A, which operated a mine in Armenia. The Danish FI had entered into a bilateral contract directly with Company A that required the company to meet certain requirements of the IFC Performance Standard. This contract required Company A

[74] NCP Netherlands, *Bart Stapert, attorney vs. Mylan,* Final Statement, 11 April 2016, https://www.oecdguidelines.nl/notifications/documents/publication/2016/4/11/bart-stapert-attorney-vs-mylan (last accessed 27 May 2024).

[75] NCP Netherlands, *Bart Stapert, attorney vs. Mylan,* Final Statement, 11 April 2016, p. 3, https://www.oecdguidelines.nl/notifications/documents/publication/2016/4/11/bart-stapert-attorney-vs-mylan (last accessed 27 May 2024).

[76] NCP Netherlands, *Bart Stapert, attorney vs. Mylan,* Final Statement, 11 April 2016, pp. 3–4, https://www.oecdguidelines.nl/notifications/documents/publication/2016/4/11/bart-stapert-attorney-vs-mylan (last accessed 27 May 2024).

[77] NCP Netherlands, *Bart Stapert, attorney vs. Mylan,* Final Statement, 11 April 2016, p. 5, https://www.oecdguidelines.nl/notifications/documents/publication/2016/4/11/bart-stapert-attorney-vs-mylan (last accessed 27 May 2024).

[78] In some NCP cases, at the request of the parties involved, the NCP may hide the actual name of the institution.

[79] NCP Denmark, *Two NGOs vs. Danish Financial Institution*, Final Statement, 19 June 2018,, https://ncp-danmark.dk/sites/default/files/2021-03/Decision_19_june_2018.pdf (last accessed 27 May 2024); NCP France, *Unite here vs. Natixis and NGAM in the United States of America*, Detailed Report 05 December 2017, https://www.tresor.economie.gouv.fr/Articles/422bdea0-4e4a-4bf4-8e44-c8a471316fe4/files/06015fda-82da-4d1d-a0ce-358ced22aca8 (last accessed 27 May 2024); NCP Australia, *Equitable Cambodia (EC) and Inclusive Development International (IDI) vs. Australian and New Zealand Banking Group Limited (ANZ Group) and its group entity ANZ Royal Bank (Cambodia) Limited (ANZ Royal)*, Final Statement, 27 June 2018, https://ausncp.gov.au/sites/default/files/inline-files/11_AusNCP_Final_Statement.pdf (last accessed 27 May 2024).

to have the social and environmental impact assessments carried out by a third party and to report on the monitoring to the Danish FI in a timely manner. In addition to this contract, prior to the start of the project, the Danish FI conducted extensive stakeholder consultation involving local officials, NGOs and representative citizens from the towns near the mine, and received input from stakeholders on the implementation of the plans. In addition, the Danish FI visited the mines on site, received complaints from stakeholders and met with stakeholders directly to follow up on the complaints. Also, the Danish FI visited Armenia to meet with the company's management because Company A was not meeting contractual requirements regarding social and environmental impacts. After the company responded inadequately, the Danish FI decided to terminate the agreement. This case may be one of the best examples of what FIs can do to meaningfully engage with companies and stakeholders and use their influence to meet their own responsibilities towards human rights and the environment. The case also illustrates the OECD's recommended practice of 'early warning systems' and active stakeholder engagement.

In addition to case of the Danish FI, the case against ANZ under the Australian NCP may also demonstrate the responsibility of FIs to remedy the harms associated with them. In this case, ANZ initially refused to accept responsibility for the alleged impact of its investments after being accused of providing a loan for the sugar plant project in Cambodia that forcibly evicted local communities. However, by highlighting the fact that ANZ approved a loan despite the known widespread protests against the project, the Australian NCP underlined ANZ's lack of human rights due diligence conduct.[80] Later, under pressure from the public, it agreed to remediate the harm and compensate the affected people.[81] ANZ publicly announced that it will commit to its human rights policies and agreed to pay out the profits earned from the loan for the sugar plantation project in Phnom Penh.[82] This might be one of the few cases where FIs have admitted that they have profited from investments linked to human rights abuses and acknowledge their responsibility for remediation. In the French NCP case, French bank Natixis and one of its asset managers, Natixis Global Asset Management (NGAM), are accused of failing to properly leverage their US subsidiary, real estate management company AEW Capital Management (AEW).[83] AEW manages real estate assets, including the Westin Long Beach Hotel,

[80] NCP Australia, *Equitable Cambodia (EC) and Inclusive Development International (IDI) vs. Australian and New Zealand Banking Group Limited (ANZ Group) and its group entity ANZ Royal Bank (Cambodia) Limited (ANZ Royal),* Final Statement, 27 June 2018, para 37,, https://ausncp.gov.au/sites/default/files/inline-files/11_AusNCP_Final_Statement.pdf (last accessed 27 May 2024).

[81] Dickison, M (2021), *In 'Watershed Moment,' Bank Compensates 'Blood Sugar' Victim Families*, VOD English News,https://vodenglish.news/in-watershed-moment-bank-compensates-blood-sugar-victim-families/ (last accessed 20 April 2023).

[82] Dickison, M (2021), *In 'Watershed Moment,' Bank Compensates 'Blood Sugar' Victim Families*, VOD English News, https://vodenglish.news/in-watershed-moment-bank-compensates-blood-sugar-victim-families/ (last accessed 20 April 2023).

[83] NCP France, *Unite here vs. Natixis and NGAM in the United States of America*, Detailed Report, 5 December 2017,, https://www.tresor.economie.gouv.fr/Articles/422bdea0-4e4a-4bf4-8e44-c8a471316fe4/files/06015fda-82da-4d1d-a0ce-358ced22aca8 (last accessed 27 May 2024).

which allegedly violates the rights of hotel employees by engaging in anti-union practices and denying their collective bargaining rights. After a thorough review of the two companies' relationships with other companies, the French NCP concluded that NGAM and Natixis had failed to exercise due diligence on their subsidiary and that they should use their influence over AEW to ensure that AEW exercised due diligence in this particular case and its activities in general.[84] After the proceedings of French NCP started, both Natixis and NGAM contacted their US subsidiary about alleged violations by the hotel, which resulted in the hotel management being sold to another company that immediately recognised the hotel workers' labour unions.

Regarding the role of FIs in climate change, several institutions have come under fire from CSOs for financing fossil fuels while failing to adequately disclose their clear commitment to the Paris Agreement. The recent cases before the NCPs of Australia, the Netherlands and Poland against ANZ, ING and the PZU Group provide an insight into the role of FIs in reducing greenhouse gas emissions through their investment activities, in particular their specific climate change approaches, including measuring, target-setting and steering.[85] In the case of ING in particular, the Dutch NCP recognises that financed emissions are indirect and therefore difficult to measure and control. It, therefore, advises ING to step up its efforts to consider immediate goals alongside long-term sustainable climate goals and to regularly review and adjust its measurements and targets in line with the Paris Agreement. The NCP also stressed that the lack of a methodology or an internationally recognised standard should not prevent companies from making continuous efforts to measure and disclose environmental impacts to strengthen their efforts towards a sustainable environment. This statement could be even more strongly based on the corporate responsibility for the environment and sustainability contained in the OECD Guidelines. As the NCP highlighted, while there is a lack of clear guidance for companies, especially FIs, on what is expected of them to reduce GHG emissions, the requirements of the UNGPs, the OECD Guidelines and other regulations broadly encourage companies to step up their efforts to achieve climate goals and align their decision-making with the SDGs. In the case of ANZ, which allegedly invests in fossil fuels that are causing the climate crisis like the Australian bushfires in 2020, the complainants also demand that ANZ be fully transparent in disclosing its greenhouse gas emissions, which should cover all its financial activities. However, the Australian NCP found that existing regulations such as the OECD Guidelines and UNGPs are very broad and have

---

[84] NCP France, *Unite here vs. Natixis and NGAM in the United States of America*, Detailed Report, 5 December 2017, https://www.tresor.economie.gouv.fr/Articles/422bdea0-4e4a-4bf4-8e44-c8a471316fe4/files/06015fda-82da-4d1d-a0ce-358ced22aca8 (last accessed 27 May 2024).

[85] NCP Australia, *Friends of the Earth, Egan, Dodds and Simons vs. ANZ Group,* Final Statement, 15 December 2021, https://ausncp.gov.au/sites/default/files/2021-12/AusNCP_Final_Statement_Friends_of_Earth_0.pdf (last accessed 27 May 2024); NCP Netherlands, *Oxfam Novib, Greenpeace Netherlands, BankTrack and Friends of the Earth Netherlands (Milieudefensie) vs. ING*, Final Statement, 19 April 2019, https://www.oecdguidelines.nl/latest/news/2019/04/19/final-statement-dutch-ncp-specific-instance-4-ngos-versus-ing-bank (last accessed 27 May 2024); NCP Poland, *Development Yes, Open Pit No' vs. Group PZU S.A*, Final Statement, 26 July 2019, https://mneguidelines.oecd.org/database/instances/0006.htm (last accessed 27 May 2024).

limited wording in relation to climate change and do not include specific disclosure or assessment requirements.[86] Therefore, the NCP concluded that ANZ had fully complied with its obligations under the current requirements of the Guidelines. This case demonstrates the need of the revision of the OECD Guidelines (2011) in order to raise expectations for the company to respond proactively and manage climate-related risks. Following this experience and consultation with experts, the updated 2023 Guidelines significantly improved the recommendations for companies to adapt to international climate and biodiversity agreements.[87] This case emphasised that climate risk disclosure must be transparent and fully progressive given the urgency of the climate emergency and it must require FIs to disclose the types of information they are required to disclose.

Concerning sustainable development, certain cases, although not specifically targeting FIs, could help to further clarify the role of FIs in relation to sustainability. The cases relating to ENRC, Rockwool, Perenco Group and Bollore Group, the UK, Danish and French NCPs analysed whether the companies' actions were in line with the SDGs.[88] In relation to Rockwool's social and environmental impact assessments, for example, the Danish NCP emphasised that the impacts that are the focus of the assessments must be on people, the environment and society as sustainable development goals. Furthermore, in both cases against the Perenco and Bollore groups, the French NCP stated that they should be aware of their significant impact on the progress of sustainable development in the local community and recommended that they provide information on the direct and indirect impact of their activities on employment and the economy of their project region. In the case of the Bollore and Socapalm, the French NCP found that the company should have been aware of the impact of its project on local communities, particularly on their livelihoods and incomes, as they received little compensation for resettlement under

---

86 NCP Australia, *Friends of the Earth, Egan, Dodds and Simons vs. ANZ Group*, Final Statement, 15 December 2021, paras 3, 20, and 41, https://ausncp.gov.au/sites/default/files/2021-12/AusNCP_Final_Statement_Friends_of_Earth_0.pdf (last accessed 27 May 2024).

87 OECD (2023), Key Updates on OECD Guidelines for Multinational Enterprises on Responsible Business Conduct, https://mneguidelines.oecd.org/targeted-update-of-the-oecd-guidelines-for-multinational-enterprises.htm (last accessed 25 July 2023).

88 NCP UK, *RAID vs. ENRC*, Final Statement, 01 February 2016, https://assets.publishing.service.gov.uk/media/5dd2a0a140f0b606ee65ea84/BIS-16-156-raid-and-enrc-final-statement-after-complaint.pdf (last accessed 27 May 2024); NCP Denmark, *West Virginians for Sustainable Development vs. Rockwool International A/S and its subsidiary Rockwool North America Inc.*, Final Statement, 3 June 2021, https://mneguidelines.oecd.org/database/instances/dk0019.htm (last accessed 27 May 2024); NCP France, *CED Cameroon (Cameroon Centre for the Environment and Development), the FOCARFE (Cameroon Foundation of Rational Actions and Training for the Environment, the French association Sherpa and the German NGO Misereor. vs. Socapalm*, Final Statement, 3 June 2013, https://www.tresor.economie.gouv.fr/Institutionnel/Niveau3/Pages/bd7a00fc-6949-450b-bc40-aa09ac044ab0/files/08d3f300-c97d-4b7b-9621-308e6d1cde5b (last accessed 27 May 2024); NCP France, *Avocats Sans Frontières and I WATCH vs. Perenco*, Final Statement, 26 January 2022, https://www.tresor.economie.gouv.fr/Institutionnel/Niveau3/Pages/3c98c1c4-0d82-4fd2-9f7e-94b924152f2c/files/abb8db3e-2ff1-4986-b84c-ed4afeb2666c (last accessed 27 May 2024).

domestic law.[89] Specifically, the NCP stated that it could have created more jobs and income opportunities for the local population after they received a small compensation for the resettlement of their land. The French NCP, therefore, considers that the Bollore Group has not fulfilled the SDG-related obligations set out in the Guidelines. The French NCP statements show that while the company's actions might comply with national law, they should be fully in line with the SDGs objectives and that the company has a clear responsibility to contribute to progress on the SDGs in the countries where it operates. Finally, regarding the case against ENRC, the complainants argued that the resettlement of the local community of Kisankala takes longer and affects the social and environmental rights of the local community. ENRC countered that the resettlement of Kisankala should only take place to the extent that it is reasonable and necessary for the development phase of the project. UK NCP concluded that the deliberate postponement and suspension of resettlement is contrary to the Guidelines' requirements to promote sustainability and advised the company to consider and mitigate the negative impacts of the suspension on affected communities.[90] Based on the implications of these cases, there is an urgent need for a further conceptualisation of the requirements that companies need to meet to consider how their actions affect the progress towards sustainable development.

3.2 *Current Challenges in OECD Cases that Need to Be Addressed to Further Clarify the Human Rights and Environmental Responsibilities of FIs*

This section focuses on the current challenges arising from the examination of these OECD cases that need to be considered and addressed to improve and clarify the FIs' human rights and environmental obligations. It highlights the existing difficulties in the handling of NCP cases that hinder the further development of the FI's human rights and environmental responsibilities. Also, it addresses the lack of clear guidance on specific actions to be taken by FIs to fulfil their responsibilities under the UNGPs and the Guidelines. Looking at the cases discussed above, some NCPs, particularly the Australian and Dutch NCPs, fulfilled their role in successfully handling the cases and achieved outcomes that were acceptable to both parties.[91] Through their

---

[89] NCP France, *CED Cameroon (Cameroon Centre for the Environment and Development), the FOCARFE (Cameroon Foundation of Rational Actions and Training for the Environment, the French association Sherpa and the German NGO Misereor. vs. Socapalm*, Final Statement, 3 June 2013, pp. 1–2, https://www.tresor.economie.gouv.fr/Institutionnel/Niveau3/Pages/bd7a00fc-6949-450b-bc40-aa09ac044ab0/files/08d3f300-c97d-4b7b-9621-308e6d1cde5b (last accessed 27 May 2024).

[90] NCP UK, *RAID vs. ENRC*, Final Statement, 01 February 2016, para 55, https://assets.publishing.service.gov.uk/media/5dd2a0a140f0b606ee65ea84/BIS-16-156-raid-and-enrc-final-statement-after-complaint.pdf (last accessed 27 May 2024).

[91] NCP Australia, *Friends of the Earth, Egan, Dodds and Simons vs. ANZ Group*, Final Statement, 15 December 2021, https://ausncp.gov.au/sites/default/files/2021-12/AusNCP_Final_Statement_Friends_of_Earth_0.pdf (last accessed 27 May 2024); NCP Netherlands, *Lok Shakti Abhiyan,*

authoritative statements, which adequately address whether the actions of the FIs are in line with the Guidelines, the NCPs managed the FIs to acknowledge their responsibility for the negative effects directly linked to their investments.

These successful cases were a good start for the NCP to further strengthen expectations of FIs regarding human rights and the environment. However, other cases that also helped to clarify the responsibility of FIs for their human rights and the environmental impacts could have been elaborated on in more detail. While the Dutch NCP defined the expected behaviours of various FIs such as the state export credit agency and the bank in the cases against ADSB and Rabobank, it failed to thoroughly investigate whether both institutions adequately fulfilled their responsibilities under the Guiding Principles and failed to link their inadequate fulfilment of responsibilities to the alleged harm.[92] In both cases, the NCP considered that these FIs were directly linked to the harm without considering the fact that their negligence and failure to exercise adequate due diligence may have contributed to the harm. However, these cases were dealt with before the OHCHR provided an interpretation regarding the FIs' human rights responsibility, which explains how direct links can become a contribution to harm. However, the role and involvement of FI in the alleged harms were not considered in the NCP proceedings in further instances after this interpretation was developed. This could be because some NCPs strategically do not focus on the errors and failures of the FIs, but rather promote positive communication between the parties to achieve better results. In its own words, the Dutch NCP stated in the case against ING, […a determination of whether or not ING complied with the OECD Guidelines (to 'disclose (…) greenhouse gas emissions (…) to cover direct and indirect, current and future, corporate and product emissions') is not helpful to the future process between the parties, nor does it reflect the efforts ING is making to steer its portfolio towards the goals of the Paris Agreement…].[93] However, without a clear determination of whether or not the company has complied with the Guiding Principles, NCPs lose their role in providing redress to victims and advising companies on their human rights responsibilities in line with international human rights law, and there is a risk that companies will not take their

KTNC Watch, Fair Green and Global Alliance, Forum for Environment and Development vs. ABP/APG, Final Statement, 18.09.2013, https://www.oecdguidelines.nl/latest/news/2013/9/18/publication-final-statement-posco-a.o.---lok-shakti-abhiyan-a.o (last accessed 27 May 2024).

[92] NCP Netherlands, *Friends of the Earth Europe and Friends of the Earth Netherlands/ Milieudefensie vs. Rabobank*, Final Statement, 15 January 2016, https://www.oecdguidelines.nl/notifications/documents/publication/2016/1/15/fs-foe-milieudefensie-rabobank (last accessed 27 May 2024); NCP Netherlands, *Both ENDS, Associação Fórum Suape Espaço Socioambiental, Conectas Direitos Humanos and Colônia de Pescadores do Município do Cabo de Santo Agostinho vs. Atradius Dutch State Business*, Final Statement, 30 November 2016, https://www.oecdguidelines.nl/notifications/news/2016/11/30/final-statement-both-ends-associacao-forum-suape-vs-atradius-dutch-state-business (last accessed 27 May 2024).

[93] NCP Netherlands, *Oxfam Novib, Greenpeace Netherlands, BankTrack and Friends of the Earth Netherlands (Milieudefensie) vs. ING*, Final Statement, 19 April 2019, https://www.oecdguidelines.nl/notifications/documents/publication/2019/04/19/ncp-final-statement-4-ngos-vs-ing (last accessed 27 May 2024).

responsibilities seriously.[94] Moreover, as OECD Watch noted, the possibility of a final statement finding non-compliance with the Guiding Principles will make their involvement in dispute resolution more likely.[95]

Instead of determining the non-compliance by companies, NCPs use different mediation methods, in particular the forward-looking approach and the dialogue-based approach that Dutch and Swiss NCPs usually use, which is not conducive for NCPs to successfully investigate the case and help remedy the harm. About the forward-looking approach, this is particularly evident in the case of Rabobank, ADSB and ING, where the NCP did not take account of the responsibility of the FIs to remedy the existing harms outlined in the complaints. In the case of ING, the NCP specifically stated that it will apply the forward-looking approach, which does not focus on past actions and allegations, but on possible improvements in the future to address the issues raised.[96] Although this approach can be good for developing current practises of FIs for the future, it undermines the accountability of FIs to address existing alleged harms. The Swiss NCP also applied this approach in the cases against Credit Suisse and BWK Group by not focusing on the responsibility of the FIs involved for the allegations made by the complainant, but by closing these cases with the mere promise of the FIs to update their policies and improve their practises.[97] The damaging side of this approach became clear in the case of the Swiss NCP against Credit Suisse. This case concerns human rights violations related to the North Dakota Access Pipeline (NDAP) project. The complainant alleged that Credit Suisse had not conducted human rights due diligence and had failed to actively encourage its investment partners to prevent or mitigate the negative impacts of the project. Following the mediation process, Credit Suisse agreed to incorporate the concept of Free, Prior, Informed Consent (FPIC) into its internal policies and to expect its clients to work with affected stakeholders under the requirements of the IFC Performance Standard. However, there was no actual progress or results after this case. A year later, another NGO also filed a complaint against Credit Suisse for

---

[94] Van't Hoort and Lambooy (2018) *Effective or Not? Crucial role of effectiveness in specific instances*, in OECD Guidelines for Multinational Enterprises: A Glass Half Full, pp. 67, 73.

[95] OECD Watch (2017) *Our Campaign Demands For Policymakers: We Need Effective NCPs Now* https://www.oecdwatch.org/wp-content/uploads/sites/8/2017/11/OECD-Watch_-Campaign_demands.pdf (last accessed 23 April 2023).

[96] NCP Netherlands, *Oxfam Novib, Greenpeace Netherlands, BankTrack and Friends of the Earth Netherlands (Milieudefensie) vs. ING*, Final Statement, 19 April 2019, p. 6, https://www.oecdguidelines.nl/notifications/documents/publication/2019/04/19/ncp-final-statement-4-ngos-vs-ing (last accessed 27 May 2024).

[97] NCP Switzerland, *the Society for Threatened Peoples Switzerland vs. Credit Suisse,* Final Statement, 16 October 2019, https://www.seco.admin.ch/seco/en/home/Aussenwirtschaftspolitik_Wirtschaftliche_Zusammenarbeit/Wirtschaftsbeziehungen/nachhaltigkeit_unternehmen/nkp/Statements_zu_konkreten_Faellen.html (last accessed 27 May 2024); NCP Switzerland, *the Society for Threatened Peoples vs. BKW Group*, Final Statement, 26 August 2021, https://www.seco.admin.ch/seco/en/home/Aussenwirtschaftspolitik_Wirtschaftliche_Zusammenarbeit/Wirtschaftsbeziehungen/nachhaltigkeit_unternehmen/nkp/Statements_zu_konkreten_Faellen.html (last accessed 27 May 2024).

the same allegations at the US NCP.[98] Disappointingly, the US NCP rejected the case on the grounds that mediation would not contribute because the same dialogue had already been conducted by the Swiss NCP.

In the recent cases against UBS, BKW and ING in the Swiss and Dutch NCPs, the NCPs, without themselves deciding on the company's compliance or non-compliance with the Guiding Principles, left the determination of the FIs' responsibilities in relation to their involvement in the alleged damages to the dialogue between the parties.[99] Without a clear authoritative determination, this kind of dialogue-based approach to determining the role of the FI based on dialogue between the parties will not be successful, as hardly any FI will fail to recognise its responsibility without pressure, strong persuasion and interpretation based on international law. The recent BankTrack benchmark shows that banks tend to be evasive when asked about specific human rights violations.[100] In response to BankTrack's enquiries about human rights violations, out of 50 institutions, 12 banks did not respond, while 16 responded but never confirmed their links to the impact or alleged concerns.[101]

While a handful of documents and reports have been produced since 2014 explaining how FIs' financial activities can be linked to and contribute to negative impacts, FIs are still unwilling to acknowledge their role and responsibility. This is demonstrated by the recent case related to ING in the Dutch NCP in 2022, where ING explicitly expressed that they were related to the alleged negative impacts, but did not cause or contribute to them, so the bank is not responsible to participate in or remedy the remediation.[102] In the final statement, the Dutch NCP noted that the parties did not reach a common conclusion on whether ING contributed to or

---

[98] NCP United States, *Divest Invest Protect, Indigenous Peoples Law and Policy Program, Women's Earth and Climate Action Network vs. Credit Suisse*, Final Statement, 31 August 2021,, https://www.state.gov/specific-instance-between-divest-invest-protect-indigenous-peoples-law-and-policy-program-womens-earth-and-climate-action-network-and-credit-suisse/ (last accessed 27 May 2024).

[99] NCP Switzerland, *the Society for Threatened Peoples vs. BKW Group*, Final Statement, 26 August 2021, https://www.seco.admin.ch/seco/en/home/Aussenwirtschaftspolitik_Wirtschaftliche_Zusammenarbeit/Wirtschaftsbeziehungen/nachhaltigkeit_unternehmen/nkp/Statements_zu_konkreten_Faellen.html (last accessed 27 May 2024);

NCP Switzerland, *Society for Threatened Peoples vs. UBS Group AG*, Final Statement, 20 December 2021, https://www.seco.admin.ch/seco/en/home/Aussenwirtschaftspolitik_Wirtschaftliche_Zusammenarbeit/Wirtschaftsbeziehungen/nachhaltigkeit_unternehmen/nkp/Statements_zu_konkreten_Faellen.html (last accessed 27 May 2024); NCP Netherlands,*Milieudefensie/Friends of the Earth Netherlands, WALHI/Friends of the Earth Indonesia and SDI/Friends of the Earth Liberia vs. ING*, Final Statement, 7 April 2022, https://www.oecdguidelines.nl/notifications/documents/publication/2022/04/07/foe-ing-final-statement (last accessed 27 May 2024).

[100] The BankTrack (2022) BankTrack Global Human Rights Benchmark 2022 https://www.banktrack.org/download/global_human_rights_benchmark_2022/global_human_rights_benchmark_2022_2.pdf (last accessed 23 April 2023).

[101] The BankTrack (2022) BankTrack Global Human Rights Benchmark 2022 https://www.banktrack.org/download/global_human_rights_benchmark_2022/global_human_rights_benchmark_2022_2.pdf (last accessed 23 April 2023), p. 7.

[102] NCP Netherlands, *Milieudefensie/Friends of the Earth Netherlands, WALHI/Friends of the Earth Indonesia and SDI/Friends of the Earth Liberia vs. ING*, Final Statement, 7

was directly related to the impact through the business relationship. At the end of the final statement, the NCP emphasised that a direct link can be converted into a contribution if FI is aware of the situation but has ignored the problem and has not taken appropriate measures to mitigate the impact. However, it did not take a determination on this itself. In the UBS case, where the Swiss NCP used dialogue-based approaches to discuss the role of FIs in relation to the allegations made in the case, the company also avoided reflecting on its activities that were linked to the harm, stating that this type of case could only be resolved through the multi-stakeholder approach.[103] Although the complainant insisted that the company could address the alleged harm in some way and change its policies and actions, the company insisted on the multi-stakeholder approach and the case was closed without clearly establishing the company's responsibility for this particular case. This shows that these mediation approaches are not suitable for NCPs if they are truly ambitious and expect to create a platform that enables effective redress. Perhaps in the future, the question of whether these mediation strategies are appropriate for dealing with companies and human rights violations should be analysed more.

Apart from not being able to determine compliance or non-compliance of the companies' actions in relation to the alleged harms, the NCPs also fail to effectively monitor the FIs' obligations agreed in the mediation process. More than one complaint has been lodged with the Australian, Dutch, Swiss and US NCPs against FIs such as ANZ, ING, Credit Suisse and NBIMs, but there are no clear commitments and changes resulting from the mediation procedures. As mentioned earlier, US NCP simply refused to take up the case without follow-up with Credit Suisse about its approach to the NDAP.[104] While there has been some progress in the actions of these FIs, particularly ANZ and ING, which are top performers in the BankTrack benchmark for compliance with UNGP requirements.[105] However, assessed by BankTrack, they are better at responding to requests, but not good at taking effective action on related impacts.[106] This means that ANZ and ING, although the mediation process has helped them to respond to the allegations and improve their communication

April 2022, https://www.oecdguidelines.nl/notifications/documents/publication/2022/04/07/foeing-final-statement (last accessed 27 May 2024).

[103] NCP Switzerland *Society for Threatened Peoples vs. UBS Group AG*, Final Statement, 20 December 2021, https://www.seco.admin.ch/seco/en/home/Aussenwirtschaftspolitik_Wirtschaftliche_Zusammenarbeit/Wirtschaftsbeziehungen/nachhaltigkeit_unternehmen/nkp/Statements_zu_konkreten_Faellen.html (last accessed 27 May 2024).

[104] NCP United States, *Divest Invest Protect, Indigenous Peoples Law and Policy Program, Women's Earth and Climate Action Network vs. Credit Suisse*, Final Statement, 31 August 2021,, https://www.state.gov/specific-instance-between-divest-invest-protect-indigenous-peoples-law-and-policy-program-womens-earth-and-climate-action-network-and-credit-suisse/ (last accessed 27 May 2024).

[105] The BankTrack (2022) BankTrack Global Human Rights Benchmark 2022, https://www.banktrack.org/download/global_human_rights_benchmark_2022/global_human_rights_benchmark_2022_2.pdf (last accessed 23 April 2023), p. 7.

[106] The BankTrack (2022) BankTrack Global Human Rights Benchmark 2022, https://www.banktrack.org/download/global_human_rights_benchmark_2022/global_human_rights_benchmark_2022_2.pdf (last accessed 23 April 2023), p. 54.

strategies, are still struggling to acknowledge their responsibility and take effective action against the associated impacts. However, the NBIM, which has received a total of 4 complaints under the Norwegian NCP, was able to change its attitude towards its responsibility for negative impacts, as the recent case with Mcdonalds' shows.[107] The NBIM agreed to influence the company (Mcdonald's) to take action against gender-based violence and harassment. The NBIM also agreed to work directly with NGOs and trade unions to share information on the company's performance in addressing and mitigating negative impacts.[108]

As regards the provision of clear guidance, NCPs still have difficulties in assessing the quality of FIs' actions, in particular, whether they have adequately identified the impact on their clients, whether they have adequately involved the stakeholders involved and, finally, whether they have adequately addressed complaints about the negative impact of the project in which they have invested. Although the above-mentioned strategies used by some NCPs influence this outcome, the cases analysed in this chapter clearly show that there is a lack of clear criteria and expectations under international regulations that NCPs can apply to determine the effectiveness of the FIs' human rights and environmental responsibilities. In most cases, NCPs use general language in the "Conclusions" and "Recommendations" sections of the closing statements when asking companies to actively engage with stakeholders and improve their ability to influence them.[109] It appears that while the NCPs recommendations call on FIs to use and increase their leverage over the companies in which they invest, there are still no clear criteria for determining what constitutes appropriate or effective leverage that should be exercised by FIs and what types of direct and indirect impacts related to specific human rights issues should trigger collective responsibility and action by investors.

In addition, several cases against government export credit agencies, including United Kingdom Export Finance (UKEF), New Zealand Permanent Trustees Ltd, and Korean Export–Import Bank of Korea (KEXIM) under the UK, New Zealand and Korean NCPs, held that these institutions do not fall within the scope of the Guidelines as they are not considered multinational enterprises within the meaning of the Guidelines. In the case against the UKEF, Global Witness stated that the UKEF [...as a public FI, plays a key role in enabling fossil fuel projects and providing larger amounts of capital for these projects...], and referred to the other NCP statements which also examined actions of export credit agencies such as the ADSB under the

---

[107] NCP Norway: *Trade Unions IUf, EFFAT-IUF, SEIU and UGT vs. Norges Bank. Investment Management (NBIM),* Final Statement, 22 April 2022, https://files.nettsteder.regjeringen.no/wpuploads01/sites/263/2022/04/FinalStatement_4tradeunions-vs.-NBIM_ENG.pdf (last accessed 27 May 2024).

[108] NCP Norway: *Trade Unions IUf, EFFAT-IUF, SEIU and UGT vs. Norges Bank. Investment Management (NBIM),* Final Statement, 22 April 2022, para 4, https://files.nettsteder.regjeringen.no/wpuploads01/sites/263/2022/04/FinalStatement_4tradeunions-vs.-NBIM_ENG.pdf (last accessed 27 May 2024).

[109] For instance, NCP Japan, *Market Forces vs. Mizuho Financial Group, Inc., Sumitomo Mitsui Banking Corporation and Mitsubishi UFJ Financial Group, Inc,* Final Statement, 15 January 2021, https://www.mofa.go.jp/files/100138168.pdf (last accessed 27 May 2024).

Dutch NCP. However, UKEF argued that it is in a different situation compared to other export credit agencies, as it is a ministerial government department with no resources of its own, issuing guidelines on behalf of the Minister for International Trade and fulfilling a statutory purpose. UK NCP did not explore further this particular argument that the UKEF does not apply to the Guidelines, but simply dismissed the case. OECD Watch stated that it disagrees with this statement because state export credit agencies do engage in and facilitate commercial activities that fall within the scope of the OECD Guidelines and that dismissing complaints against ECAs undermines state leadership in promoting RBC through its own state-affiliated entities.[110] These statements by the UK, Korean and New Zealand NCPs regarding export credit agencies differ from those of the Danish and Dutch NCPs and also contradict the meaning of the UNGPs, which state that all investment companies such as public pension funds, sovereign wealth funds and development finance institutions are responsible for respecting human rights like any other business.[111] Moreover, WGBHR stated that UNGPs apply equally to investment entities such as public pension funds, sovereign wealth funds and development finance institutions are responsible for respecting human rights like any other business enterprises.

4 Conclusion

This chapter showed that despite the significant progress made in raising awareness among FIs of their responsibilities to address human rights and environmental impacts connected to their financial services and products, there is still a lack of clear statement, both in substantive and procedural aspect, in the international framework to clearly define the actions expected of FIs in relation to negative impacts. Although several guidance documents have been developed to guide FIs in their progress on human rights and the environment and to interpret their involvement in related harms, these guidance documents lack substance and come across as mere practical advice. Moreover, current initiatives and guidelines require FIs not only to adopt human rights policies and to exercise due diligence on their clients but also to proactively engage in the SDGs. Thus, as discussed in this chapter, the existing framework needs to be strengthened to clearly define the critical responsibilities and contributions of

---

[110] NCP UK, *Global Witness vs. UK Export Finance*, Initial assessment, 9 September 2020, https://www.gov.uk/government/publications/global-witness-complaint-to-the-uk-ncp-about-uk-export-finance/initial-assessment-global-witness-complaint-to-the-uk-ncp-about-uk-export-finance (last accessed 27 May 2024); NCP New Zealand, *Mr and Mrs C/Southern Response vs. NZ Permanent Trustees Ltd*, Final Statement, 9 March 2016,, https://www.mbie.govt.nz/dmsdocument/1670-mr-and-mrs-c-southern-response-pdf (last accessed 27 May 2024); OECD Watch (2019), *KTNC Watch* et al. *vs KEXIM Violations of FPIC, consultation at Philippine Jalaur dam*, 18 January 2019,, https://www.oecdwatch.org/complaint/ktnc-watch-et-al-vs-kexim/ (last accessed 27 May 2024).

[111] OECD Watch (2020), *Global Witness vs. UK Export Finance UK Export Finance fails climate commitments, disclosures* September 2020, https://www.oecdwatch.org/complaint/global-witness-vs-uk-export-finance/ (last accessed 24 April 2023).

FIs if they are to accelerate their progress on human rights, climate change and sustainability. To date, however, the discourse on business and human rights has rarely discussed the relationship of FIs to human rights and the environment based on international law. Although the responsibility of FIs for human rights and the environment has been examined in more than 20 cases under the OECD NCP system, its implications on international law have not been adequately discussed. This chapter, therefore, analysed each case relating to FIs for its alleged link to various human rights and environmental harms. The research showed that some of the cases examined provided a critical analysis of the commitment of FIs to human rights and some successful cases were presented as good practices that could potentially raise the expectations of FIs in terms of sufficient due diligence, the exercise of leverage and the remediation of associated harm. However, certain mediation approaches used by some NCPs hinder progress in conceptualising FI in the areas of human rights and the environment. Therefore, the NCP case handling system should be urgently redesigned if it is truly aimed at contributing to the development of finance sector and human rights framework and providing victims with an effective platform for redressing their harm.

See Table 1.

Table 1 Cases that target the FIs' responsibility towards human rights and the environment

No	The final statement date (descending)	OECD case	NCP	Alleged human rights abuse/issues	Outcome
1	April 2022	FoE Netherlands, WALHI, SDI, FoE Indonesia, and FoE Liberia against ING	NCP Netherlands	Climate change	No agreement
2	April 2022	IUF, EFFAT-IUF, SEIU and UGT against Norges Bank Investment Management (NBIM)	NCP Norway	Gender violence/ harassment at workplace	Agreement
3	January 2022	Jalaur River for the People's Movement, the People's Solidarity for Participatory Democracy and the KTNC against Export–Import Bank of Korea (KEXIM) and Daewoo	NCP Korea	Negative social and environmental impacts on the local community due to the mining project	Rejected
4	December 2021	Friends of Earth, Egan, Dodds and Simons against ANZ Group	NCP Australia	Climate change	No agreement
5	December 2021	Society for Threatened People against UBS Group	NCP Switzerland	Forced labour	No agreement
6	August 2021	Society for Threatened People against BWK Group	NCP Switzerland	FPIC, Indigenous People's rights	No agreement
7	August 2021	Divest-Invest Project, Indigenous People's Law and Policy Program, Women's Earth and Climate Action Network against Credit Suisse	NCP United States	FPIC, Negative social and environmental impacts on the local community	Rejected
8	January 2021	Market Forces against Mizuho Financial Group, Inc., Sumitomo Mitsui Banking Corporation and Mitsubishi UFJ Financial Group, Inc	NCP Japan	Negative social and environmental impacts on the local community	No agreement

(continued)

Table 1 (continued)

No	The final statement date (descending)	OECD case	NCP	Alleged human rights abuse/issues	Outcome
9	September 2020	Global Witness against UK Export Finance	NCP United Kingdom	Climate change	Rejected
10	November 2019	STP against Credit Suisse	NCP Switzerland	FPIC, Negative social and environmental impacts on the local community	Agreement
11	July 2019	Development Yes – Open Pit Mines No! Foundation against Group PZU SPA	NCP Poland	Climate change, right to a clean, healthy and sustainable environment	Agreement
12	April 2019	Oxfam Novib, Greenpeace Netherlands, BankTrack and Friends of the Earth Netherlands (Milieudefensie) versus ING	NCP Netherlands	Climate change	Completed
13	Dezember 2018	Complaint by IC and IDI against ANZ Group	NCP Australia	Forced eviction, negative social and environmental impacts on the local community	Agreement
14	June 2018	Two NGOs against the Ministry of Finance	NCP Denmark	Negative social and environmental impacts on the local community	Completed
15	December 2017	Unite Here against Natixis and NGAM	NCP France	Violation of Workers' Rights in the hotel business	Agreement
16	November 2016	Both ENDS et al. against Atradius Dutch State Business	NCP Netherlands	Violations against local communities, environmental damage	No agreement reached

(continued)

Table 1 (continued)

No	The final statement date (descending)	OECD case	NCP	Alleged human rights abuse/issues	Outcome
17	April 2016	Bart Stapert Attorney against Mylan	NCP Netherlands	Pharmaceutical companies supply of lethal injections to US prisons for executions	Agreement
18	February 2016	RAID against ENRC	NCP United Kingdom	Negative social and environmental impacts on the local community, land grabbing	No agreement
18	January 2016	FoE Europe and FoE Netherlands against Rabobank	NCP Netherlands	Environmental and social negative impacts in palm oil industry	No agreement
19	July 2015	United Steel Workers and Birlesik Metal against NBIM	NCP Norway	Violation of labour rights	
20	September 2013	Lok Shakti Abhiyan, KTNC Watch, Fair Green and Global Alliance, Forum for Environment and Development against ABP/APG	NCP Netherlands	Negative social and environmental impacts on the local community; Indigenous people's rights	Agreement
21	May 2013	Lok Shakti Abhiyan, KTNC Watch, Fair Green and Global Alliance, Forum for Environment and Development against POSCO and NBIM	NCP Norway	Negative social and environmental impacts on the local community; Indigenous people's rights	No agreement

References

Bhatt K, Erdem Türkelli G (2021) OECD national contact points as sites of effective remedy: new expressions of the role and rule of law within market globalization? Bus Human Rights J 6(3):423–448

Bohoslavsky JB (2020) Complicity of international financial institutions in violation of human rights in the context of economic reforms. Columbia Human Rights Law Rev 52(1):203–250

Bordignon M (2022) Ensuring financial sector compliance with human rights: from the UNGPs to complicity. In Marx A, Van Calster G, Wouters J et al. (eds) Research handbook on global governance, business and human rights. Edward Elgar Publishing 2022, pp 381–394

Buhmann K (2018) Analysing OECD national contact point statements for guidance on human rights due diligence: method, findings and outlook. Nordic J Human Rights 36(4):390–410

Evans J (2016) The record of international financial institutions on business and human rights. Bus Human Rights J 1(2):327–332

Macchi C, Bernaz D (2021) Business, human rights and climate due diligence: understanding the responsibility of banks. Sustainability 13(15):8391

Mohr K, Riquelme M, Quick PM (2022) Double materiality for financial institutions survey findings and recommendations. BSR. https://www.bsr.org/reports/BSR_Issue_Brief_Materiality_Survey_December_2022_final.pdf (last accessed 7 April 2023)

OECD (2014) OECD Due diligence in the financial sector: adverse impacts directly linked to financial sector operations, products or services by a business relationship. Global Forum on Responsible Business Conduct

OECD (2019) OECD Due Diligence for Responsible Corporate Lending and Securities Underwriting: Key considerations for banks implementing the OECD Guidelines for Multinational Enterprises., OECD Publishing, Paris

OECD (2022) OECD responsible business conduct due diligence for project and asset finance transactions 14. OECD Publishing, Paris

OECD (2017) OECD responsible business conduct for institutional investors: key considerations for due diligence under the OECD Guidelines for Multinational Enterprises

OHCHR (2013) Advise regarding the UNGPs and the finance sector' response to the request from the chair of the OECD working party on responsible business conduct

OHCHR (2013) The application of the guiding principles on business and human rights to minority shareholdings of institutional investors

OHCHR (2017) Response to request from banktrack for advice regarding the application of the UN guiding principles on business and human rights in the context of the banking sector 5

Ruggie JG (2017) Comments on Thun group of banks discussion paper on the implications of UN guiding principles 13 & 17. In a Corporate and Investment Banking Context' Harvard Kennedy School

Täger M (2021) Double materiality: what is it and why does it matter?. LSE, Grantham Research Institute on Climate Change and the Environment. https://www.lse.ac.uk/granthaminstitute/news/double-materiality-what-is-it-and-why-does-it-matter/ (last accessed 17 April 2023)

Talmon S (2012) Jus Cogens after Germany v. Italy: substantive and procedural rules distinguished. Leiden J Intern Law 4(25):979–1002

Van Ho T (2021) Defining the relationships: "cause, contribute, and directly linked to" in the UN guiding principles on business and human rights. Hum Rights Q 43(4):625–658

Van Ho T, Alshaleel MK (2018) The mutual fund industry and the protection of human rights. Hum Rights Law Rev 18(1):1–29

Van't Hoort S, Lambooy T (2018) Effective or Not? Crucial role of effectiveness in specific instances. In: OECD (2018) OECD Guidelines for Multinational Enterprises: A Glass Half Full, pp 67–76

Measuring the Effectiveness of OECD National Contact Points: A Critical Review

The Future of Supervision Mechanisms Under the OECD Guidelines for Multinational Enterprises on Responsible Business Conduct

Jernej Letnar Černič

Abstract The OECD Guidelines for Multinational Enterprises for Responsible Business Conduct are a quasi-legal document imposing obligations on the state to regulate the activities of multinational enterprises when doing business at home and outside the Member States of the OECD. This chapter discusses the current state of the OECD Guidelines for Responsible Business Conduct and their added value for rights holders concerning corporate adverse human rights conduct. It first describes the origins and background of adopting the document and then moves to analyse the supervision mechanisms of the OECD Guidelines. As such, it concentrates on the added value of the specific instance procedures before the National Contact Points (NCPs). In this regard, it also analyses the role of the OECD Investment Committee and its peer review mechanism of the NCPs. As a result, it argues that the OECD Governing body should strengthen enforcement mechanisms under the OECD Guidelines.

1 Introduction

The Organization for Economic Co-operation and Development (OECD) is an international organization promoting trade and investment, consisting of Members mainly from the Global North.[1] The OECD Guidelines for Multinational Enterprises for Responsible Business Conduct are among the earlier business and human rights

The author acknowledges the financial support from the Slovenian Research and Innovation Agency (project "Corporate accountability, human rights, and climate change: Towards coherent and just Slovenian and international legal order", ID J5-50171)

J. Letnar Černič (✉)
Faculty of Government and European Studies, New University, Kranj, Slovenia
e-mail: jernej.letnar@fds.nova-uni.si

[1] OECD, List of OECD Member countries - Ratification of the Convention on the OECD, https://www.oecd.org/about/document/ratification-oecd-convention.htm (last accessed 30 April 2024).

O. Davaanyam and M. Krajewski (eds.), *Exploring Corporate Human Rights Responsibilities in OECD Case Law*, Interdisciplinary Studies in Human Rights 14,
https://doi.org/10.1007/978-3-031-75717-4_5

documents.[2] The OECD adopted them as part of the OECD Declaration on Investment as a response to the early failures to adopt any documents at international levels that would bind companies to respect and protect human rights.[3] They exemplify authoritative normative standards in business and human rights.[4] The OECD Guidelines restate binding international obligations of states in business and human rights.

The OECD Guidelines have, in the past decades, provided a basis for the OECD to draft and adopt an array of specific due diligence guides to particular sectors. As they provide the basis for the enforcement of state and corporate human rights obligations, they have provided hope for rights-holders to achieve at least some kind of justice for rights-holders.[5] The OECD Guidelines established administrative legal procedures before the National Contact Points to enforce corporate accountability for business-related human rights abuses.[6] In the last decade, National Contact Points (NCPs) in some member states have turned to a robust enforcement system of adequate supervision of multinational enterprises. Nonetheless, there are opportunities for improvement of such a system.

This chapter looks at the future of the OECD Guidelines and explores how the OECD can enhance its enforcement mechanisms. It is divided into six parts. After the introduction, Sect. 2 describes and analyses the backdrop of the Guidelines. After that, Sect. 3 critically discusses supervision systems under the OECD Guidelines. Section 4 studies the peer review supervision mechanism of the NCPs. Finally, Sect. 5 explores possible reform of the supervision mechanism and argues for an increased role of the OECD Investment Committee. As such, this chapter discusses what is the added value of OECD Guidelines for Multinational Enterprises in business and human rights and what should be the future of its supervision mechanism. Firstly, its monitoring system encourages the deterrence of adverse business-related human rights impacts. Secondly, it provides one of the rare opportunities to enforce corporate accountability for business-related human rights abuses. Nonetheless, this chapter argues that its supervision mechanism needs to respond to the coherence gap among different NCPs, enhance peer-review monitoring, and strengthen the role of the investment committee. It also explores how NCPs can complement novel Business and Human Rights normative approaches.

---

[2] OECD (2023b), *OECD Guidelines for Multinational Enterprises on Responsible Business Conduct*, adopted 8 June 2023, OECD.

[3] OECD (1976), *OECD Declaration on International Investment and Multinational Enterprises.* For a historical account: Van't Foort S (2017), 195–214.

[4] Ramasastry A (2015) 237–259.

[5] Bhatt K, Erdem Türkelli G (2021), 423–448.

[6] Buhmann K (2018), 390–410; OECD (2022a, b, c, d, e, f) *Annual report on the Activity of National Contact Points for Responsible Business Conduct*, https://mneguidelines.oecd.org/annual-report-on-the-activity-of-national-contact-points-for-responsible-business-conduct-2021.pdf (last accessed 30 April 2024).

2 The Backdrop of the OECD Guidelines

The OECD Guidelines for Multinational Enterprises were established in 1976 as a platform for business and human rights standards, updated in 2001, 2011, and 2023.[7] The United Nations Guiding Principles on Business and Human Rights (UNGPs on Business and Human Rights) have in 2011 set a multi-layered normative framework of protection, respect, and remedy in the case of business-related human rights abuses.[8] The UNGPs on Business and Human Rights provide that states carry primary obligations to respect, protect, and fulfil human rights. States are to provide access to remedy to rights holders in the case of business-related human rights abuses.[9] The UNGPs provide that States must first respect their territory's business and human rights standards. Secondly, many commentators in academia argue that states also have obligations to ensure that companies respect human rights standards when they do business outside the borders. They have to ensure that their private companies comply with human rights. The second pillar provides that businesses are also responsible for respecting human rights. As such, companies shall respect, protect and fulfil human rights. They are to control their supply chains and compensate rights holders when there are abuses and violations.

The 20 founding member states established on 14 December 1960 the Organisation for Economic Co-operation and Development.[10] In 2024, the OECD had 38 members, mostly from Global North, but only in the last decade or two have states from Latin America and Central and Eastern Europe joined.[11] The OECD Guidelines do not define the concept of multinational enterprises. As a result, some civil society organizations have interpreted multinational enterprises to include local companies. The OECD Guidelines include chapters on disclosure, human rights, employment, environment combating bribery, consumer interests, science, technology, taxation, and competition.[12] They reflect different dimensions of public policies. However, what is the added value of the OECD Guidelines? Perhaps its enforcement mechanisms under the NCPs? Are the NCP valuable tools, or just bureaucratic tools for public functionaries employed in the OECD and high up in the ministries of economies of the OECD Member States? Also, what is the impact of the NCPs in seeking justice for the rights-holders, particularly compared with social movements such as demonstrations and protests? Arguably, sometimes, social movements appear

---

[7] Backer L C (2011), 69–172.

[8] United Nations Human Rights Council (HRC) (2011), *Guiding Principles on Business and Human Rights: Implementing the United Nations "Protect, Respect and Remedy" Framework*, A/HRC/17/31 (21 March 2011).

Wettstein F et al. (2019), 54–65; Parella K (2020) 168–173; Ruggie J G (2007), 819–840; Ruggie J G et al. (2021), 179–197.

[9] Ruggie J G (2007).

[10] OECD, List of OECD Member countries.

[11] OECD, List of OECD Member countries.

[12] OECD (2023a, b), *Guidelines for Multinational Enterprises on Responsible Business Conduct*, adopted 8 June 2023, OECD, https://doi.org/10.1787/81f92357-en.

much more successful than the enforcement mechanisms under the OECD Guidelines or any other legal mechanisms.

The OECD Guidelines draw on diligence requirements from UNGPs on Business and Human Rights. They restate the text from principles 15 to 17 of the UNGPs on Business and Human Rights.[13] First; businesses should ensure respect for human rights in their operations and beyond.[14] Second, the OECD Guidelines ask businesses to avoid causing and contributing to adverse effects of their activities.[15] Thirdly, they seek ways to prevent and mitigate adverse human rights impacts.[16] Fourthly, they also ask companies to produce statements on human rights and carry out human rights due diligence, introduce indicators and human risk avoidance systems, and provide for remediation.[17]

The OECD Guidelines have triggered the adoption of new domestic human rights due diligence laws.[18] Many have been adopted in northern European countries and at the EU level. Furthermore, the EU has been promoting extraterritorial policies in the third countries.[19] As a result, the OECD Guidelines were translated into one of the few enforcement mechanisms in businesses and human rights. What is the added value of the Guidelines for multinational enterprises, and what do they bring to businesses and human rights as a field, whether they should focus more on prevention, deterrence, accountability, or both? States are primarily responsible for protecting against business-related human rights abuses. States are mostly obliged to establish a normative framework that obliges companies to consider non-financial indicators in their operations, such as protecting human rights and the environment and respecting good corporate governance practices. Under the UNGPs on Business and Human Rights, states are asked to lead by example on business and human rights and ensure that state-owned enterprises incorporate due diligence and access to remedies in their internal policies. It is questionable if (all) national authorities can effectively supervise the implementation of recommendations.

---

[13] HRC (2011), *Guiding Principles on Business and Human Rights: Implementing the United Nations "Protect, Respect and Remedy" Framework*, A/HRC/17/31 (21 March 2011), Principles 15–17.

[14] HRC (2011), *Guiding Principles on Business and Human Rights: Implementing the United Nations 'Protect, Respect and Remedy' Framework*, A/HRC/17/31, adopted 21 March 2011, HRC. Principles 15–17.

[15] HRC (2011), *Guiding Principles on Business and Human Rights: Implementing the United Nations 'Protect, Respect and Remedy' Framework*, A/HRC/17/31, adopted 21 March 2011, HRC. Principles 15–17. Van Ho T (2021), 625–658.

[16] HRC (2011), *Guiding Principles on Business and Human Rights: Implementing the United Nations 'Protect, Respect and Remedy' Framework*, A/HRC/17/31, adopted 21 March 2011, HRC. Principles 15–17.

[17] HRC (2011), *Guiding Principles on Business and Human Rights: Implementing the United Nations 'Protect, Respect and Remedy' Framework*, A/HRC/17/31, adopted 21 March 2011, HRC. Principles 15–17.

[18] NCP Netherlands, *NUON Energy NV vs. FNV Eamshaven*, Final Statement, 5 February 2014, https://www.oecdguidelines.nl/latest/news/2014/2/5/publication-final-statement-nuon-%E2%80%93-fnv.

[19] Ratnaningsih E (2023) 110,008–1/9.

3 Supervision Systems of the OECD Guidelines

NCPs under the OECD Guidelines are part of so-called state non-judicial grievance mechanisms, complementing the judicial mechanisms under principle 25 for UNGPs on Business and Human Rights. They also complement the mechanisms of national human rights institutions and ombudsman' offices. Moreover, they were adopted as recommendations and include conditional language, which some commentators have criticized.[20] The OECD Guidelines also refer to the international human rights obligations of countries where they operate.

Are there recommendations or quasi-legal documents that can be enforced in the courts? Some case law of NCPs suggests that guidelines are both recommendations and quasi-legal documents.

Over fifty OECD Member states must comply with the OECD Guidelines for multinational enterprises. They have to establish national contact points (NCPs). NCPs are supervisory mechanisms that monitor the implementation of the OECD Guidelines in domestic systems.[21] Only a few states have established the NCPs as independent public agencies with self-standing funding, which are not directly under the influence of the Ministry of Economy or Ministry of Industry. Many challenges exist, particularly in those countries that generally need help with the quality of state institutions. States with deficient functioning the NCPs are those with general systematic and general rule of law problems. They are not judicial organs. One could describe them as quasi-judicial organs. They are non-judicial grievance systems. However, their main task is mediating between rights holders and duty holders, individuals, civil society organizations, and companies. How many rights-holders are familiar with the possibility of lodging specific instance procedures before NCPs?

The conclusion of the specific instances process is the final statement, which is backed by an agreement between the rights holders and duty-holders, where the company commits to certain acts, and the rights holders also sign that agreement. It is not a process that would lead to, in most cases, sanctions and administrative fines. It is not a process where individual rights holders can access judicial mechanisms to appeal a decision before the administrative courts. It is a mechanism with some quasi-judicial and judicial mechanisms traits. The due diligence process is very similar to the UNGP diligence process, which involves identifying and assessing the actual and potential adverse human rights impacts.[22] The procedure includes an initial assessment, good offices, and a final assessment. The second stage includes dialogue and

---

[20] Letnar Černič J (2021), 11–16.

[21] OECD (2023a, b), *Guidelines for Multinational Enterprises on Responsible Business Conduct*, https://doi.org/10.1787/81f92357-en, procedures: Decision of the Council on the Guidelines for Multinational Enterprises on Responsible Business Conduct, p. 58.

[22] See, for example, NCP United Kingdom, *Lawyers for Palestinian Human Rights vs. J.C. Bamford Ltd*, Final Statement, 12 November 2021, https://www.gov.uk/government/publications/lawyers-for-palestinian-human-rights-complaint-to-uk-ncp-about-jcb/final-statement-lawyers-for-palestinian-human-rights-complaint-to-uk-ncp-about-jcb#:~:text=The%20UK%20NCP%20concluded%20that,diligence%20in%20its%20supply%20chain.

mediation between parties. Initial assessments are steps of alternative dispute resolution.[23] The procedure for the NCPs usually ends with an agreement that both parties sign. It is not a decision that states a company has violated the OECD Guidelines. There will only be a recommendation, even though commentators argue that the NCP's supervision system should be turned into proper judicial mechanisms.

As a result, the specific instance procedure ends with the final quasi-binding statement. What does the final statement include? It consists of the resolution of the dispute. Sometimes, there would be an agreement between the parties concerned. Nonetheless, NCPs often do not accept merits examination of specific instances.[24] Some NCPs find violations of the OECD Guidelines.[25] Other NCPs also decide whether the company has met expectations in the OECD Guidelines. Some statements also include provisions for remedies and sanctions.[26] There is also supervision of implementation. Some NCPs have asked their government to cease the existing

[23] OECD (2023a, b), *Guidelines for Multinational Enterprises on Responsible Business Conduct*, https://doi.org/10.1787/81f92357-en, procedures: Decision of the Council on the Guidelines for Multinational Enterprises on Responsible Business Conduct, p. 58.

[24] NCP Korea, *Korean Civil Society in Solidarity with Rohingya, Korean Transnational Corporation Watch and Justice for Myanmar vs. Inno Group*, Initial Assessment, 14 July 2021, http://www.ncp.or.kr/servlet/kncp/eng/4001 (last accessed 29 May 2024).

[25] NCP Sweden, *Jijnjevaerie Saami village vs. Statkraft SCA Vind AB (SSVAB)*, Final Statement, 9 February 2016, https://www.government.se/contentassets/b08309e008a84c39aa491b0451cea50d/final-statement-jijnjevaerie-saami-village--statkraft-sca-vind-ab-ssvab-norway-and-sweden-oecd-ncp.pdf; NCP Switzerland, *TUK Indonesia vs. Roundtable for Sustainable Palm Oil*, Final Statement, 5 June 2019, https://www.seco.admin.ch/seco/en/home/Aussenwirtschaftspolitik_Wirtschaftliche_Zusammenarbeit/Wirtschaftsbeziehungen/nachhaltigkeit_unternehmen/nkp/Statements_zu_konkreten_Faellen.html; NCP Switzerland, *Society for Threatened Peoples Switzerland vs. BKW Group*, Final Statement, 26 August 2021, https://www.seco.admin.ch/seco/en/home/Aussenwirtschaftspolitik_Wirtschaftliche_Zusammenarbeit/Wirtschaftsbeziehungen/nachhaltigkeit_unternehmen/nkp/Statements_zu_konkreten_Faellen.html.

[26] NCP United Kingdom, *Bahrain Institute for Rights and Democracy vs. HPG*, Final Statement, 8 December 2021, https://www.gov.uk/government/publications/bird-complaint-to-uk-ncp-about-hpower-group-limited-hpg-company-a-and-company-b/final-statement-bahrain-institute-for-rights-and-democracy-bird-complaint-to-the-uk-ncp-about-hpower-group-limited-hpg; NCP United Kingdom, *Crude Accountability vs. KPO Consortium*, Final Statement, 30 November 2017, https://www.gov.uk/government/publications/crude-accountability-complaint-to-uk-ncp-about-kpo-consortium; NCP United Kingdom, *Global Legal Action Network vs. Anglo American Plc*, on-going, specific instance submitted 18 January 2021, https://www.gov.uk/government/publications/glan-complaint-to-uk-ncp-about-anglo-american/initial-assessment-global-legal-action-network-complaint-to-the-uk-ncp-about-anglo-american.

or planned business projects due to human rights and environmental risks.[27] Additionally, some NCPs have introduced diligent supervisory processes so that after the agreement is reached after six months or twelve months, they follow up and monitor whether the agreement has been complied with. It is a mechanism that mostly civil society uses. It has some advantages, particularly for strategic litigation concerning business-related human rights impacts that would not otherwise be examined for business-related human rights violations.

NCPs very rarely deliver findings of noncompliance. NCPs have so far examined 401 complaints.[28] In only a small proportion of cases, NCPs found non-compliance with the Guidelines.[29] Sanctions are very rare. Only a few NCPs have delivered statements with sanctions. For instance, the Canadian NCP delivered a sanction against the company, which was found to violate the OECD Guidelines.[30] The sanction was the withdrawal of diplomatic support from the Canadian government concerning promoting business activity.[31]

Many countries need more staff to deal with their complaints. There is some evidence to the contrary, like Denmark, Netherlands, Germany, and some other countries have sufficient staff employed. Another current problem in many countries is this perception of or lack of impartiality. Should a governmental ministry be tasked with promoting the economy and investment and maintaining and managing the NCPs? If unsatisfied with the result, can the rights-holders challenge the NCP's decision before any appeals body? OECD Guidelines allow for a review of the NCP's final statement before the OECD Investment Committee.[32] Nonetheless, only a few

---

[27] NCP Belgium, *Greenpeace India vs. Dredging International*, Final Statement, 11 March 2011, https://economie.fgov.be/nl/themas/ondernemingen/een-onderneming-beheren-en/maatschappelijk-verantwoord/oeso-richtlijnen-voor/nationaal-contactpunt-belgie/berichten-nationaal (last accessed 29 May 2024); NCP Brazil, *Forum Suape* et al. *vs. Van Oord*, Final Statement, 30 November 2016, https://www.oecdguidelines.nl/latest/news/2016/11/30/final-statement-both-ends-associacao-forum-suape-vs-atradius-dutch-state-business (last accessed 29 May 2024). See, in more detail: Davaanyam and Krajewski (2023), *Guardians of Rights? The Role of Government in Promoting Responsible Business Conduct under the Updated OECD Guidelines for Multinational Enterprises*. OECD Watch, Blog symposium co-organised by OECD Watch and NOVA School of Law, 30 November 2023, https://www.oecdwatch.org/guardians-of-rights-the-role-of-governments/ (last accessed 30 April 2024).

[28] OECD Watch, Complaints, https://www.oecdwatch.org/complaints-database/ (last accessed 30 April 2024).

[29] Buhmann (2018).

[30] NCP Canada, *Canada Tibet Committee vs. China Gold Int. Resources*, Final Statement, 1 April 2015, https://www.international.gc.ca/trade-agreements-accords-commerciaux/ncp-pcn/statement-gyama-valley.aspx?lang=eng.

[31] NCP Canada, *Canada Tibet Committee vs. China Gold Int. Resources*, Final Statement, 1 April 2015, https://www.international.gc.ca/trade-agreements-accords-commerciaux/ncp-pcn/statement-gyama-valley.aspx?lang=eng.

[32] OECD (2023a, b) *Guidelines for Multinational Enterprises on Responsible Business Conduct*, https://doi.org/10.1787/81f92357-en, procedures: Decision of the Council on the Guidelines for Multinational Enterprises on Responsible Business Conduct, p. 61. More specifically, the procedure notes that»consider a substantiated submission by an Adherent, an advisory body (BIAC or TUAC) or OECD Watch on whether an NCP is fulfilling its responsibilities about its handling of specific

appeals have ever been submitted. As such, ensuring the rule of law has been a challenge, including providing impartiality and independence. Visibility, perhaps, is another challenge.

If a company commits at the end to a final agreement that will establish an internal grievance mechanism, this is undoubtedly a good step. Changes in business culture are another positive outcome. Business culture is crucial in one case, from an NCP to a business culture change. Rights-holders turn to the NCPs and guardians as they are few effective and accessible fast procedures. The OECD Guidelines pursue different aims than only justice seeking justice. The OECD Guidelines engineer corporate culture and promote adopting business and human rights standards in domestic and regional systems.[33] They are primarily aimed at the companies, not the victims. Right-holders should be realistic about what one can achieve with submission-specific instances. More specifically, the main objective could be to gather public attention and awareness of the proceedings. One of the advantages of the OECD Guidelines is that you can also bring a specific instance parallel to judicial proceedings against the company for alleged environmental degradation.

In essence, the procedure before NCPs has the nature of the administrative, legal procedure, even though it is based on arbitration and mediation. The OECD Guidelines use very vague language from the point of view of human rights law. They use this language of impact, whereas they rarely mention human rights or abuses. One of the critical questions is where to submit the complaint and which rights the victim will refer to. Rights-holders should possess documentation that proves the alleged abuse of business-related human rights. The procedure has many challenges in all phases, including initial assessment, good offices, and a conclusion with a final

---

instances. The Committee will approve the response by consensus. The Adherent whose NCP is the subject of a substantiated submission will participate in the process in good faith, and is expected to join the consensus except in exceptional circumstances«, p. 61, Procedures, II, 2(b).

[33] Regulation (EU) 2017/821 of the European Parliament and of the Council of 17 May 2017 laying down supply chain due diligence obligations for Union importers of tin, tantalum, and tungsten, their ores, and gold originating from conflict-affected and high-risk areas, OJ L 130, 19.5.2017; Directive (EU) 2022/2464 of the European Parliament and of the Council of 14 December 2022 amending Regulation (EU) No 537/2014, Directive 2004/109/EC, Directive 2006/43/EC, and Directive 2013/34/EU, as regards corporate sustainability reporting (Text with EEA relevance), PE/35/2022/REV/1, OJ L 322, 16.12.2022; HRC (2011), *Guiding Principles on Business and Human Rights: Implementing the United Nations 'Protect, Respect and Remedy' Framework*, UN Doc. A/HRC/17/31, adopted 21 March 2011; Act on Corporate Due Diligence in Supply Chains, Bundestag, 16 July 2021; Modern Slavery Act 2018 (No. 153, 2018), Australia, 12 October 2018; The California Transparency in Supply Chains Act of 2010 (SB 657); Modern Slavery Act 2015, UK Public General Acts 2015 c. 30; Loi 2017–399 du 27 Mars 2017 relative au devoir de vigilance des sociétés mères et des entreprises donneuses d'ordre, Official Gazette of the Republic of France, 27 March 2017, article L. 225–102-4; European Commission (2022), *Proposal for a Directive the European Parliament and of the Council on Corporate Sustainability Due Diligence and amending Directive* (EU) 2019/1937, COM/2022/71 final. UN, Committee on Economic, Social and Cultural Rights (CESCR) (1998), *General Comment No. 9: The Domestic Application of the Covenant*, UN Doc. E/C.12/1998/24, 3 December 1998; UN,CESCR (2017) *General Comment No. 24 on State Obligations Under the International Covenant on Economic, Social and Cultural Rights in the Context of Business Activities*, UN Doc. E/C.12/GC/24, 10 August 2017; OECD (2022a, b, c, d, e, f) Stocktaking Report on the OECD Guidelines for Multinational Enterprises.

statement. The procedure has been challenged several times from the rule of law perspective, particularly from the perspective of rights holders.

How many rights-holders are familiar with lodging specific instance procedures before NCPs? What should one expect from the Guidelines? Should they function as a deterrent mechanism, or should it be a preventive mechanism? There is also a question of how to align the NCPs with enforcement mechanisms under the Corporate Sustainability Due Diligence Directive (EU CSDDD). The language of the final statements of the NCPs often has much to be improved and reformed. It is often very vague from the legal point of view.[34]

Nonetheless, many civil society organisations and rights-holders have placed a fate in the NCPs to bring justice for human rights violations. Another critical question is, given the difference in the quality and resources of different national contact points, how do you respond to the coherence gap among other national contact points? Over fifty states that adhere to the OECD Guidelines should have set up NCPs, but only a few are functioning well. There are very few that are very efficient. Also, it is critical to consider how NCPs can complement novel approaches in business and human rights, particularly concerning mandatory due diligence in domestic systems of some European states and the newly adopted EU Directive on corporate sustainability due diligence. One can anticipate that some of the problems with the functioning of some NCPs will be repeated concerning the functioning of national authorities, which will be charged with implementing the recently adopted EU CSDDD.

Several NCPs, which mainly operate in state or public administrations of the OECD Member States, are dormant. Nonetheless, they often turn a blind eye to business-related human rights abuses. As such, the Enforcement Mechanisms under the OECD Guidelines have struggled to provide meaningful justice for rights-holders for some time. Nonetheless, without NCPs, the Guidelines would be without teeth. As such, they provide some supervision as to the businesses' compliance but also state the Guidelines for multinational enterprises. However, there are several challenges regarding the functioning of the NCPs. One is composition and organization, as well as the competencies. One often mentions business, human rights, and conflict of interest questions. There is clear evidence from some countries of the collision of corporate and governmental interests from the work of the NCPs. Another issue, which civil society organizations often highlight, but which has also been raised by the rights holders, which is the impartiality or lack thereof, and how to ensure the impartial functioning of the NCPs, which is a structural, organizational problem as most of the NCPs are part of public administration, in some cases, state administration. As a result, it is challenging to ensure the right of a fair procedure. There have been many proposals on how to remedy that, such as moving away the NCPs from

[34] See, for example, NCP Netherlands, *Oxfam Novib, Greenpeace Netherlands, BankTrack and Friends of the Earth Netherlands (Milieudefensie) vs. ING*, Final Statement, 19 April 2019, https://www.oecdguidelines.nl/latest/news/2019/04/19/final-statement-dutch-ncp-specific-instance-4-ngos-versus-ing-bank (last accessed 29 May 2024); NCP Netherlands, *Former employees of Bralima vs. Bralima and Heineken*, Final Statement, 18 August 2017, https://www.oecdguidelines.nl/latest/news/2017/08/18/final-statement-notification-former-employees-bralima-vs.-bralima-heineken.

the state administration and creating expert bodies that would also be financially independent of the government.

4 Peer Review Supervision of the NCPs

Peer reviews are a procedure conducted by the Secretariat of the OECD. Peer review refers to a procedure where representatives of other OECD member states and staff from the OECD Responsible Business Secretariat in Paris examine the functioning of an NCP and deliver recommendations to improve their performance, fairness, and impartiality. Let us look at some of the objectives of peer review. The peer review procedure aims to "assess that the functioning and operation of the NCPs are following the core criteria set out in the Procedural Guidance;", "identify the NCP's strengths and positive results as well as any gaps and possibilities for improvement;", "make recommendations for improvement in line with the Guidelines;" "serve as a learning tool for reviewed and participating NCPs. The overarching goal is to promote functional equivalence of all NCPs and to ensure that the network of NCPs operates to its full capacity in helping implement the Guidelines."[35] After the visit, the Secretariat prepares the final peer review report. It includes "An assessment of the conformity of the NCP's operations with the core criteria and core aspects of the NCP mandate…" and provides recommendations on the reforms of NCPs.[36] The state party is obliged to submit a follow-up within one year.[37]

The peer-review conclusions provide interesting insights concerning the NCP's independence, impartiality, and funding resources. Let us look at conclusions from some recent peer reviews of NCPs. The OECD noted in a peer-review report on Sweden, "Staff resources of the NCP should be at least maintained, or ideally reinforced, to provide, for example, one full-time government member to manage the NCP secretariat."[38] It added, "The NCP should revise its Rules of Procedure in accordance with the Procedural Guidance, to ensure predictability, transparency, and impartiality in the specific instance process."[39] In the 2022 peer review report on Slovenia, the recommendation was to enhance the role of the inter-ministerial working group and advisory body.

[35] OECD (2021a, b) National Contact Point Peer Reviews: Core Template, https://mneguidelines.oecd.org/national-contact-point-peer-reviews-core-template.pdf (last accessed 30 April 2024), p. 7.

[36] OECD (2021a, b) National Contact Point Peer Reviews: Core Template, https://mneguidelines.oecd.org/national-contact-point-peer-reviews-core-template.pdf, p. 11.

[37] OECD (2021a, b) National Contact Point Peer Reviews: Core Template, https://mneguidelines.oecd.org/national-contact-point-peer-reviews-core-template.pdf, p. 11.

[38] OECD (2022a) OECD Guidelines for Multinational Enterprises National Contact Point Peer Reviews: Sweden, https://mneguidelines.oecd.org//national-contact-point-peer-reviews-sweden.pdf (last accessed 30 April 2024), p. 18.

[39] OECD (2022a) OECD Guidelines for Multinational Enterprises National Contact Point Peer Reviews: Sweden, https://mneguidelines.oecd.org//national-contact-point-peer-reviews-sweden.pdf, p. 38.

More specifically, it noted, "the NCP should enhance the roles of the interministerial working group and advisory body, particularly with more meetings of the bodies individually and together."[40] It added: "The NCP should address concerns related to the perception of impartiality of the NCP through substantive changes or improved communication on the NCP structure".[41] In the report on Brazil's NCP, the OECD recommended fostering communication to prevent conflict of interest. It noted that "the NCP should better communicate about measures taken to foster its impartiality, such as the applicable framework regarding conflict of interests, the NCP's decision-making procedures, or its practice to decide by consensus."[42] The OECD observed in the report on Australia, that "arrangements should be made regarding coordination between Examiners to avoid inconsistent decisions while protecting the independence of each Examiner. A clear, transparent and objective process should also be designed for assigning cases to Examiners, taking into account relevant factors."[43] Similarly, the OECD observed in a peer review report on Peru that "The NCP should address concerns related to its impartiality through substantive changes and communication on the NCP's structure and operating rules. This could be notably accomplished through updated official documentation clarifying meeting and decision-making rules, and provisions on conflict of interests."[44]

In 2023, the OECD submitted in a peer review report concerning Morocco that "[t]he human resources of the NCP Secretariat should be reinforced, notably through additional staff with expertise on responsible business conduct. The NCP should also take measures to ensure continuity in case of staff changes in the future, notably through a handover strategy involving the interagency body. The interagency body and the NCP Chair should also better support the NCP Secretariat in achieving the NCP's double mandate."[45] It added that "the interagency structure of the NCP and its high-level Chair are important opportunities for the NCP's authority, visibility and access to expertise. Government representatives and stakeholders agree on the need to elevate the profile of the NCP within government … and improve

---

[40] OECD (2022b) OECD Guidelines for Multinational Enterprises National Contact Point Peer Reviews: Slovenia, https://mneguidelines.oecd.org//national-contact-point-peer-reviews-slovenia.pdf (last accessed 30 April 2024), p. 7.

[41] OECD (2022b) OECD Guidelines for Multinational Enterprises National Contact Point Peer Reviews: Slovenia, https://mneguidelines.oecd.org//national-contact-point-peer-reviews-slovenia.pdf, p. 7.

[42] OECD (2022c) OECD Guidelines for Multinational Enterprises National Contact Point Peer Reviews: Brazil, https://mneguidelines.oecd.org//national-contact-point-peer-reviews-brazil.pdf (last accessed 30 April 2024), p. 7.

[43] OECD (2022d) OECD Guidelines for Multinational Enterprises National Contact Point Peer Reviews: Australia, https://mneguidelines.oecd.org//national-contact-point-peer-reviews-australia.pdf (last accessed 30 April 2024), p. 44.

[44] OECD (2023a) OECD Guidelines for Multinational Enterprises National Contact Point Peer Reviews: Peru, https://mneguidelines.oecd.org//ncps/national-contact-point-peer-reviews-peru.pdf (last accessed 30 April 2024), p. 19.

[45] OECD (2023a, b) OECD Guidelines for Multinational Enterprises National Contact Point Peer Reviews: Morocco, https://mneguidelines.oecd.org//ncps/national-contact-point-peer-reviews-morocco.pdf (last accessed 30 April 2024), p. 20.

processes to guarantee the impartiality of the NCP and communication around those processes. Morocco should consider ways to upgrade the level of institutionalization and bolster the authority, transparency, and perception of impartiality of the NCP…".[46] Concerning the Korean NCP, the OECD noted, "the NCP should provide concrete recommendations that respond specifically to the issues in question and, as relevant, reference recommendations of the Guidelines and due diligence guidance. The NCP should also consider following up on specific instances where recommendations are issued to assess whether they have been responded to."[47]

Despite these theoretical goals, many NCPs face numerous challenges in the daily operation of public administration, from ensuring transparent operation to fair decision-making. As highlighted above, many of them suffer from often allegedly dependent and non-transparent decision-making. NCPs must gain the population's trust through open and honest work and a willingness to expose themselves to the supervision of civil society and other state institutions.

5 Reform of the Supervision Mechanism

Proper, independent, impartial, public, professional, and meritorious operation of supervisory institutions is the key to adequate supervision of companies' due diligence obligations.[48] Since NCP decides on such vital issues in business and human rights, it must be composed of people who have internalized its values and are distinguished by professionalism, meritoriousness, and transparency. State supervisory institutions can only realize the postulates of equal and fair supervision through their self-government's transparent and honest operation. Despite these theoretical goals, many OECD Member states face numerous challenges in the daily operation of public administration, from ensuring transparent operation to fair decision-making.[49] Some NCPs often suffer from allegedly dependent and non-transparent decision-making. Supervisory institutions must gain the population's trust through open and honest work and a willingness to expose themselves to the supervision of civil society and other state institutions.

A substantive submission can be sent to the Investment Committee if the rightsholders disagree with an NCP's final statement. Nevertheless, there is still much room for improvement. The Investment Committee could be more diligent in providing decisions concerning substantive submissions. On the other hand, there are several dilemmas concerning the case law of NCPs and supervision of implementing the

---

[46] OECD (2023a, b) OECD Guidelines for Multinational Enterprises National Contact Point Peer Reviews: Morocco, https://mneguidelines.oecd.org//ncps/national-contact-point-peer-reviews-morocco.pdf, p. 20.

[47] OECD (2021a) OECD Guidelines for Multinational Enterprises National Contact Point Peer Reviews: Korea, https://mneguidelines.oecd.org/oecd-guidelines-for-multinational-enterprises-national-contact-peer-reviews-korea.pdf (last accessed 30 April 2024), p. 6.

[48] Michalakea T (2022).

[49] Ingrams and Booth (2023).

OECD Guidelines. The OECD Member States should ensure that governmental, political, or business interests do not capture NCPs.[50] Indeed, NCPs are part of the state and public administration. Undoubtedly, it is challenging to insist on independence in the workings of administrative organs. Still, impartiality should be a minimum, which all NCPs should comply with, as well as the fairness of procedures. Additionally, confidentiality has always been a challenge in procedures before the NCPs, as generally, in business and human rights, businesses are reluctant to keep their information public. There are rare findings of non-compliance in very few final statements with findings of violations and sanctions.

How can the supervision of the OECD Committee improve? OECD will always submit that OECD Guidelines are recommendations. However, there are some issues where they could improve their work, particularly concerning the follow-up of peer review, including different stakeholders in the peer review and including their comments and suggestions in the final report; not all the comments that civil society in academia submit to the peer review are heeded. The main challenge is achieving the enforceability of OECD Guidelines in business and human rights.[51] Civil society places a lot of hope or faith in the mechanism as there is a lack of similar, successful mechanisms to enforce business-related human rights abuses.[52] At least in civil society and academia, the NCPs are often considered a mechanism that has been partially successful, in contrast to some other international mechanisms, in bringing cases against corporations, notwithstanding some domestic cases.[53]

It is important to strengthen them and protect the human dignity of right-holders. As a result, OECD member states should proceed to reform the OECD Investment Committee, which should perform its functions in a way that harmonizes different approaches of the NCPs. The OECD Investment Committee could also sanction the NCPs that perform poorly, particularly those in Central and Eastern Europe and perhaps in some countries of Latin America. As for the future of the OECD Guidelines, what could be some proposals on how to improve and strengthen the function of the OECD Guidelines?

The first step is maintaining the flexibility and predictability of procedures, making them clear and transparent, publishing the concerns of the rights holders, and letting them know where to turn. Moreover, promoting OECD Guidelines is essential among civil society and stakeholders. After more than 20 years of functioning, only a few hundred cases have been resolved. One issue that civil society needs to be more mindful of is the promotion of the NCPs among rights holders.

Second, one could argue for a proposal to harmonize procedural practices of all NCPs. Typical suspects of best practices are NCPs from Sweden, Norway, Netherlands, UK, Sweden, Switzerland, and Germany, among others. As such, uniform procedural rules should be developed for all NCPs. Accordingly, the OECD Committee could supervise a more uniform, harmonized application of procedural

[50] Letnar Černič J (2021); Letnar Černič J (2022), 1–23.

[51] Ingrams M G (2023); 427–433.

[52] Schuler G (2008), 1753–1778.

[53] Simon Perillo P (2022), 36–56; Bhatt K, Erdem Türkelli G (2021).

guidance and strengthen peer review among national contact points. There are many good examples from different NCPs who resorted to more experienced NCPs' assistance. For example, the South Korean NCP improved after it consulted the Dutch NCP.[54] As a result, some examples of synergies exist, but much more could have been done.

Third, another proposal is to create an independent, impartial supervisory mechanism of Guidelines, perhaps to strengthen the OECD Committee to make it more efficient and to appoint OECD Committee Experts from all areas of business and human rights, not only from governments but also from companies and civil society. Ombudsman-like mechanisms are another example. It would be helpful to adopt good practices from financial ombudsman mechanisms in some European countries that deal with complaints against businesses and certain business sectors.

Finally, what should be NCPs' complementary role to the existing and recently created mandatory due diligence supervisory mechanisms? How can the NCPs complement national or competent authorities in implementing, for example, the Conflict Minerals Regulation or the newly adopted EU CSDDD, particularly how to strengthen supervision processes? In many countries, the problem is that weak institutions and the weak rule of law hamper the implementation of OECD Guidelines. As a result, much work must be done in a national environment.

All in all, the room for improvement of the OECD Guidelines is the widest in the enforcement area. Several NCPs have strengthened their proceedings' independence, impartiality, and fairness in the last decade. However, the practice of different NCPs remains variable. As a result, rights-holders in other member states of the OECD need equal access to fair, impartial, and independent proceedings before NCPs concerning business-related human rights and environmental violations. Notably, there is a need for more uniformity, impartiality, and independence in many NCPs. Politics and corporate interests have undermined several of them in the past. The prospects for a similar body outside state institutions could be promising. As a result, the industry and sector private transnational bodies may prove more effective in complementing the role and functions of state institutions.

6 Conclusion

Rights-holders have, for decades, argued in vain for effective remedies for business-related human rights abuses both at domestic and international levels. They have often suffered due to an imbalance of powers in business-related human rights abuses. All too often in public administrations, one can observe formalism, authoritarianism, and the absence of a discursive evaluation of arguments. For NCPs to function well, they must open to the public, as this is the only way to increase ordinary people's trust in

[54] OECD Watch, State of Remedy 2022: Examining Outcomes of Complaints Concluded in 2022, Exploring Highlights for Remedy under the Updated OECD Guidelines, 19 July 2023, https://www.oecdwatch.org/state-of-remedy-2022/ (last accessed 30 April 2024).

their operation. Proper, independent, impartial, public, professional, and meritorious operation of supervisory institutions is the key to adequate supervision of companies' due diligence obligations. Since NCPs decide on such vital issues in business and human rights, they must be composed of persons who have internalized its values and are distinguished by professionalism, meritoriousness, and transparency. State supervisory institutions can only realize the postulates of equal and fair supervision through their government's transparent and honest operation. This chapter analysed and discussed the normative frameworks for implementing the OECD Guidelines for Multinational Enterprises on Responsible Business Conduct. It discussed how the implementation mechanisms could be improved and harmonized, enabling rights-holders access to remedies in case of alleged business-related human rights abuses. The peer review mechanism of the NCPs could strengthen enforcement mechanisms under the OECD Guidelines. All in all, enforcement mechanisms before NCPs could provide meaningful justice for rights-holders only if the OECD Member States and the OECD Investment Committee can close the coherence gap among different NCPs by harmonizing procedural rules and introducing the possibility of full-fledges sanctions of companies and providing them with effective right to remedies.

References

Journal Articles

Backer LC (2011) From Institutional misalignments to socially sustainable governance: the guiding principles for the implementation of the United Nations protect, respect and remedy and the construction of inter-systemic global governance. Pacific McGeorge Glob Bus Devel Law J 25(1):69–172

Bhatt K, Erdem Türkelli G (2021) OECD national contact points as sites of effective remedy: new expressions of the role and rule of law within market globalization? Bus Human Rights J 6(3):423–448

Buhmann K (2018) Analyzing OECD national contact point statements for guidance on human rights due diligence: method, findings and outlook. Nordic J Human Rights 36(4):390–410

Ingrams MG (2023) The 2023 update of the OECD guidelines sets stronger standards for companies but weak expectations for governments – high and lowlights from the new text. Bus Human Rights J 8(3):427–433

Letnar Černič J (2021) The divergent practices of NCPs under OECD guidelines for multinational enterprises: time for a more uniform approach? Intern Labor Rights Case Law J 7(1):11–16

Letnar Černič J (2022) The human rights due diligence standard-setting in the European Union: bridging the gap between ambition and reality. Global Bus Law Rev 10(1):1–23

Michalakea T (2022) Anti-corruption and transitional justice: a distinction without a difference. Human Rights Law Rev 22(2) https://doi.org/10.1093/hrlr/ngac014

Parella K (2020) Hard and soft law preferences in business and human rights. AJIL Unbound 114:168–173

Ramasastry A (2015) Corporate social responsibility versus business and human rights: bridging the gap between responsibility and accountability. J Human Rights 14(2):237–259

Ratnaningsih E (2023) Responsibilities of multinational corporations in their business in global supply chains in Indonesia: a case study approach. AIP Conf Proc 2594(1):110008–1/9

Ruggie JG (2007) Business and human rights: the evolving agenda. Am J Intern Law 101(4):819–840

Ruggie JG, Rees C, Davis R (2021) Ten years after: from UN guiding principles to multi-fiduciary obligations. Bus Human Rights J 6(2):179–197
Schuler G (2008) Effective governance through decentralized soft implementation: the OECD guidelines for multinational enterprises. German Law J 9(11):1753–1778
Simon Perillo P (2022) The role of the OECD guidelines for multinational enterprises and the national contact points in shaping the future of corporate accountability. Intern Comm Law Rev 24(1–2):36–56
Van Ho T (2021) Defining the relationships: "cause, contribute, and directly linked to" in the UN Guiding principles on business and human rights'. Hum Rights Q 43(4):625–658
Van't Foort S (2017) The history of national contact points and the OECD guidelines for multinational enterprises. Rechtsgeschichte - Legal History 25:195-214
Wettstein F, Giuliani E, Santangelo GD, Stahl GK (2019) International business and human rights: a research agenda. J World Bus 54(1):54–65

Cases

NCP Belgium (2011) Greenpeace India vs. Dredging International, Final Statement by the Belgian National Contact Point for the OECD Guidelines for Multinational Enterprises
NCP Brazil (2016) *Forum Suape et al. vs. Van Oord*, Final Statement
NCP Canada (2015) *Canada Tibet Committee vs. China Gold Int. Resources*, Final Statement
NCP Korea (2021) Korean Civil Society in Solidarity with Rohingya, Korean Transnational Corporation Watch and Justice for Myanmar vs. Inno Group, Initial Assessment
NCP Netherlands (2017) *Former employees of Bralima vs. Bralima and Heineken*, Final Statement
NCP Netherlands (2019) *Friends of the Earth Netherlands (Milieudefensie) vs. ING*, Final Statement
NCP Netherlands (2019) *Oxfam Novib, Greenpeace Netherlands, BankTrack and Friends of the Earth (Netherlands) vs. ING bank*, Final statement
NCP Sweden (2016) *Jijnjevaerie Saami village vs. Statkraft SCA Vind AB (SSVAB)*, Final Statement
NCP Switzerland (2021) *Society for Threatened Peoples Switzerland vs. BKW Group*, Final Statement
NCP United Kingdom (2017) *Bahrain Institute for Rights and Democracy vs. HPG*, Final Statement, 8 December 2021.NCP United Kingdom, *Crude Accountability vs. KPO Consortium*, Final Statement
NCP United Kingdom (2021) *Global Legal Action Network vs. Anglo American Plc*, on-going, specific instance submitted
NCP United Kingdom (2021) *Lawyers for Palestinian Human Rights vs. J.C. Bamford Ltd*, Final Statement

OECD Legal Instruments

OECD (1976) OECD Declaration on International Investment and Multinational Enterprises
OECD (2021) National Contact Point Peer Reviews: Core Template, https://mneguidelines.oecd.org/national-contact-point-peer-reviews-core-template.pdf (last accessed 30 April 2024)
OECD (2021a) OECD Guidelines for Multinational Enterprises National Contact Point Peer Reviews: Korea, https://mneguidelines.oecd.org/oecd-guidelines-for-multinational-enterprises-national-contact-peer-reviews-korea.pdf (last accessed 30 April 2024)
OECD (2022) Annual report on the Activity of National Contact Points for Responsible Business Conduct, https://mneguidelines.oecd.org/annual-report-on-the-activity-of-national-contact-points-for-responsible-business-conduct-2021.pdf (last accessed 30 April 2024)

OECD (2022a) OECD guidelines for multinational enterprises national contact point peer reviews: Sweden. https://mneguidelines.oecd.org//national-contact-point-peer-reviews-sweden.pdf (last accessed 30 April 2024)

OECD (2022b) OECD guidelines for multinational enterprises national contact point peer reviews: Slovenia. https://mneguidelines.oecd.org//national-contact-point-peer-reviews-slovenia.pdf (last accessed 30 April 2024)

OECD (2022c) OECD Guidelines for Multinational Enterprises National Contact Point Peer Reviews: Brazil. https://mneguidelines.oecd.org//national-contact-point-peer-reviews-brazil.pdf (last accessed 30 April 2024)

OECD (2022d) OECD Guidelines for Multinational Enterprises National Contact Point Peer Reviews: Australia. https://mneguidelines.oecd.org//national-contact-point-peer-reviews-australia.pdf (last accessed 30 April 2024)

OECD (2023) OECD Guidelines for Multinational Enterprises National Contact Point Peer Reviews: Morocco. https://mneguidelines.oecd.org//ncps/national-contact-point-peer-reviews-morocco.pdf (last accessed 30 April 2024)

OECD (2023a) OECD guidelines for multinational enterprises national contact point peer reviews: peru, https://mneguidelines.oecd.org//ncps/national-contact-point-peer-reviews-peru.pdf (last accessed 30 April 2024)

OECD (2023b) OECD Guidelines for Multinational Enterprises on Responsible Business Conduct

OECD, List of OECD Member countries - Ratification of the Convention on the OECD. https://www.oecd.org/about/document/ratification-oecd-convention.htm (last accessed 30 April 2024)

Legislation

Act on corporate due diligence in supply Chains, Bundestag, 16 July 2021

Directive (EU) 2022/2464 of the European Parliament and of the Council of 14 December 2022 amending Regulation (EU) No 537/2014, Directive 2004/109/EC, Directive 2006/43/EC, Directive 2013/34/EU, as regards corporate sustainability reporting (Text with EEA relevance), PE/35/2022/REV/1, OJ L 322, 16.12.2022, 15–80

Loi 2017–399 du 27 Mars 2017 relative au devoir de vigilance des sociétés mères et des entreprises donneuses d'ordre, Official Gazette of the Republic of France, 27 March 2017, article L. 225–102–4

Modern Slavery Act 2015, UK Public General Acts2015 c. 30

Modern Slavery Act 2018 (No. 153, 2018), Australia, 12 October 2018

Regulation (EU) 2017/821 of the European Parliament and of the Council of 17 May 2017 laying down supply chain due diligence obligations for Union importers of tin, tantalum and tungsten, their ores, and gold originating from conflict-affected and high-risk areas, OJ L 130, 19.5.2017, 1–20

The California Transparency in Supply Chains Act of 2010 (SB 657)

UNHRC (2011) The Guiding Principles on Business and Human Rights: Implementing the United Nations 'Protect, Respect and Remedy' Framework, UN Doc. A/HRC/17/31

United Nations Human Rights Council, Guiding Principles on Business and Human Rights: Implementing the United Nations "Protect, Respect and Remedy" Framework, A/HRC/17/31 (21 March 2011)

Others

Davaanyam O, Krajewski M (2023) Guardians of Rights? The Role of Government in Promoting Responsible Business Conduct under the Updated OECD Guidelines for Multinational Enterprises, OECD Watch, Blog symposium co-organised by OECD Watch and NOVA School of Law, 30 November 2023, https://www.oecdwatch.org/guardians-of-rights-the-role-of-governments/ (last accessed 30 April 2024)

European Commission, Proposal for a Directive the European Parliament and of the Council on Corporate Sustainability Due Diligence and amending Directive (EU) 2019/1937, COM/2022/71 final

Ingrams MG, Booth K (2023) Hardening soft law: Strategic use of the OECD Guidelines to achieve meaningful outcomes. Columbia FDI Perspectives, No. 351

OECD (2022) Stocktaking Report on the OECD Guidelines for Multinational Enterprises

OECD Watch, Complaints, https://www.oecdwatch.org/complaints-database/ (last accessed 30 April 2024)

OECD Watch (2023) State of Remedy 2022: Examining Outcomes of Complaints Concluded in 2022, Exploring Highlights for Remedy under the Updated OECD Guidelines. https://www.oecdwatch.org/state-of-remedy-2022/ (last accessed 30 April 2024)

NCP Netherlands (2014) *NUON Energy NV vs. FNV Eemshaven*, Final Statement

NCP Switzerland (2019) *TUK Indonesia vs. Roundtable for Sustainable Palm Oil*, Final Statement

UN, CESCR, General Comment No. 24 (2017) on State Obligations Under the International Covenant on Economic, Social and Cultural Rights in the Context of Business Activities, UN Doc. E/C.12/GC/24

UN (1998) CESCR, General Comment No. 9: The Domestic Application of the Covenant, UN Doc. E/C.12/1998/24

Degrees of Remedy: Understanding Remedy Outcomes at the OECD National Contact Points

Kari Otteburn

Abstract Nonjudicial mechanisms such as the National Contact Points (NCPs) for the Organization of Economic Cooperation and Development Guidelines for Multinational Enterprises on Responsible Business Conduct play a prominent role in access to remedy for victims of extraterritorial human rights abuses resulting from business activities. Yet, a body of research has cast doubt on their effectiveness, highlighting numerous challenges of procedure and design. Considerably less attention, however, has been paid to remedy outcomes through nonjudicial mechanisms. In particular, the appropriateness of outcomes has not been evaluated vis-à-vis the alleged violations. This chapter presents and analyzes a new dataset of remedy outcomes for transnational business-related human rights abuses at the NCPs. The findings demonstrate that NCPs are fairly effective at providing access to minor forms of remedy but are unable to provide appropriate remedy for severe violations. As the remedial landscape evolves alongside new mandatory rules for corporate conduct, these findings may help better situate nonjudicial mechanisms within the remedial architecture.

1 Introduction

While it is well-established in international human rights law that victims of human rights abuses have the right to an effective remedy,[1] when those abuses are committed by businesses in the course of conducting business, particularly across borders, the

K. Otteburn (✉)
Leuven Centre for Global Governance Studies, KU Leuven, Leuven, Belgium
e-mail: kari.otteburn@kuleuven.be

[1] This right is set out in United Nations General Assembly (UNGA) (1948), *Universal Declaration of Human Rights* (UDHR), A/RES/217A adopted 10 December 1948, Article 8, and confirmed in UNGA (1966), International Covenant for Civil and Political Rights (ICCPR), A/RES/2200A, adopted 16 December 1966, entered into force 23 March 1976, Article 2, in addition to numerous regional treaties on human rights (e.g. Council of Europe (CoE) (1950), European Convention on Human Rights (ECHR), adopted 4 November 1950, Article 13, and Organization of American States (OAS) (1969), American Convention on Human Rights (ACHR), adopted 22 November 1969, Article 25.

O. Davaanyam and M. Krajewski (eds.), *Exploring Corporate Human Rights Responsibilities in OECD Case Law*, Interdisciplinary Studies in Human Rights 14,
https://doi.org/10.1007/978-3-031-75717-4_6

calculus for accessing remedy changes significantly. Considerable research has shed light on manifold barriers that victims of transnational business-related human rights abuses face in accessing remedy in national and international legal fora.[2] In this context, nonjudicial mechanisms have been relied upon to provide additional avenues for access to remedy. The United Nations Guiding Principles on Business and Human Rights (UNGP),[3] which has formed the normative foundation for businesses' responsibilities toward human rights since its adoption in 2011, envisions a prominent role for nonjudicial mechanisms in complementing and supplementing judicial mechanisms in the provision of access to remedy. To this end, a variety of diverse state- and non-state-based nonjudicial mechanisms have emerged or been revamped in recent years as the right to effective remedy as well as the existing barriers to access to remedy have become the focus of greater attention by states and regional and international organizations.[4]

Though nonjudicial mechanisms were never meant to replace judicial ones, the often insurmountable barriers to accessing remedy for extraterritorial business-related human rights abuses through courts have made it so that legal avenues are generally out of reach for most victims. In practice, nonjudicial mechanisms are the only available option—even for very grave allegations. Despite this, and while a growing body of research has begun to assess nonjudicial mechanisms in providing access to remedy,[5] what remedy *outcomes* actually look like through nonjudicial mechanisms remains unclear. In particular, most accounts have generally left aside questions regarding the appropriateness of remedy outcomes, which relies on an assessment of 'degree' in two senses: the degree of severity (or gravity) of the alleged violations handled by nonjudicial mechanisms and the degree of remedy outcomes afforded by these mechanisms.

If nonjudicial mechanisms are indeed to play a role—however significant—in the remedial architecture, either as a stop-gap measure as they are now or supplemental to courts as envisioned by the UNGP, these questions matter. While gravity of cases[6] and the appropriateness of remedies[7] have long been subjects of inquiry in international law, these topics have more or less been sidestepped with respect to

---

[2] Human Rights Council (HRC) (2016), *Improving Accountability and Access to Remedy for Victims of Business-Related Human Rights Abuse*, A/HRC/32/19, adopted 10 May 2016; Marx et al. (2019), Skinner et al. (2013), George and Laplante (2017), Prihandono (2011).

[3] HRC (2011), *Guiding Principles on Business and Human Rights: Implementing the United Nations 'Protect, Respect and Remedy' Framework*, A/HRC/17/31, adopted 21 March 2011.

[4] For example, the Office of the High Commissioner for Human Rights (OHCHR) Accountability and Remedy Project (ARP) launched in 2014, https://www.ohchr.org/en/business/ohchr-accountability-and-remedy-project (last accessed 8 May 2024) has carried out a sweeping exploration of access to remedy through judicial mechanisms, state-based nonjudicial mechanisms, and non-state-based nonjudicial mechanisms; see also G20, G20 Leaders' Declaration: Shaping an interconnected world, 8 July 2017, https://www.consilium.europa.eu/media/23955/g20-hamburg-leaders_-communiqu%C3%A9.pdf (last accessed 10 June 2023).

[5] See Sect. 2.1

[6] Deguzman (2012), Lopez (2020), Pues (2017).

[7] Shelton (2005); Article 15, General Assembly resolution 60/147, *Basic Principles and Guidelines on the Right to a Remedy and Reparation for Victims of Gross Violations of International Human*

nonjudicial mechanisms in the field of business and human rights. Despite a long-standing consensus in public international law that remedy outcomes should aim to restore a victim to the situation they would have been in had the violation not occurred (the so-called 'Chorzów standard of full reparation')[8] and should be 'proportional to the gravity of the violations and the harm suffered',[9] the same standards are generally not applied to remedy outcomes for extraterritorial human rights abuses resulting from business activities.

Yet if we are to take seriously that victims of transnational business-related human rights abuses possess internationally recognized human rights, which entail that the rights-holder has access to an effective remedy (including reparations), remedy outcomes through nonjudicial mechanisms should be evaluated using the same criteria. While previous research has demonstrated that nonjudicial mechanisms often fail to operate effectively and, as a result, access to remedy through these mechanisms has been rather limited,[10] most studies have been limited in scope to a handful of case studies,[11] and overall the type and severity of transnational business-related human rights abuses nonjudicial mechanisms can reliably handle and the form and appropriateness of the possible remedy outcomes available through nonjudicial mechanisms remain unknown.

This chapter therefore proposes a rights-centered perspective to conceptualize and assess the alleged complaints and remedy outcomes for one of the most prominent and frequently used nonjudicial mechanisms: the National Contact Points (NCPs) for the Organization for Economic Cooperation and Development (OECD) Guidelines for Multinational Enterprises on Responsible Business Conduct (OECD Guidelines).[12] To do so, it introduces a new dataset comprising all cases concerning an instance of transnational business-related human rights abuse that were concluded at the NCPs between 2012 and 2021. The 81 cases are scored on several factors previously sidestepped including the gravity of the alleged violation, the degree of remedy sought by the rights-holders, and the degree of remedy ultimately achieved.

Based on an analysis of this data, the chapter formulates several novel insights as to how cases of varying degrees of gravity are handled by the NCP system as well

---

Rights Law and Serious Violations of International Humanitarian Law, adopted 16 December 2005, UNGA.

[8] PCIJ, *The Factory at Chorzów (Germany v Poland)* Permanent Court of International Justice(13 September 1928), Merits 47. See also the commentary to Article 34, *Draft Articles on the Responsibility of States for Internationally Wrongful Acts with Commentaries*, adopted 2001, International Law Commission.

[9] UNGA (2005),, *Basic Principles and Guidelines on the Right to a Remedy and Reparation for Victims of Gross Violations of International Human Rights Law and Serious Violations of International Humanitarian Law*, A/RES/60/147, adopted 16 December 2005, Article 15.

[10] Thompson (2017), Haines and Macdonald (2019), Otteburn (2023), HRC (2018), *Improving accountability and access to remedy for victims of business-related human rights abuse through State-based non-judicial mechanisms*, A/HRC/38/20, adopted 14 May 2018; Daniel C et al. (2015), Bhatt and Erdem Türkelli (2021), Wielga and Harrison (2021), Bugalski (2016).

[11] Van Huijstee and Wilde-Ramsing (2020).

[12] OECD (2023), *Guidelines for Multinational Enterprises on Responsible Business Conduct*, adopted 8 June 2023, OECD.

as the adequacy of remedies achieved and how the system meets the expectations of rights-holders. Overall, the findings show that the NCP system—and likely nonjudicial mechanisms more broadly—only offers rights-compatible access to remedy for allegations of transnational business-related human rights abuses that require more limited forms of remedy and is therefore unsuitable for allegations of grave abuses. But the reverse of this is also true: the mechanism frequently facilitates access to a minor forms of remedy for less severe violations. Because the NCPs present considerable institutional diversity, the findings are likely to have important implications for the use of nonjudicial mechanisms more generally as remedy institutions, particularly as part of a broader system of remedy—implications that are especially relevant as negotiations are ongoing at regional and international levels concerning mandatory due diligence legislation.

This chapter proceeds as follows. The next section sets the scene by considering the role of nonjudicial mechanisms as remedy institutions and the right to effective remedy for transnational business-related human rights abuses, as well as conceptualizing gravity and degree of remedy. The dataset is then introduced in Sect. 3 alongside the methodology for its collection and coding. This data is then analyzed and discussed. A conclusion follows.

2 Right to Remedy for Transnational Business-Related Human Rights Abuses

2.1 *The Role of Nonjudicial Mechanisms*

Though they take different institutional forms, draw their mandates from diverse sources, and follow a wide range of procedures, overall nonjudicial mechanisms offer a non-legal but 'routinized' process through which 'grievances concerning business-related human rights abuse can be raised and remedy can be sought'.[13] They are typically employed to monitor compliance with various non-binding, voluntary, or 'soft law' standards or guidance related to responsible business conduct, such as company codes of conduct, voluntary or industry regulatory standards, or national or international guidelines on business conduct such as the OECD Guidelines. Scheltema identifies five general types of nonjudicial mechanisms: (1) company or project-level grievance mechanisms; (2) mechanisms linked to industry and multistakeholder initiatives; (3) national mechanisms based in government; (4) national mechanisms

[13] HRC (2011), *Guiding Principles on Business and Human Rights: Implementing the United Nations 'Protect, Respect and Remedy' Framework*, A/HRC/17/31, adopted 21 March 2011, Commentary to Principle 25.

that are state-supported but independent of government; and (5) regional and international mechanisms.[14] The OHCHR gives a number of examples,[15] including labour tribunals, national human rights institutions or ombudsmen offices,[16] the NCPs for the OECD Guidelines, company-level grievance mechanisms, grievance mechanisms set up by multistakeholder initiatives or voluntary sustainability standards and accountability mechanisms of development finance institutions (DFIs).

Beyond merely taking the burden off of courts, proponents of nonjudicial mechanisms argue that informal types of dispute resolution, often centered around mediation, can be superior to adjudication in many cases, allowing for greater empowerment of the victims who have an equal place at the mediation table and for creativity in reaching solutions to complex issues and even systemic change[17]—this resonates strongly with the movement for restorative justice in criminal justice and human-rights based approaches (HRBA) to development, both of which emphasize the importance of the participation of victims.[18] In addition, nonjudicial mechanisms are thought to be more flexible and accessible than judicial mechanisms, capable of facilitating solutions before a problem escalates and requires recourse to judicial fora.[19]

Though the UNGP encourage the use of nonjudicial mechanisms to complement and support—but not replace—judicial mechanisms in providing access to remedy,[20] the inaccessibility of legal avenues of redress has made nonjudicial mechanisms the primary and, in many cases, only fora for addressing transnational business-related human rights abuses. They are thus increasingly required to address serious allegations, including those involving modern slavery, deaths, child labour, and forced evictions.

Yet, despite their centrality to the remedial architecture for human rights violations arising from transnational business activity, growing research on nonjudicial mechanisms—including the grievance mechanisms of multistakeholder initiatives,[21] accountability mechanisms of DFIs including the inspection panel and the Office of

---

[14] Scheltema (2013).

[15] Second and third reports of the ARP: HRC (2018), *Improving accountability and access to remedy for victims of business-related human rights abuse through State-based nonjudicial mechanisms*, A/HRC/38/20, adopted 14 May 2018, https://www.ohchr.org/en/business/ohchr-accountability-and-remedy-project (last accessed 8 May 2024), HRC (2020), *Improving accountability and access to remedy for victims of business-related human rights abuse through non-State-based grievance mechanisms*, A/HRC/44/32, adopted 19 May 2020, https://www.ohchr.org/en/business/ohchr-accountability-and-remedy-project (last accessed 8 May 2024).

[16] See also Reif (2022).

[17] Rees (2010).

[18] On restorative justice and human rights, see Skelton (2018); on HRBA, see Miller and Redhead (2019).

[19] Van Huijstee and Wilde-Ramsing (2020).

[20] HRC (2011), *Guiding Principles on Business and Human Rights: Implementing the United Nations 'Protect, Respect and Remedy' Framework*, A/HRC/17/31, adopted 21 March 2011, Commentary to Principle 27.

[21] See Wielga and Harrison (2021), Daniel et al. (2015), MSI Integrity (2020).

Compliance Advisor Ombudsman of the World Bank,[22] the NCPs for the OECD Guidelines,[23] national human rights institutions,[24] company-level grievance mechanisms[25] and others—has demonstrated an inconsistent, often poor, record with regard to the provision of access to remedy.[26] These studies point out numerous institutional and procedural deficiencies in these mechanisms that prevent their effective functioning as remedy institutions. Moreover, it is increasingly recognized that there may be upper limits to the remedial potential of nonjudicial mechanisms.[27]

While some have skirted this challenge by pointing out the fact that, very often, nonjudicial mechanisms are the only available option,[28] a better understanding of the possibilities and limits of nonjudicial mechanisms with regard to the provision of remedy is crucially needed. Not least if they expected to (continue to) form part of a larger system of remedy envisioned by the UNGP.[29] This idea of a remedial division of labour has taken hold. Ideally, this vision sees more severe cases as reserved for the courts, with nonjudicial mechanisms capable of picking up the slack for cases that are less grave or require non-legal solutions or providing an option for early intervention through dialogue. This hierarchy has been further emphasized by the OHCHR Accountability and Remedy Project (ARP): the second and third ARP reports on nonjudicial mechanisms note that since not all types of remedies may be available through nonjudicial mechanisms, states must take care to carefully demarcate the roles and responsibilities of state and non-state-based nonjudicial and judicial mechanisms based on 'the type, nature and severity of different business-related human rights harms' while recognizing that 'effective judicial mechanisms are at the core of ensuring access to remedy.'[30] Relatedly, the Committee on Economic, Social and Cultural Rights (CESCR) of the OHCHR emphasizes this point in one of two general comments (GC) that concern business and human rights,[31] stating that

---

[22] See for example, Bugalski (2016), Bhatt (2020), chapter 4.

[23] Daniel et al (2015), Ingrams et al. (2021), Buhmann (2020), Balaton-Chrimes and Haines (2017), Bhatt and Erdem Türkelli (2021).

[24] Prihandono et al. (2021), Wolfsteller (2022).

[25] Knuckey and Jenkin (2015), Thompson (2017).

[26] Haines and Macdonald (2020), Van Huijstee and Wilde-Ramsing (2020), Scheltema (2013), HRC (2018), *Improving accountability and access to remedy for victims of business-related human rights abuse through State-based nonjudicial mechanisms*, A/HRC/38/20, adopted 14 May 2018; HRC (2020), *Improving accountability and access to remedy for victims of business-related human rights abuse through non-State-based grievance mechanisms*, A/HRC/44/32, adopted 19 May 2020.

[27] Otteburn (2023).

[28] Van Huijstee and Wilde-Ramsing (2020).

[29] HRC (2011), *Guiding Principles on Business and Human Rights: Implementing the United Nations 'Protect, Respect and Remedy' Framework*, A/HRC/17/31, adopted 21 March 2011, Commentary to Principle 26.

[30] HRC (2020), *Improving accountability and access to remedy for victims of business-related human rights abuse through non-State-based grievance mechanisms*, A/HRC/44/32, adopted 19 May 2020, 8–9.

[31] Reif (2022).

means of redress should 'preferably take the form of ensuring access to independent and impartial judicial bodies,'[32] citing a previous GC to add that 'other means [of ensuring accountability] used could be rendered ineffective if they are not reinforced or complemented by judicial remedies'.[33] Scholars, too, have subscribed to this notion. A compelling metaphor by van Huijstee and Wilde-Ramsing explains that 'judicial mechanisms are the spine of the remedy system: they form the core and handle the most serious cases' whereas nonjudicial mechanisms 'are like the fingertips: they are more sensitive and can reach into places that are inaccessible to the spine, solving problems and providing remedy early and creatively before a major disaster occurs'.[34] While this hierarchy is currently not operational due to major existing barriers to seeking effective remedy for transnational business-related human rights abuses through judicial mechanisms, if hope remains for a comprehensive remedial system to function in the future, it will be important and necessary to define the parameters for nonjudicial mechanisms within this system.

This, however, is complicated by considerable ambiguity with regard to what constitutes an effective remedy *outcome* in the context of human rights abuses committed by businesses.

2.2 Understanding Effective Remedy Outcomes

It has been increasingly acknowledged that existing frameworks for understanding effective remedy in the context of transnational business-related human rights abuses, and especially nonjudicial mechanisms, are inadequate. In the business and human rights context, the most authoritative and far-reaching concept of effective remedy is provided by the UNGP. However, as others have noted, the UNGP focus primarily on procedural criteria for remedy, paying less attention to what constitutes effective remedy outcomes, and in particular the substantive outcomes that aim to repair the harm caused to the victim(s)[35] (hereafter, 'reparations'). The UNGP provides a list of eight criteria for effective remedy, of which seven relate to procedure and only one has to do with outcomes, which specifies that outcomes and remedies be 'rights-compatible' and 'accord with internationally recognized human rights.'[36]

[32] OHCHR (2017), *GC No. 24, on State obligations under the International Covenant on Economic, Social and Cultural Rights in the context of business activities*, E/C.12/GC/24, adopted 10 August 2017, Para. 39.

[33] OHCHR (2017), *GC No. 24, on State obligations under the International Covenant on Economic, Social and Cultural Rights in the context of business activities*, E/C.12/GC/24, adopted 10 August 2017, Para. 39, citing CESCR (1998), *GC No. 9, The domestic application of the Covenant*, E/C.12/1998/24, adopted 3 December 1998.

[34] Van Huijstee and Wilde-Ramsing (2020).

[35] Otteburn (2023), Buhmann (2023).

[36] HRC (2011), *Guiding Principles on Business and Human Rights: Implementing the United Nations 'Protect, Respect and Remedy' Framework*, A/HRC/17/31, adopted 21 March 2011, Principle 31.

However, the UNGP do stipulate that the goal of remedy is 'to counteract or make good any human rights harms that have occurred' and that substantively remedies can take various forms 'apologies, restitution, rehabilitation, financial or non-financial compensation and punitive sanctions (whether criminal or administrative, such as fines), as well as the prevention of harm through, for example, injunctions or guarantees of non-repetition.'[37]

This framework faces several shortcomings that have been noted by many scholars. In light of this, a handful of scholars have made various proposals for assessing and measuring whether an outcome can be considered effective remedy. This has led to the articulation of proposals for additional criteria[38] for evaluating remedy outcomes, such as the cessation of ongoing violations,[39] reparation of the harm that has occurred,[40] inclusion or consideration of the preferences and satisfaction of the stakeholders or claimants,[41] enforceability,[42] and whether outcomes have a transformative or deterrent component that helps address systemic problems or prevent similar abuses from occurring in the future.[43]

Despite this, it remains that the definition and contours of effective remedy outcomes have not yet been fully unpacked for transnational business-related human rights abuses. In particular, these proposals, have generally left aside (both intentionally and unintentionally) two key deficiencies in the conceptualization of reparations for human rights abuses arising from exterritorial business activity, which are an important means to restore justice, recognize and remedy the suffering of victims, and deter further harm.[44]

First, it is unclear to what extent reparations should counteract the harm to be considered effective. In international law, the most widely accepted understanding of reparations is that they are expected to 'wipe out all the consequences of the illegal act and reestablish the situation which would, in all probability, have existed if that act had not been committed.'[45] In other words, remedial outcomes should 'aim to place an aggrieved party in the same position as he or she would have been in had no injury occurred.'[46] This Chorzów standard of 'full reparation' is sought or claimed across numerous areas of international law, even if it is not always applied in

---

[37] HRC (2011), *Guiding Principles on Business and Human Rights: Implementing the United Nations 'Protect, Respect and Remedy' Framework*, A/HRC/17/31, adopted 21 March 2011, Commentary to Principle 25.

[38] Van Huijstee and Wilde-Ramsing (2020) provide a convenient overview of these proposals, 485.

[39] Wielga and Harrison (2021), Daniel et al. (2015).

[40] Wielga and Harrison (2021), Daniel et al. (2015).

[41] HRC (2014), *Report of the Working Group on the Issue of Human Rights and Transnational Corporations and Other Business Enterprises*', A/HRC/26/25, adopted 5 May 2014,; Thompson (2017), Bhatt and Erdem Türkelli (2021).

[42] Bhatt and Erdem Türkelli (2021).

[43] Scheltema (2017).

[44] Shelton (2005), Naidu and Torpey (2012).

[45] PCIJ, *The Factory at Chorzów (Germany v Poland)* (13 September 1928), Merits 47.

[46] Shelton (2005), 10.

practice.[47] In national legal systems, it is almost always the case that full reparation is due to the victim from the wrongdoer with the aim of 'making good' the injury that was caused to the victim.[48]

However, the UNGP lack specific guidance as to the extent of reparation due to a victim of transnational business-related human rights abuse; so while it uses the same phrasing as international law ('make good'), its meaning is not clear to many end-users of the UNGP—namely rights-holders and businesses—who lack familiarity with international law. Indeed, potential forms of substantive remedy outcomes are presented without any hierarchy or order, giving the impression that the forms of reparations are equally valid and perhaps even roughly interchangeable; the UNGP do not specify that the appropriate form of remedy be determined in proportion to the alleged harm. Yet the options proposed—apologies, restitution, rehabilitation, financial or non-financial compensation, and punitive sanctions (whether criminal or administrative, such as fines), and the prevention of harm through, for example, injunctions or guarantees of non-repetition—can hardly be understood as providing equivalent levels of repair, nor can they be considered appropriate for all cases. In international law, it is well understood that 'reparation should be proportional to the gravity of the violations and the harm suffered'.[49] Indeed a clearly defined hierarchy of reparations has emerged[50]: restitution (restoring a victim to their original state) is sought first; next, compensation is sought to make up the difference when full restitution cannot be provided; and lastly, different forms of satisfaction are sought when restitution and/or compensation cannot fully 'make good' a harm caused.

Second, and relatedly, while the second pillar of the UNGP considers the gravity—or 'severity'—of human rights impacts to be a determinant for a company's prioritization in addressing actual or potential abuses, the UNGP framework does not call for take into account the gravity of the alleged violation when it comes to access to remedy. Indeed, such consideration of an impact's severity is entirely left out of the third pillar. Yet, consideration of the gravity of an alleged violation is necessary for determining the appropriate level of remedy. However, despite the importance of the concept of gravity—gravity is referred to in determining admissibility for certain courts (e.g. International Criminal Court), in establishing proportionality for sanctions,[51] or for justifying an investigation by a UN body or even military intervention[52]—the concept is nevertheless indeterminate in international law.[53] Moreover,

---

[47] Torres (2021).

[48] See Shelton (2005), chapter 2.

[49] UNGA (2005), *Basic Principles and Guidelines on the Right to a Remedy and Reparation for Victims of Gross Violations of International Human Rights Law and Serious Violations of International Humanitarian Law*, A/RES/60/147, adopted 16 December 2005, Article 9(15).

[50] See International Law Commission (ILC) (2001), *Articles on Responsibility of States for Internationally Wrongful Acts*, Articles 34–38.

[51] E.g., UNGA (2005), *Basic Principles and Guidelines on the Right to a Remedy and Reparation for Victims of Gross Violations of International Human Rights Law and Serious Violations of International Humanitarian Law*, A/RES/60/147, adopted 16 December 2005.

[52] Deguzman (2012), Lopez (2020), Pues (2017).

[53] Deguzman (2012), Lopez (2020), Pues (2017), Altwicker-Hámori et al. (2016).

what is considered as constituting a grave breach of international law varies by context, and gravity is most often articulated by using examples of grave breaches, rather than criteria. In international human rights law, the examples of what constitutes a grave breach varies by enforcement body, and without a clear definition, UN bodies have been accused of using political rather than legal criteria to decide which breaches are grave.[54]

In the absence of clear or well-established indicators for assessing gravity, this chapter proposes a proxy measure for gravity: the extent of harm. There is precedent for such a choice: in a systematic mapping of how gravity is determined by international courts and other bodies of international law, Lopez notes that the extent of the harm is nearly always used to determine the gravity of a violation and elaborates that '[h]arm is sufficient to classify a violation as grave under two circumstances: (1) when the harm of a single violation to a limited number of individuals is extremely acute, or (2) when the violation is so widespread or systematic that the cumulative harm is severe.'[55] The acuteness or seriousness of a violation is frequently understood in terms of the irreversibility of the harm, with irreversibility sometimes used interchangeably with seriousness.[56] We therefore suggest that irreversibility of harm is a useful way to measure the acuteness of a violation, and number of victims can stand in for whether the violation is particularly widespread.

By introducing these criteria for effective remedy—(1) the degree of remedy outcome(s) achieved and (2) the gravity of the alleged violation—this paper takes a rights-centered approach that is based on internationally recognized human rights, and among these, the right to remedy. It is reasonable to situate our search for the meaning of the right to remedy for abuses resulting from transnational business activities within the broader discussion that has more or less already taken place within international law. First, victims of transnational business-related human rights abuse need not rely on the UNGP to make a claim for a right to effective remedy. In fact, a 'right to remedy' is not once mentioned in the UNGP—a strange omission considering this right is well-established in international human rights law. However, this right is enshrined in the Universal Declaration of Human Rights (UDHR),[57] the International Covenant on Civil and Political Rights (ICCPR),[58] and numerous regional human rights such as the EU Charter on Fundamental Rights (ECHR),[59]

[54] Lopez (2020), 594.

[55] Lopez (2020), 604.

[56] Trouwborst (2009).

[57] UNGA (1948), UDHR, A/RES/217A (III), adopted 10 December 1948, Article 8 establishes a right to recourse at a competent national tribunal for violations of fundamental rights.

[58] UNGA (1966), A/RES/2200A, ICCPR, 2200A, adopted 16 December 1966, entered into force 23 March 1976, Article 2(3) establishes a right to recourse, an 'effective remedy', to individuals for a violation of their rights as laid out in the covenant.

[59] CoE (1950), ECHR, adopted 4 November 1950, Article 13 establishes the right to recourse, 'remedy before a national authority', and in the event that reparations provided by the national authority are insufficient, Article 41 establishes right to reparation 'just satisfaction' to cover the difference.

the American Convention on Human Rights (ACHR),[60] and others. This right is also evident in the jurisprudence of the corresponding courts, which often order various forms of substantive remedies. That a particular human rights abuse is committed by a business does not alter or lessen this right—even if the duty-bearer of this right is the state and not the party responsible for a violation.

Though remedy in the business and human rights context has been viewed, conceived, and measured differently from remedy in international human rights law up until this point—a phenomenon that is likely the result of deliberate efforts to downplay the responsibility of businesses—this chapter starts from the assumption that the right to remedy is blind to the public or private nature of the violator. Indeed the UNGP themselves draw upon principles and concepts of international law and the concept of remedy articulated in the UNGP is no exception: the list of substantive options provided in the UNGP echoes almost perfectly the list of possibilities provided for in the 'Basic Principles and Guidelines on the Right to a Remedy and Reparation for Victims of Gross Violations of International Human Rights Law and Serious Violations of International Humanitarian Law' (the Van Boven/Bassiouni Principles), adopted by the UN General Assembly in 2005, which include 'restitution, compensation, rehabilitation, satisfaction and guarantees of non-repetition'.[61] The next sections, therefore, proceed under the assumption that remedy outcomes from nonjudicial mechanisms should be assessed using the same criteria as for judicial ones.

3 Case Selection, Methodology and Data Collection

3.1 Case Selection

This chapter focuses on human rights cases handled by the NCPs of the OECD Guidelines for several reasons. Of state-based nonjudicial mechanisms, the OECD NCPs are among the most visible and widely used.[62] The OECD Guidelines are unique in that victims of transnational business-related human rights abuse (or, more often, victims' representatives) can bring claims, called 'specific instances,' directly against a multinational enterprise headquartered in one of the 51 states adhering to the Guidelines, regardless of where the alleged violation occurred.

The Guidelines, adopted alongside the OECD Declaration on International Investment and Multinational Enterprises in 1976, outline responsible business conduct

---

[60] OAS (1969), ACHR, adopted 22 November 1969, Article 7(6) establishes the right to recourse while Article 63(1) establishes the right to reparation.

[61] UNGA (2005), *Basic Principles and Guidelines on the Right to a Remedy and Reparation for Victims of Gross Violations of International Human Rights Law and Serious Violations of International Humanitarian Law*, A/RES/60/147, adopted 16 December 2005.

[62] HRC (2021), *Guiding Principles on Business and Human Rights at 10: Taking Stock of the First Decade*, A/HRC/47/39, adopted June 2021, 20.

across several fields including environmental protection, employment and industrial relations, corruption and others. Since the fifth revision in 2011, the Guidelines include a chapter on human rights and integrate the concept of risk-based due diligence. The sixth revision in June 2023 further strengthened the human rights chapter, including guidance on paying increased attention to those who may be at increased risk, such as indigenous peoples and human rights defenders, and guidance on heightened due diligence for operating in situations of armed conflict. Though human rights is among the newest areas of guidance in the Guidelines, it has elevated the Guidelines as an international human rights instrument and has made the NCPs the de facto international grievance mechanism for not only the Guidelines but the UNGP,[63] with which the Guidelines are explicitly aligned. Accordingly, the NCPs have increasingly been understood to be 'remedy mechanisms' and as such, a *raison d'être* of the NCPs is seen as supporting 'access to remedy on a global scale by providing a platform for mediation and conciliation.'[64] The NCPs are expected to ensure that those negatively affected by a company's business activities can access remedy or obtain redress, which can take the form of 'financial compensation or reparation, or through apologies, recognition of guilt, or guarantees of non-repetition.'[65]

3.2 Data Collection

We compiled a novel dataset of all specific instances alleging human rights violations that were accepted and concluded[66] at an NCP between 2012 and 2020, according to the OECD Database of Specific Instances.[67] 2012 was chosen as a starting point because it is the first full year following the update of the OECD Guidelines in 2011 which saw the addition of the human rights chapter and the concept of due diligence. According to the OECD Specific Instances Database, in total, 84 cases were filed and concluded during the time period. Three cases that were accepted and concluded during this time period were left out of the study because the NCP closed the specific instance without offering good offices, either due to the complaint being withdrawn early in the process or upon further review. In total, 81 cases were included in the analysis, comprising specific instances concluded by 24 NCPs.

---

63 Otteburn and Marx (2022).

64 See OECD (2020), http://mneguidelines.oecd.org/ncps/ncps-at-20/ (last accessed 31 December 2023).

65 OECD (2020), Providing access to remedy 20 years and the road ahead, https://mneguidelines.oecd.org/NCPs-for-RBC-providing-access-to-remedy-20-years-and-the-road-ahead.pdf, 7.

66 While many barriers to access to justice actually precede the successful filing of a case, preventing the claim from being made or accepted in the first place, this paper focuses on substantive outcomes of the specific instance process and therefore focuses on only those specific instances that were concluded.

67 OECD, Database of specific instances, https://mneguidelines.oecd.org/database/ (last accessed 31 December 2023).

NCPs typically publish on their websites an initial and final statement, and occasionally and intermediate and/or follow-up statement. Data for the analysis was primarily collected from these statements. In a few cases, when the official statements lacked necessary information, additional information was sought from press releases issued by the complainant or respondent.

3.3 Methodology

To assess whether the remedy outcomes of the NCP specific instances can be understood as 'effective remedy' as articulated in Sect. 2, this chapter engages in a two-step analysis of our dataset that allows for the evaluation of remedy outcomes at the NCPs through a rights-centered lens. First, our concept of effective remedy is operationalized into replicable criteria by which we score the remedy outcome(s) of each specific instance. We also operationalize two other concepts of remedy described in Sect. 2—the minimal definition utilized by the UNGP and one that attempts to approximate rights-holder satisfaction—to allow for comparison of different concepts of effective remedy. As a first analytical step, we provide a descriptive quantitative analysis of this data. Second, we carry out a case study of the cases that our first analysis revealed as exceptional (three in total).

In the first step, the substantive outcomes of the cases were scored in NVIVO for several variables. Scores were either awarded on a graded scale of 0–3 (0 being the lowest score, 3 being the highest) or on a binary basis (0 for absence, 1 for presence), as described below.

To measure effective remedy in line with the rights-centered approach taken by this chapter (see Sect. 2), it is necessary to determine whether a remedial outcome may 'counteract or make good' an alleged harm in line with the way this is interpreted in international law, which entails that the remedy outcome be commensurate with the gravity of the violation. This definition of effective remedy relies on a hierarchy of remedy outcomes as described in the previous section, and requires that both the gravity of the alleged violation and the degree of remedy achieved be individually assessed as follows:

Degree of remedy achieved: This chapter utilizes the approach taken by the ILC, which organizes forms of reparations hierarchically.[68] According to this hierarchy, forms of restitution, including rehabilitation—examples include return of lands, reinstatement of dismissed workers, repair of damaged homes—are regarded as the most sufficient and are scored 3. Compensation, while considered secondary to restitution and is to be used when damages cannot be made good by restitution, is scored 3 when restitution is not possible and compensation represents the highest form of available remedy, especially when combined with other forms of remedy such as guarantees of non-repetition and acknowledgment of guilt. On the other hand,

[68] ILC (2001), *Articles on Responsibility of States for Internationally Wrongful Acts*, Articles 34–7, See also Antoine C. Buyse (2008).

compensation is awarded 2 when restitutive forms of remedy remain possible but are not pursued, or when compensation is minor or symbolic. Satisfaction, including cessation of ongoing activities, public apologies, revelation of the truth, and guarantees of non-repetition,[69] including commitments of corporate policy changes and punitive measures, is scored as 1. If no reparative outcome is achieved, a case is scored as 0. Where multiple outcomes are achieved, the highest is scored.

Gravity of alleged violation: As discussed above, gravity is an indeterminate concept in international law.[70] Measuring gravity poses a considerable challenge for human rights violations due to the diversity of human rights abuses resulting from business activities and the diversity and frequent precarity of victims, which may amplify the effects of human rights abuse. Nevertheless, to arrive at a systematic measurement, we had to take a rather technical approach. We scored alleged violations based on the degree of irreversibility of the violation, which allows for replicability and consistency in measuring the extent of harm as a proxy for gravity (see Sect. 2 for a justification of this choice) based on available information, admittedly at the expense of nuance. Cases alleging a violation leading to irreversible harm, such as death, irreversible environmental destruction, forced displacement, child labour, slavery, loss of limb, long-term illness, are scored 3 (most grave). Violations causing partly reversible harm are scored 2 (moderate), such as destruction of property, emotional/psychological trauma, lack of free, prior and informed consent (FPIC), damage to sacred lands or cultural or religious monuments, and loss of livelihood. Mostly reversible harms are scored 1 (least grave), including financial loss, inadequate working conditions, invasion of privacy, temporary stress and discomfort, and obstruction to freedom of association. Reversible violations are those for which cessation of ongoing activities can immediately resolve the issue with no lasting harm, such as a lack of transparency, lack of access to information, and an insufficient grievance mechanism, and are scored 0. Scored this way, our measurement also assures that rights widely regarded as non-derogable (for example the right to life, the prohibition of slavery, and the prohibition of torture[71]) and violations impinging on a person's physical and mental integrity are considered more grave, in line with the reasoning used by many courts.[72]

In addition, other variables were scored for comparison and contextual reasons. One measures whether a remedy is achieved following the minimal criteria of the UNGP (see Sect. 2). The others attempt to approximate the perspective of the rightsholder, which scholars have proposed as an important indicator for effective remedy (see Sect. 2). Because for many cases, the final opinions of the rights-holders are unknown, this paper considers both the degree of remedy sought by claimants as well

[69] Some courts and instruments of international law separate satisfaction from guarantees of non-repetition (see, for example UN Commission on Human Rights, *Report of the Special Rapporteur on the Question of Torture Submitted in Accordance with Commission Resolution 2002/38*, E/CN.4/2003/68), but for simplicity, we follow the ILC in considering guarantees of non-repetition as a form of satisfaction.

[70] Lopez (2020).

[71] CoE (1950), ECHR, adopted 4 November 1950, Article 15.

[72] Altwicker-Hámori et al. (2016).

as whether the outcomes sought by the claimant in the specific instance submission match with the outcomes achieved. These variables are scored as follows:

Remedial outcome achieved: This score indicates whether the specific instance resulted in an outcome that is included among the 'bouquet of remedies' (i.e. the substantive options for remedy) listed in the UNGP, which are 'apologies, restitution, rehabilitation, financial or non-financial compensation and punitive sanctions (whether criminal or administrative, such as fines), as well as the prevention of harm through, for example, injunctions or guarantees of non-repetition'.[73] It is a binary score because the UNGP do not propose a hierarchy among these substantive outcomes.

Degree of remedy sought: This is graded using an identical scale to degree of remedy achieved (see above).

Equivalence of actual outcome and sought outcome: This score assessed whether the outcomes sought by the claimant are commensurate with the outcomes achieved through the specific instance. A case is scored as 0 when no outcome is achieved or when outcomes achieved do not match the desired outcomes. For example, if a claimant filed by a trade union requests reinstatement of dismissed workers, monetary compensation, and recognition of the union, and the specific instance results in the NCP's determination that the respondent's actions violated the Guidelines, the case would receive a 0, even though it resulted in an outcome that could be considered a form of remedy. If a case with the same requested outcomes resulted in recognition of the union, but not compensation or the reinstatement of workers, it would be scored a 1. If a case results in two or more of the claimants' requested outcomes, but not all, it is scored 2. When outcomes achieved are fully in line with outcomes requested, the case receives a full score (3).

4 Analysis

The analysis proceeds as follows. First, we assess the results of each variable across the body of 81 cases through descriptive quantitative analysis. Second, we take a closer look at the three individual cases with exceptional outcomes.

[73] HRC (2011), *Guiding Principles on Business and Human Rights: Implementing the United Nations 'Protect, Respect and Remedy' Framework*, A/HRC/17/31, adopted 21 March 2011, Principle 25.

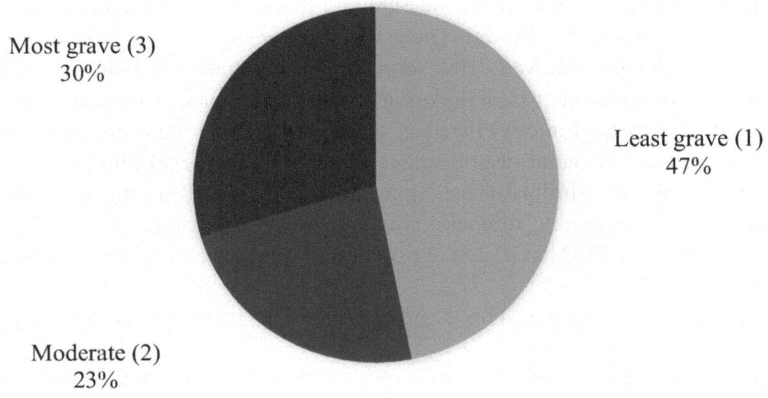

Fig. 1 Total cases by degree of gravity 2012–2020

4.1 Descriptive Quantitative Analysis

4.1.1 Gravity

NCPs are frequently engaged to handle instances of severe human rights abuse, which represent nearly one third of total cases. Of the 81 cases, 38 (47%) were scored 1 (least grave), 19 (23%) were scored 2 (moderate) and 24 (30%) were scored 3 (most grave). See Fig. 1.

4.1.2 Degree of Remedy Sought

Complainants sought a high degree (3) of remedy in 33 cases (40%), moderate degree (2) in 9 cases (12%), and a low degree of remedy in 39 cases (48%). Put differently, in more than half of the cases, the claimants sought either restitution (e.g. return of lands, reinstatement of workers) or compensation.

The gravity of the alleged violation does seem to influence the degree of remedy sought. In particular, satisfaction or a low degree of remedy is sought less often and compensation (moderate degree of remedy) is sought more often for cases dealing with grave cases than for cases dealing with mostly reversible violations. This is not the case for moderately grave cases, for which restitution (high degree of remedy) is sought in the majority of cases. The increased emphasis on compensation alone for cases dealing with the gravest violations may reflect the perceived impossibility or difficulty in achieving restitution for severe abuses. When the degree of gravity of the violation was low, claimants most frequently sought a low degree of remedy (a form of satisfaction). See Fig. 2.

We turn now to consider the various aspects of the remedies achieved in the 81 cases.

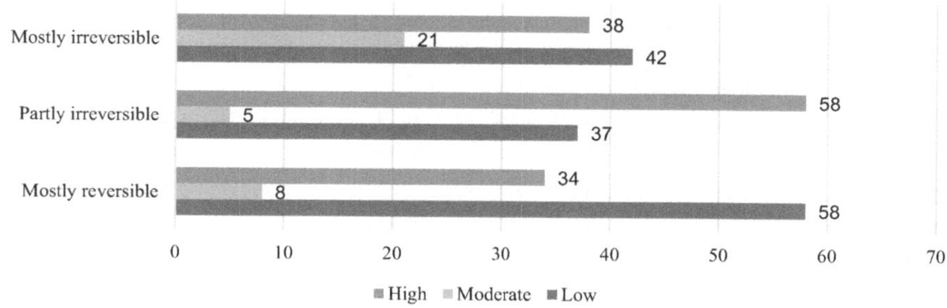

Fig. 2 Degree of remedy sought by gravity of case (percent) 2012–2020

4.1.3 Remedial Outcome (Any) and Degree of Remedy Achieved

53 of accepted cases (65%) can be considered to have provided some form of a remedial outcome based on the list of options outlined by the UNGP.

However, while the NCPs often facilitated a form of remedy, the vast majority of remedial outcomes offered a low degree of remedy. Of the 53 cases that provided some form of remedial outcome (hereafter, 'remedy cases'), 43 cases (84% of remedy cases, 53% of total accepted cases) resulted in a minimal form of remedy (scored 1, hereafter 'low remedy' or 'low degree of remedy'), typically a form of satisfaction such as the expression of a commitment to review or update corporate policy or acknowledgement by the NCP that a certain activity was not in line with the Guidelines. Seven cases (13% of remedy cases, nine percent of total cases) were scored 2, having led to some form of symbolic or minor compensation (hereafter, 'moderate remedy' or 'moderate degree'). Only three of the 81 total cases (six percent of remedy cases, 4% of total) resulted in a form of restitution, the highest degree of remedy (scored 3, 'high remedy' or 'high degree').

The remedy outcomes look roughly similar across cases of varying levels of gravity. A remedy outcome (based on the UNGP definition) was achieved in 63% of the most grave cases (compared with 64% of total cases). However, when we look at the breakdown of remedy cases by degree of remedy, the picture changes for the most grave cases: cases of moderate or low gravity were somewhat more likely to achieve a moderate or higher degree remedy (26 and 11% respectively) than were the gravest cases (4%). However, as noted, the overall number of cases that resulted in a moderate or high degree of remedy were low. See Table 1.

The three instances of high remedy were evenly split among the three levels of gravity, with one case for each level of gravity. Aside from this one case among the most grave cases, all of the other 23 gravest cases led to no remedy or the lowest degree of remedy. The single grave case that resulted in a high degree of remedy—Equitable Cambodia (EC) and Inclusive Development International (IDI) v ANZ Banking Group (2014)—will be examined in more depth below.

Table 1 Degree of remedy outcomes achieved by degree of gravity of violation for cases 2012–2020, percentages based on 81 total cases

	Remedy cases			
Gravity of violation	No remedy achieved (0)	Low remedy achieved (1)	Moderate remedy achieved (2)	High remedy achieved (3)
Most grave (3)	9 (11%)	14 (17%)	0	1 (1%)
Moderate (2)	6 (7%)	8 (10%)	4 (5%)	1 (1%)
Least grave (1)	14 (17%)	20 (25%)	3 (4%)	1 (1%)
Total cases	29 (36%)	42 (52%)	7 (9%)	3 (4%)

4.1.4 Equivalence of Actual Outcome and Sought Outcome

We turn now to examine whether and to what extent the outcomes sought by the claimants were achieved by the claimants. This could function as a simplistic (rough) proxy for rights-holder satisfaction with remedy outcomes. More importantly for our purposes, it allows us to explore whether the degree of outcomes achieved might have to do with the degree of outcomes sought.

39 of the 81 cases (48%) did not result in the achievement of any sought outcomes. Another 17 cases (21%) were scored 1, indicating that they resulted in a single minor outcome that was sought by the claimants, but generally did not succeed in meeting the claimants' demands. 12 cases (15%) resulted in more than one sought outcome being achieved, though the outcomes still fell short of the claimants' demands. In 13 cases (16%), however, the degree of remedy awarded to the claimants was in line with the degree of remedy requested by the claimants. See Fig. 3.

In other words, in a very reasonable 31% of concluded cases, claimants' demands were fully or substantially met through the NCP process with regard to remedy outcomes. This is, of course, at odds with existing research on the OECD NCPs, which paints an overall bleak picture of access to remedy through the NCPs.[74]

The data offer some clues to this puzzle. Perhaps unsurprisingly, the expectations of the claimants appear to influence whether and to what extent the claimants' demands are met. Cases in which the degree of remedy sought was low were more likely to result in full equivalence between sought and achieved outcomes; in 9 of the 13 cases that resulted in full equivalence between sought and achieved outcomes, a low degree of remedy was sought by claimants. Indeed, cases in which claimants sought low remedy were considerably more likely to have had their expectations fully met by the process (23% of total cases) than those who sought high remedy, whose expectations were met fully in only 6% of cases. Of the 32 cases in which claimants sought a high degree of remedy, only two led to outcomes fully meeting the claimants' expectations: International Union of Food, Agriculture, Hotel, Restaurant, Catering, Tobacco and Allied Workers' Associations (IUF) v Starwood Hotels & Resorts Worldwide (2015) and one which we have met before, EC and IDI v ANZ Banking Group (2014) (both discussed below). On the other hand, for the vast majority (25)

[74] Otteburn (2023), Daniels et al. (2015), Ingrams et al (2021), Bhatt et al. (2021).

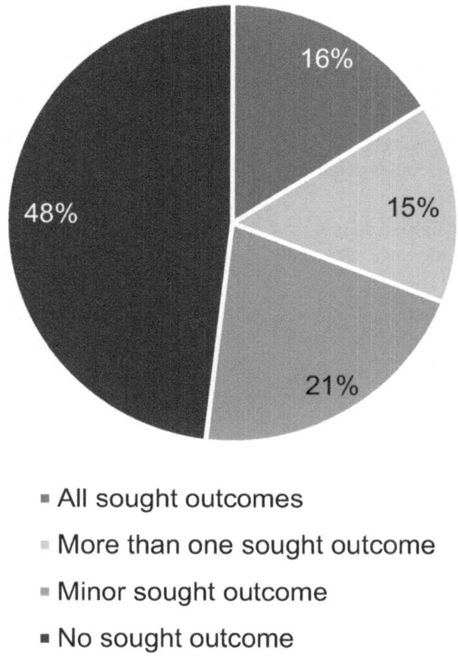

Fig. 3 Achievement of sought outcomes for cases filed 2012–2020

of these 32 'high expectations' cases, the NCP process led to outcomes not or mostly not aligned with claimants' expectations or no outcome at all (score of 0 or 1). On the other side of the same coin, 56% of claimants with high expectations achieved none of their sought outcomes compared to 36% of claimants who sought low remedy. Hence, whether the rights-holder's expectations are met in a particular case seems to be directly linked to whether their kept their expectations low, and in fact, claimants who kept their expectations low were more likely to get at least some form of remedy than those who held moderate or high expectations. See Table 2.

4.2 External Pressure: Explaining the Exceptional Cases

Overall, the quantitative analysis has pointed to three success cases—the three cases that exceptionally led to a high degree of remedy—to which we now turn our attention. As we saw above, these three cases each involve a violation of a different degree of gravity. Claimants in all three cases sought a high degree of remedy. These three cases thus include the other exceptional cases with regard to gravity (the one grave case that resulted in high remedy) and also concerning equivalence of sought and achieved outcomes (the three cases for which claimants held high expectations that also led to a high degree of remedy). See Table 3 for an overview of cases.

Table 2 Degree of remedy outcomes achieved by degree of outcomes sought for cases 2012–2020

	Low degree sought (1)	Moderate degree sought (2)	High degree sought (3)	Total cases by outcomes achieved
No sought outcomes achieved (0)	**14**	**7**	**18**	39
Minimal sought outcomes achieved (1)	**10**	**0**	**7**	17
Substantial sought outcomes achieved (2)	**6**	**1**	**5**	12
All sought outcomes achieved (3)	**9**	**1**	**3**	13
Total cases by degree sought	39	9	33	

Table 3 Overview of exceptional cases

Case	Gravity	Sought outcome	Achieved outcome
International Union of Food, Agriculture, Hotel, Restaurant, Catering, Tobacco and Allied Workers' Associations v Starwood Hotels & Resorts Worldwide (filed 2015, concluded 2016)	Low (1)	High (3)	High (3)
Former employees of Bralima vs. Bralima and Heineken (filed 2015, concluded 2017)	Moderate (2)	High (3)	High (3)
Equitable Cambodia and Inclusive Development International v ANZ Banking Group (filed 2014, concluded 2020)	High (3)	High (3)	High (3)

4.2.1 EC and IDI v ANZ

Equitable Cambodia (EC) and Inclusive Development International (IDI) v ANZ Banking Group (2014) concerned allegations of the forced eviction of more than 600 families, loss of livelihood, and child labour for the operation of a sugar plantation and refinery by a Cambodian developer, for which ANZ had provided a loan. The specific instance at the Australian NCP first concluded in June 2018 with a gentle rebuke from the NCP that suggested ANZ's conduct was not in line with the Guidelines:

'The AusNCP considers that in this case it is difficult to reconcile ANZ's decision to take on PPS as a client with its own internal policies and procedures—which appear to accord with the OECD Guidelines—as the potential risks associated with this decision would likely have been readily apparent.'[75]

Finding this remedial outcome to fall far short of redress and inadequate to improve the situation of the displaced families,[76] IDI and EC, with the support of other non-governmental organizations OECD Watch and BankTrack, continued to put pressure on ANZ. Moreover, the specific instance was settled during a time when ANZ was facing additional pressure from the Australian government following a fact-finding commission that had revealed widespread misconduct,[77] and ANZ's Chief Executive Officer (CEO) was forced to respond to queries related to the complaint by EC and IDI during a parliamentary hearing related to the commission.[78] During the hearing, the CEO testified that the bank would provide compensation,[79] but later backtracked on this promise leading to further pressure and campaigning from the claimants.[80] The results of the NCP specific instance and the lack of redress for the Cambodian victims were subsequently widely reported by the media, both in Australia and abroad.[81]

---

[75] NCP Australia, *EC and IDI vs. ANZ,* Final Statement, 27 June 2018, https://ausncp.gov.au/sites/default/files/2023-01/11_AusNCP_Final_Statement.pdf (last accessed 31 December 2023).

[76] IDI, ANZ bank issued rare rebuke by Australian oversight body, 11 October 2018 https://web.archive.org/web/20210227005416/https://www.inclusivedevelopment.net/sugar/anz-issued-rare-rebuke-by-australian-oversight-body/ (last accessed 31 December 2023); ANZ loan to controversial Cambodian sugar firm criticized by Australia, Reuters, 11 October 2018, https://www.reuters.com/article/us-anz-bank-cambodia-idUSKCN1ML0K2 (last accessed 31 December 2023).

[77] ANZ Bank chief Shayne Elliott grilled by MPs in Canberra, News.com.au, 12 October 2018, https://www.news.com.au/finance/business/banking/anz-bank-chief-shayne-elliott-grilled-by-mps-in-canberra/news-story/9a7236eb48bf97dbeb44f3567239d220 (last accessed 31 December 2023).

[78] Robertson H, ANZ boss says bank will consider compensating Cambodians forced off farms for sugar plantation, ABC News, 12 October 2018, https://www.abc.net.au/news/2018-10-12/anz-rebuked-over-loan-to-cambodian-sugar-firm/10370648 (last accessed 31 December 31, 2023); Danckert S, "I misspoke": ANZ boss backflips on compensation comments, The Sydney Morning Herald, 12 October 2018, https://www.smh.com.au/business/banking-and-finance/i-misspoke-anz-boss-backflips-on-compensation-comments-20181012-p509ai.html (last accessed 31 December).

[79] Robertson H, ANZ boss says bank will consider compensating Cambodians forced off farms for sugar plantation, ABC News, 12 October 2018, https://www.abc.net.au/news/2018-10-12/anz-rebuked-over-loan-to-cambodian-sugar-firm/10370648 (last accessed 31 December 31, 2023); Danckert S, "I misspoke": ANZ boss backflips on compensation comments, The Sydney Morning Herald, 12 October 2018, https://www.smh.com.au/business/banking-and-finance/i-misspoke-anz-boss-backflips-on-compensation-comments-20181012-p509ai.html (last accessed 31 December).

[80] IDI, ANZ Declines to do the Right Thing for Displaced Cambodian Farmers, 18 December 2018, https://web.archive.org/web/20190920103312/https://www.inclusivedevelopment.net/anz-declines-to-do-the-right-thing-for-displaced-cambodian-farmers/ (last accessed 10 June 2023).

[81] See for example, ANZ loan to controversial Cambodian sugar firm criticized by Australia, Reuters, 11 October 2018; Baker R and McKenzie N, ANZ failed to meet human rights standards: government report, The Sydney Morning Herald, 11 October 2018, https://www.smh.com.au/business/banking-and-finance/anz-failed-to-meet-human-rights-standards-in-cambodia-government-report-20181011-p508z2.html (last accessed 31 December 2023); Chakrya K, ANZ mulling payout to sugar project victims, Phnom Penh Post, 1 November 2018, https://www.phnompenhpost.com/national/anz-mulling-payout-sugar-project-victims (last accessed 31 December 2023).

A follow-up meeting was arranged at the request of the parties almost two years following the closure of the specific instance, leading to an agreement between the parties in which ANZ committed to not only improve its due diligence processes, but also provide the gross profits from the loan to the affected communities.

An award of compensation is rare in the NCP system. Moreover, this case was the only case that both was scored as 'irreversible' (3) and also resulted in a form of remedy beyond satisfaction. However, the NCP process itself led only to a low remedy outcome (satisfaction), though this outcome was leveraged by the claimants and others to pressure ANZ to reach a new agreement on compensation for the displaced families.

4.2.2 Former Employees v Bralima and Heineken

Three former employees of Bralima, a subsidiary of Heineken situated in the Democratic Republic of the Congo (DRC), filed a complaint at the Dutch NCP in December 2015 on behalf of 168 former Bralima employees alleging unfair and under-compensated mass dismissals between 1999 and 2003.[82] The NCP carried out a fact-finding mission and conducted interviews with former employees before arranging professional mediation between the parties at the Dutch embassy in Uganda, allowing for a neutral setting that kept travel costs low for the DRC-based parties. The NCP proactively consulted with a Congolese lawyer, experts and the former employees themselves before and after the mediation, in preparation of the final statement. Ultimately an agreement was reached between the parties that included compensation for the former employees and a commitment to updating corporate policy.

Concluded in 2017, this case has been the subject of considerable focus, even being 'used as a proverbial poster child for the potential of NCPs to provide effective remedy to rights-holders within a rule of law framework when business enterprises are involved in wrongdoings'.[83] However, as pointed out by Bhatt and Erdem Türkelli in their study of this case, the success of the case partly rests on the considerable publicity that surrounded the proceedings.[84] The authors point out that the case 'mobilized Dutch and international media attention around the labour violations but also focused on broader legal and accounting measures Heineken had taken to minimize tax liabilities in Africa'.[85] Like the case against ANZ, the case's success in facilitating a high level of remedy appears to be dependent (at least in part) on external factors, such as media attention.

---

[82] NCP Netherlands, *Former employees of Bralima vs. Bralima and Heineken*, Final Statement, 18 August 2017, https://www.oecdguidelines.nl/latest/news/2017/08/18/final-statement-notification-former-employees-bralima-vs.-bralima-heineken (last accessed 31 December 2023).

[83] Bhatt and Erdem Türkelli (2021), 436.

[84] Bhatt and Erdem Türkelli (2021).

[85] Bhatt and Erdem Türkelli (2021), 438.

4.2.3 IUF v Starwood

IUF's complaint against Starwood filed at the United States (US) OECD NCP alleged anti-union activity including disciplinary actions against and termination of employees for union participation and failure to recognize the union or engage in collective bargaining at affiliate Sheraton hotels in the Maldives and Ethiopia.[86] Despite contesting these allegations, Starwood agreed to participate in the mediation process, which was conducted through the US Federal Mediation and Conciliation Service at the engagement of the NCP. The mediation sessions, held over four months, ultimately led the parties to reach an agreement in April 2016, the contents of which were not made public but were considered satisfactory to both parties.

Though this case received significantly less attention than the other two, the International Labour Organization (ILO) pointed to the case as an example for the use of the OECD NCP system for trade union action[87] and the OECD provided the case as an example of the flexibility of the NCP system to successfully address issues where other mechanisms might fail.[88] This case, dealing with a alleged violation of low gravity, seems ideally suited to the NCP mechanism, which may explain IUF's frequent use of the system.

5 Discussion: A Difference of Degree

There are several conclusions we can draw from the above analysis. First, with regard to the NCPs as site of remedy, the data shows that the NCP system is comparatively successful at facilitating minor forms of remedy, specifically forms of satisfaction such as acknowledgement of wrongdoing by the company or by the NCP, apology, information, a commitment to update corporate policy, or a decision to discontinue certain business activities. Unfortunately, these are also—with a single exception—the only types of outcomes that were available to rights-holders for cases concerning grave violations, if any outcome is to be achieved at all. While a high or moderate degree of remedy was rare across all cases, grave cases fared worse than those of low or moderate gravity, confirming previous research based on case studies.[89] It would appear that the NCP system is vastly ill-equipped to handle grave violations

---

[86] NCP United States, *IUF vs. Starwood*, Final Statement, 12 May 2016, https://2009-2017.state.gov/e/eb/oecd/usncp/specificinstance/finalstatements/257110.htm (last accessed 31 December 2023).

[87] ILO (2020), Social dialogue, collective bargaining and responsible business conduct: Promoting the strategic use of International Instruments for trade unions' action, Geneva, https://www.ilo.org/publications/social-dialogue-collective-bargaining-and-responsible-business-conduct (last accessed 8 May 2024), p 18.

[88] OECD (2020), Providing access to remedy 20 years and the road ahead, https://mneguidelines.oecd.org/NCPs-for-RBC-providing-access-to-remedy-20-years-and-the-road-ahead.pdf, pp. 19, 48.

[89] Otteburn (2023).

of human rights and works best to provide forms of remedy that are more proportional to less grave abuses. While our study does not take into account the submissions to the NCPs that are not accepted, our findings may partly qualify previous studies that claim that remedy is rare through the NCPs[90] by demonstrating that the NCP system often leads to effective remedies for less serious allegations.

It is perhaps no surprise that the cases in which the claimants held higher expectations most often led to outcomes that did not meet the claimants' expectations. Unfortunately, however, while keeping expectations low may improve access to any solution at all, the data shows that remedy outcomes rarely exceed expectations. So, while holding low expectations is more likely to lead to at least one remedial outcome, this outcome is not likely to be an effective one. Keeping expectations low is therefore not a solution—despite the OECD's emphasis on managing submitters' expectations[91]—and merely underscores the inappropriateness of the NCPs for access to remedy for transnational business-related human rights abuses that require some form of compensation or restitution.

It is curious that the data presents a more or less consistent picture of the system's inadequacy for facilitating access to effective remedy outcomes for all types of violations. The 51 NCPs set up by the adhering countries to the OECD Guidelines have a variety of different institutional forms, varying ideas as to their purpose and function, different levels of independence, oversight, funding, and so on,[92] and yet our findings demonstrate system-wide inadequacy. A number of studies that focus on the NCPs[93] and an extensive database developed by the OECD Watch[94] have attempted to identify the ideal set of institutional design features and best practices in order to improve them as sites for access to remedy, particularly emphasizing the engagement of different stakeholders through an advisory or oversight body,[95] a neutral location within or outside government (outside a ministry devoted to export promotion or economy),[96] and the mandate to make a determination in the event mediation is unsuccessful.[97] Our analysis may cast some doubt as to what extent these institutional design adjustments can make a difference, since some of the NCPs already exhibit these features and yet the system as a whole appears ill-equipped to handle all types of remedy with which it is tasked.

---

[90] See especially Daniel et al. (2015).

[91] OECD (2020), Providing access to remedy 20 years and the road ahead, https://mneguidelines.oecd.org/NCPs-for-RBC-providing-access-to-remedy-20-years-and-the-road-ahead.pdf, p. 32.

[92] Otteburn and Marx (2022).

[93] Ingrams et al (2021), Sanchez (2015), Buhmann (2020), Daniel et al (2015).

[94] OECD Watch, NCP Evaluations, https://www.oecdwatch.org/indicator/ (last accessed 31 December 2023).

[95] Bhatt and Erdem Türkelli (2021), Ingrams et al. (2021).

[96] Ingrams et al (2021), Bhatt and Erdem Türkelli (2021).

[97] Sanchez (2015), Bhatt and Erdem Türkelli (2021), Ingrams et al. (2021), OECD Watch (2020) The State of Remedy under the OECD Guidelines: Understanding NCP Cases Concluded in 2019 through the Lens of Remedy. Briefing Paper, https://www.oecdwatch.org/wp-content/uploads/sites/8/2020/06/State-of-Remedy-2020.pdf (last accessed 31 December 2023).

But perhaps focus on other institutional features is warranted. Our case analyses suggested that for more serious violations of human rights, achieving effective remedy through the NCPs relied on the mobilization of actors outside the process—other NGOs and the media—to generate enough pressure or reputational risk that the responding company feels compelled to acquiesce to provide a higher degree of remedy. This aligns with case studies conducted by others, who have shown the potential for NCPs to facilitate mobilization in some cases.[98] Greater transparency and access to information, fewer confidentiality measures, and more funding for the NCP to carry out investigations and research may all be enabling factors for well-organized claimants to gain sufficient leverage in this regard. Indeed, these features of institutional design are often proposed for improving the NCPs as sites of remedy, and our study confirms their relevance.[99]

However, such successful mobilization has been extremely rare. As we have seen, the NCPs' record in providing effective remedy for grave violations is poor. Relatedly our analysis indicates that NCPs are less successful in providing access to any solutions at all when the rights-holder held higher expectations. Indeed, it would appear that responding companies are less amenable to engaging with the process or reaching an agreement when rights-holders' demands are high. Therefore, an alternative approach to facilitating mobilization in order to strengthen the NCPs could be to 'double down' on what they are better at: providing a platform for mediation and dialogue. This would require strengthening an entirely different set of features of the NCPs to encourage business participation without fear of reputational risk, such as actually boosting confidentiality, limiting transparency, setting standards for mediation including the engagement of a neutral professional mediator and arranging meetings in neutral locations, providing travel support and translation services, and so on. Moreover, this would also entail setting limitations on the types and severity of cases the system is able to accept: beyond simply limiting grave submissions, the system should also remain limited to cases that involve ongoing and resolvable issues and not those for which the only possible solution is compensation and/or sanctions.

While the flexibility of the NCPs is often considered a beneficial attribute,[100] it would appear that the flexibility built into nearly every aspect of the NCP system may actually trap it into not succeeding very well as either a site of remedy or site for dialogue. Choosing a path, however, ought to be done in consideration of the broader remedy landscape. Until now, rights-holders have turned to NCPs because they had no other option.[101] However, as this seems to be evolving, it is worth re-evaluating what role NCPs should play and how they should fit into this picture of remedy.

Second, there is often no way for the system to ensure remedy outcomes are commensurate with severity of the violation nor that they do enough to repair the rights-holder to the situation they would have been in had the violation not

[98] Bhatt and Erdem Türkelli (2021), Haines and Macdonald (2020).

[99] Bhatt and Erdem Türkelli (2021), Daniel et al (2015), Ingrams et al (2021).

[100] Backer (2009), Buhmann (2020).

[101] Van Huijstee and Ramsing (2020), Otteburn (2023).

occurred.[102] As we saw in the above analysis, even 'victories' in the NCP context frequently fail to produce effective remedy outcomes from a rights-centred perspective. What is worse is that, in reaching an agreement—possibly for a lower degree of remedy—the rights-holder may have to agree to not further pursue the claim, effectively prohibiting them from seeking effective remedy and forcing them to accept an inadequate solution. In other words, without neutral and authoritative adjudication, there is no guarantee that questions of degree of either severity or remedy may be appropriately considered. These insights are likely to apply to nonjudicial mechanisms more broadly. As non-legal fora typically without capacities for enforcement (like the NCPs), nonjudicial mechanisms are plagued by analogous challenges, especially facilitating commensurate levels of remedy. They often lack an adjudicator with the authority to make final decisions, evaluate the case, or determine which measures should be taken to achieve effective remedy (and accountability). For nonjudicial mechanisms that primarily function as convenors of dialogue or mediation, outcomes are either jointly determined between the parties in the form of an agreement (e.g. an agreement to reinstate dismissed workers or recognize a union) or are unilaterally decided by the responding party (e.g. stated intention to update corporate policy).

Third, with regard to evaluating effective remedy, this analysis underscores the relevance of accounting for degree of both the severity of the violation as well as the degree of remedy achieved. Ignoring the degree of remedy risks vastly overstating the remedial possibilities available to rights-holders through a given forum. Ignoring the degree of severity risks overestimating a forum's capacity for handling grave cases. Ignoring both risks that we fail to evaluate remedy based on its most essential function: its ability to repair.

Finally, the analysis also demonstrated that caution should be exercised when utilizing the rights-holders' perspective to evaluate whether a remedy is effective, as some have proposed.[103] Claimants utilizing the NCP system frequently kept their expectations for remedy outcomes low, even for very grave abuses. While this may have served a purpose in either convincing the NCP to accept the specific instance or in signaling a cooperative and non-adversarial attitude to the responding party, it lays bare a key challenge in using the rights-holder perspective as a metric for measuring effective remedy: keeping expectations low may be a function of desperation for *any* solution and an understanding that asking for 'too much' may block them from any remedy. This finding backs up an argument put forth by others[104] that the rights-holder perceptions and expectations are subject to considerable external influence. The data shows that keeping expectations low led to a greater chance that the claimant will walk away with *any* form of remedy. An understanding of this dynamic appears to have taken hold among at least a portion of the claimants—as we saw above, in almost half of the cases (48%), the claimants sought a low degree of remedy. Moreover, this picture does not significantly change for cases dealing with grave instances

[102] On the need for objective criteria, see Thompson (2017).
[103] Bhatt and Erdem Türkelli (2021), Wielga and Harrison (2021).
[104] Thompson (2017), Wettstein (2009).

of transnational business-related human rights abuse, for which 42% of claimants sought only a low degree of remedy. In other words, the rights-holder's perspective may provide more information about claimants' pessimism or pragmaticism, and less about whether a remedy is effective.

6 Conclusion

Though the right to remedy for a violation of human rights is universally recognized, when violations occur as a result of business activities, the ways in which we demand, calculate and evaluate effective remedy change. Part of this is an understandable and pragmatic response to a dire lack of options for rights-holders to exercise their rights to remedy in cases of transnational business-related human rights abuse; and part of this stems from the weak formulations of the UNGP that prioritized the buy-in of the private sector over the protection of human rights. But this chapter has proposed that effective remedy cannot be understood without reference to rights. It therefore took a rights-centred approach to the evaluation of effective remedy through a hierarchical understanding of different forms of remedy and an attention to the gravity of the alleged violations, and considers to what extent substantive remedy outcomes are achieved through one of the only mechanisms to rights-holders for instances of transnational business-related human rights abuse: nonjudicial mechanisms.

This chapter thus presented and analyzed a dataset of remedy outcomes for all cases involving an instance of transnational business-related human rights abuse handled by the OECD NCPs—which comprise one of the largest and most prominent international nonjudicial mechanisms and which have been increasingly understood and utilized as sites for access to remedy. The analysis reveals that the system almost never leads to effective remedy for cases of all levels of gravity and fares even worse when it comes to cases involving severe violations of human rights, which make up nearly one-third of total cases. Moreover, the results show that cases for which claimants held low expectations are more likely to lead to some sort of outcome, but also that the outcomes achieved rarely exceed claimants' expectations.

Ultimately, this analysis has considerable implications for nonjudicial mechanisms more generally. Different NCPs exhibit different institutional designs that reflect the gamut of institutional designs of nonjudicial mechanisms, from platforms for mediation to fact-finding commissions to quasi-judicial bodies. Yet the NCPs fail across the board to provide access to more than the most minimal forms of remedy, suggesting that other nonjudicial mechanisms are unlikely to fare better. Unless a nonjudicial mechanism provides access to an independent party with authority to consider the gravity of a particular instance of transnational business-related human rights abuse and order a form of remedy (or remedies) that is commensurate with degree of harm in order to restore the rights-holder to the position they would have been in had the harm not occurred, it is unlikely to be effective in providing access to remedy. By removing the concept of remedy outside of the internationally recognized right to remedy and by ignoring degree of both a violation's gravity and the degree of remedy, we risk that nonjudicial mechanisms perpetuate the situation in which victims of transnational business-related human rights abuses are unable to realize their rights. Further research should of course expand this database to consider remedy outcomes at other nonjudicial mechanisms at both state and non-state levels.

Recent legislation and ongoing negotiations at international (UN), regional (EU), and state levels with regard to human rights and environmental due diligence legislation may increase rights-holders' access to courts, changing the balance in the current remedial landscape. How should nonjudicial mechanisms fit into this picture? What degree of remedy can they provide, and which types of alleged violations can they be tasked with handling?

Some have pointed out that nonjudicial mechanisms are frequently the only option,[105] but continuing to rely on them to provide access to remedy—especially for grave cases—may actually make matters worse for victims or obscure the urgent need for a different solution. However, as this research has also shown, that they cannot serve as sites of effective remedy for all types of abuses does not mean that they have no role to play in a wider system of remedy. As rates of human rights abuses resulting from transnational business activities increase worldwide and business' obligations toward rights-holders become mandatory in many jurisdictions, there is a considerable risk that courts will be overwhelmed and justice therefore difficult to achieve. Nonjudicial mechanisms could handle less serious cases for which mediation or fact-finding can provide a sufficient solution. Such a hierarchical system of remedy—already envisioned by the UNGP and by other authors described in Sect. 2—will necessitate a way to assess the gravity of an alleged transnational business-related human rights abuse and determine the most appropriate forum for its handling. An ideal model for this might take the form of a centralized institution to function as a sort of clearing house. Such a system would also eliminate the considerable ambiguity for rights-holders in terms of where to seek remedy and would also cut out the possibility and challenge of forum-shopping. Another option could be to repurpose a nonjudicial mechanism such as the NCPs to serve such a function. While the mood is ripe for taking serious action to address the negative externalities of transnational business activities, this chapter demonstrates that discussions of remedy and remedial architecture should take into account questions of degree.

References

Altwicker-Hámori S, Altwicker T, Peters A (2016) Measuring violations of human rights: an empirical analysis of awards in respect of non-pecuniary damage under the european convention on human rights. Heidelberg J Intern Law (Zeitschrift Für Ausländisches Öffentliches Recht und Völkerrecht) 76(1):1–51

Backer L (2009) Rights and accountability in development ("RAID") v DAS air and global witness v Afrimex: small steps towards an autonomous transnational legal system for the regulation of multinational corporations. Melbourne J Intern Law 10(1):258–307

---

105 Van Huijstee and Wilde-Ramsing (2020).

Balaton-Chrimes S, Haines F (2017) Redress and corporate human rights harms: an analysis of new governance and the POSCO Odisha project. Globalizations 14(4):596–610

Bhatt K (2020) Concessionaires, financiers and communities implementing indigenous peoples' rights to land in transnational development projects. Cambridge University Press, Cambridge

Bhatt K, Erdem Türkelli G (2021) OECD national contact points as sites of effective remedy: new expressions of the role and rule of law within market globalization? Bus Human Rights J 6(3):423–448

Bugalski N (2016) The demise of accountability at the world bank? Am Univ Intern Law Rev 31(1):1–56

Buhmann K (2020) National contact points under OECD guidelines for multinational enterprises: institutional diversity affecting assessments of the delivery of access to remedy. In: Enneking L et al (eds) Accountability, international business operations and the law: providing justice for corporate human rights violations in global value Chains. Routledge, Abingdon, pp 38–59

Buhmann K (2023) Confronting challenges to substantive remedy for victims: opportunities for OECD national contact points under a due diligence regime involving civil liability. Bus Human Rights J 8(3):403–426

Buyse A (2008) Lost and regained? Restitution as a remedy for human rights violations in the context of international law. Heidelberg J Intern Law (Zeitschrift Für Ausländisches Öffentliches Recht und Völkerrecht) 68:129–153

Daniel C et al (2015) Remedy remains rare. OECD Watch, Amsterdam

Deguzman M (2012) How serious are international crimes? The gravity problem in international criminal law. Columbia J Transn Law 50(1):18–68

George E, Laplante L (2017) Access to Remedy. In: Deva S, Bilchitz D (eds) Building a treaty on business and human rights: context and contours. Cambridge University Press, Cambridge, pp 377–407

Haines F, Macdonald K (2020) Nonjudicial business regulation and community access to remedy. Regul Govern 14(4):840–860

Ingrams M, Wilde-Ramsing J, Fleuren J (2021) Get fit: closing gaps in the OECD guidelines to make them fit for purpose. OECD Watch, Amsterdam

Knuckey S, Jenkin E (2015) Company-created remedy mechanisms for serious human rights abuses: a promising new frontier for the right to remedy? Intern J Human Rights 19(6):801–827

Lopez R (2020) The law of gravity. Columbia J Trans Law 58(3):565–622

Marx A et al. (2019) Access to legal remedies for victims of corporate human rights abuses in third countries. Study. European Union, Brussels, https://doi.org/10.2861/566720, pp 1–134

Miller H, Redhead R (2019) Beyond "rights-based approaches"? Employing a process and outcomes framework. Intern J Human Rights 23(5):699–718

MSI Integrity (2020) Not fit-for-purpose: the grand experiment of multi-stakeholder initiatives in corporate accountability, human rights and global governance. MSI Integrity, Berkeley

Naidu E, Torpey J (2012) Reparations for human rights abuses. In: Cushman T (ed) Handbook of human rights. Routledge, Abindgon, Oxon, pp 476–490

Otteburn K, Marx A (2022) 'Seeking remedy for corporate human rights abuses: what is the contribution of the OECD national contact points? In: Marx A, Van Calster G, Wouters J (eds) Research handbook on global governance. Business and Human Rights, Edward Elgar, Cheltenham, pp 229–253

Otteburn K (2023) Reaching the limit: access to remedy through Nonjudicial mechanisms for victims of business-related human rights abuses. Intern J Human Rights 28(2):220–244

Prihandono I (2011) Barriers to transnational human rights litigation against transnational corporations: the need for cooperation between home and host countries. J Law Conf Res 3(6):89–103

Prihandono I, Hosen N, Boom K (2021) Komnas HAM's human rights jurisdiction over businesses involved in the haze crisis. Indonesia Law Rev 11(1):45–72

Pues A (2017) Discretion and the gravity of situations at the international criminal court. Intern Crim Law Rev 17(5):960–984

Rees C (2010) Mediation in business-related human rights disputes: objections, opportunities and challenges. Harvard University John F. Kennedy School of Government Corporate Social Responsibility Initiative, No. 56, hks.harvard.edu/sites/default/files/centers/mrcbg/programs/cri/files/workingpaper_56_rees.pdf (last accessed 31 December 2023)

Reif L (2022) Business and human rights: what role for national human rights institutions? In: Marx A, Van Calster G, Wouters J (eds) Research handbook on global governance. Business and Human Rights, Edward Elgar, Cheltenham, pp 253–272

Sanchez J (2015) The roles and powers of the OECD national contact points regarding complaints on an alleged breach of the OECD guidelines for multinational enterprises by a transnational corporation. Nordic J Intern Law 84(1):89–128

Scheltema M (2013) Assessing the effectiveness of remedy outcomes of nonjudicial mechanisms. Dovenschmidt Quart 1(4):190–197

Shelton D (2005) Remedies in international human rights law, 2nd edn. Oxford University Press, Oxford

Skelton A (2018) Human rights and restorative justice. In: Gavrielides T (ed), Routledge handbook on restorative justice, Routledge, Abingdon, Oxon, chapter 3

Skinner G, McCorquodale R, De Schutter O (2013) The third pillar: access to judicial remedies for human rights violations of transnational business. The International Corporate Accountability Roundtable, CORE, European Coalition for Corporate Justice. https://corporatejustice.org/wp-content/uploads/2021/04/the_third_pillar_-access_to_judicial_remedies_for_human_rights_violation.-1-2.pdf (last accessed 31 December 2023), pp 1–145

Thompson B (2017) Determining criteria to evaluate outcomes of businesses' provision of remedy: applying a human rights-based approach. Bus Human Rights J 2(1):55–85

Torres F (2021) Revisiting the Chorzów factory standard of reparation—its relevance in contemporary international law and practice. Nordic J Intern Law 90(2):190–227

Trouwborst A (2009) Prevention, precaution, logic and law—the relationship between the precautionary principle and the preventative principle in international law and associated questions. The many facets of precautionary logic. Erasmus Law Rev 2(2):105–128

Van Huijstee M, Wilde-Ramsing J (2020) Remedy is the reason: nonjudicial grievance mechanisms and access to remedy. In: Deva S, Birchall D (eds) Research handbook on human rights and business. Edward Elgar Publishing, Cheltenham, pp 471–491

Wettstein F (2009) Multinational corporations and global justice: human rights obligations of a quasi-governmental institution. Stanford University Press, Stanford

Wielga M, Harrison J (2021) Assessing the effectiveness of non-state-based grievance mechanisms in providing access to remedy for rightsholders. Bus Human Rights J 6(1):67–92

Wolfsteller R (2022) The unrealized potential of national human rights institutions in business and human rights regulation: conditions for effective engagement and proposal for reform. Human Rights Review 23(1):43–68

Improving the Effectiveness of Non-Judicial Mechanisms Under the OECD National Contact Points: Issues of Legitimacy and Accessibility

Laura Íñigo Álvarez

Abstract The effectiveness of non-judicial remedies for business-related human rights abuses can be measured based on the criteria established under UN Guiding Principle 31 which requires them to be legitimate, accessible, predictable, equitable, transparent, rights-compatible and a source of continuous learning. In this regard, current research has focused on understanding whether the OECD National Contact Points could be seen as effective non-judicial mechanism for victims of corporate abuse. Against this background, this chapter aims to assess the requirements of legitimacy and accessibility as key entry-level points to the system of NCPs. Moreover, particular attention will be given to the case of Southern European NCPs such as those in Spain and Portugal.

1 Introduction

When adverse human rights impact result from a company's activities, victims must be able to seek redress, and to this end, effective grievance mechanisms play an important role as part of both the state duty to protect and the corporate responsibility to respect. The UN Guiding Principles on Business and Human Rights (UNGPs) identified different grievance mechanisms, including judicial and non-judicial, state-based and non-state-based mechanisms that States and corporations should be able to provide in order to address and respond to business-related human rights abuse. As O'Brien points out, 'non-judicial grievance mechanisms should be seen as highly relevant to victims of business-related human rights abuses in European states, and their counsel or representatives, as well as to victims beyond Europe'.[1] In particular,

The present contribution received the support of the FCT funding in Portugal (FCT Reference UIDP/00714/2020, CEDIS, NOVA School of Law).

L. Íñigo Álvarez (✉)
NOVA School of Law and CEDIS, Lisbon, Portugal
e-mail: laura.inigo@novalaw.unl.pt

[1] O'Brien (2018), p. 141.

O. Davaanyam and M. Krajewski (eds.), *Exploring Corporate Human Rights Responsibilities in OECD Case Law*, Interdisciplinary Studies in Human Rights 14,
https://doi.org/10.1007/978-3-031-75717-4_7

non-judicial remedies remain important since they 'may provide a more immediate, accessible, affordable and adaptable point of initial recourse'.[2] In fact, the Council of Europe Recommendation on Human Rights and Business has also urged its member States to facilitate access to non-judicial grievance mechanisms and the implementation of their decisions.[3] Moreover, the updated revised draft of the Treaty on Business and Human Rights has referred to the obligation of the States to provide non-judicial mechanisms to enable victims' access to adequate, timely and effective remedy.[4]

Two main sorts of non-judicial grievance mechanisms can be identified: state-based and non-state-based mechanisms. Regarding state-based mechanisms, there are different procedures that could be used, including complaints at national human rights institutions, Ombudsman institutions, and alternative dispute resolution mechanisms. Within alternative resolution mechanisms, one of the most prominent instruments is the system of National Contact Points (NCPs) under the OECD Guidelines for Multinational Enterprises on Responsible Business Conduct ('The Guidelines').[5] The Guidelines consist of recommendations addressed by participating governments to multinational enterprises operating in or from their territory, for conduct relating to labour rights, environmental protection, human rights, consumer protection, information disclosure and the fight against corruption. To date, the Guidelines have been endorsed by 51 states, all 38 OECD Member States and 13 non-OECD members, with the recent addition of Uruguay in 2021.[6]

According to this system, all adhering states must establish an NCP at the domestic level. Victims of abuses by multinational enterprises in an adhering country and other relevant stakeholders can make complaints under the so-called 'specific instances procedure'.[7] In this procedure, the NCP plays a mediating role among multinational enterprises, trade unions, NGOs and civil society organisations, individuals or other stakeholders to settle the conflict between the parties and determine whether the Guidelines have been correctly implemented by the enterprise. As the last step, the

[2] Human Rights Council (2008), *Report of the Special Representative of the Secretary-General on the Issue of Human Rights and Transnational Corporations and Other Business Enterprises: Protect, Respect, Remedy: A Framework for Business and Human Rights*, John Ruggie, A/HRC/8/5, adopted 7 April 2008, p. 22.

[3] Council of Europe Committee of Ministers (2016), Recommendation CM/Rec (2016) 3 on Human Rights and Business, adopted 2 March 2016, available at: https://www.coe.int/en/web/ingo/human-rights-and-business (last accessed 15 May 2024).

[4] Open-ended Intergovernmental Working Group on Transnational Corporations and other Business Enterprises with respect to Human Rights (OEIGWG) (2023), *Updated draft legally binding instrument (clean version) to regulate, in international human rights law, the activities of transnational corporations and other business enterprises*, 23-27 October 2023, Articles 1.10 and 4.2.d.

[5] OECD (2023), *OECD Guidelines for Multinational Enterprises on Responsible Business Conduct*, adopted 8 June 2023, https://www.oecd.org/publications/oecd-guidelines-for-multinational-enterprises-on-responsible-business-conduct-81f92357-en.htm (last accessed 15 May 2024).

[6] See full list of adhering States to the Guidelines at OECD, OECD Declaration and Decisions on International Investment and Multinational Enterprises, https://www.oecd.org/investment/mne/oecddeclarationanddecisions.htm (last accessed 15 May 2024).

[7] See Specific instance handling under the OECD Guidelines for Multinational Enterprises, at https://mneguidelines.oecd.org/specificinstances.htm.

NCP releases a statement including the findings and the outcome of the mediation. This statement could include recommendations in relation to the implementation of the Guidelines, as well as a determination as to whether a breach occurred.

In the last years, research has focused on understanding and assessing whether these non-judicial remedies can be in fact considered an effective tool in providing remedies to victims of business-related human rights abuses.[8] Against this background, this chapter aims to assess two key elements that could have a tremendous impact on the full assessment on effectiveness, being the level of legitimacy and accessibility of the specific instance procedure under the NCPs. There are important differences among the level of performance of individual NCPs within the network, as can be observed from the fact that 10 out of 51 NCPs have dealt with more than half of all submissions and 15 NCPs have not received any case since their adherence to the Guidelines.[9] In particular, NCPs in Southern Europe, like the ones in Spain and Portugal, seem to be dragging behind in their task of promoting the Guidelines and strengthening the specific instance procedures.

Accordingly, this chapter will first address the notion of effectiveness under the UNGPs and the OECD Guidelines. Secondly, it will analyse the main challenges in terms of legitimacy and accessibility as applied to the NCP system. Thirdly, the chapter will consider the case studies of the Southern European NCPs, in particular, the Spanish and Portuguese NCPs and examine the question of legitimacy and accessibility of their procedures. Finally, the article will conclude with some recommendations as to how to improve these two elements in the network of NCPs and in the particular case of the Iberian NCPs.

2 Effectiveness Criteria According to Guiding Principle 31

Since their establishment in 2000 NCPs have handled over 650 cases.[10] Today, they still represent the only State-based non-judicial grievance mechanism specifically dealing with responsible business conduct. As explained by Buhmann, 'due to the substantive connection between the UNGPs and the OECD Guidelines, NCPs serve as de facto accountability institutions for business conduct in relation to the UNGPs'.[11] Thanks to the 2011 revision of the Guidelines, there is now a full chapter dedicated to human rights and a substantive percentage of complaints have focused since then

---

[8] See Otteburn and Marx (2022); Bhatt and Türkelli (2021); Buhmann (2020).

[9] This data will be analysed in Sect. 4 of this chapter.

[10] See OECD Database of Specific Instances at https://mneguidelines.oecd.org/database/ (last accessed 15 May 2024).

[11] Buhmann (2020), p. 38.

on different issues related to the chapter on human rights.[12] Additionally, the Guidelines were substantively updated in 2023 introducing key adjustments in relation to the environment and climate change, technology, human rights due diligence, the protection of indigenous peoples and human rights defenders, among other issues.[13]

In order to ensure the effectiveness of non-judicial grievance mechanisms, UN Guiding Principle 31 establishes a number of criteria that non-judicial remedies should be able to comply with, being legitimate, accessible, predictable, equitable, transparent, rights-compatible and a source of continuous learning.[14] These effectiveness criteria were incorporated into the OECD Guidelines' Procedural Guidance on the functional equivalence of NCPs. Consequently, the OECD Guidelines also require similar criteria, namely, visibility, accessibility, transparency and accountability, together with impartiality, predictability, equitability and compatibility with the Guidelines as required by the Procedural Guidance.[15] Moreover, as argued by Bhatt and Erdem Türkelli 'from a practical perspective, effectiveness of remedy processes and outcomes necessitates accessibility, oversight, follow-up, enforcement capabilities and alignment through coordination', adding that 'rights-holders' perspectives about the effectiveness of remedy should be prioritized to guide all practical considerations around remedy'.[16]

In this regard, the UN Working Group on Business and Human Rights has warned about the fact that despite having an effective process in place this might not always lead to an effective remedy, indicating that:

> Although several effectiveness criteria for non-judicial grievance mechanisms are stipulated in the Guiding Principles, there is no explanation of what amounts to an effective remedy. While there is a close correlation between the effectiveness of a remedial mechanism and obtaining an effective remedy, these are two separate aspects, because an effective process may not always result in an effective outcome. Accordingly, there is scope to provide guidance on the concept of an effective remedy irrespective of the type of mechanism employed by rights holders to seek redress.[17]

Likewise, the OECD Secretariat stated in its report '*20 years and the road ahead*' that there was no substantive research assessing whether NCP-facilitated outcomes

---

[12] In particular, according to the statistics of the OECD Secretariat, the human rights chapter was raised in 62% of cases since 2011. See OECD, Cases handled by the National Contact Points for Responsible Business Conduct, https://mneguidelines.oecd.org/Flyer-OECD-National-Contact-Points.pdf (last accessed 15 May 2024).

[13] The blog symposium 'Exploring New Frontiers in the updated OECD Guidelines' organized by NOVA School of Law and OECD Watch tackles different aspects related to the updated OECD Guidelines. The full list of blog posts can be found at https://novabhre.novalaw.unl.pt/category/exploring-new-frontiers-in-the-updated-oecd-guidelines/ (last accessed 15 May 2024).

[14] See Human Rights Council (2011), Guiding Principles on Business and Human Rights: Implementing the United Nations 'Protect, Respect and Remedy' Framework, A/HRC/17/31, adopted 21 March 2011, Principle 31 and its commentary.

[15] Commentary on Human Rights, para. 46 and Procedural Guidance.

[16] Bhatt and Türkelli (2021), p. 436.

[17] UN Working Group on the issue of human rights and transnational corporations and other business enterprises, *Report of the Working Group on the issue of human rights and transnational corporations and other business enterprises*, A/72/162, adopted 18 July 2017, para. 3.

consistently qualify as effective remedy.[18] In this context, OECD Watch, a global network of civil society organisations whose purpose is to inform and advise on how to use the OECD Guidelines and its grievance mechanism, has developed a project entitled 'NCP Evaluations', assessing all NCPs on 40 performance criteria linked to organisation, procedure and communication categories.[19] The aim of this project is to provide information about the functioning of NCPs, identify possible gaps in the NCP performance, and suggest ways to improve the effectiveness of both individual NCPs and the NCP system as a network.

Accordingly, several challenges that the NCP remedy system is currently facing have been identified by both the OECD Secretariat and OECD Watch. This chapter focuses on the issue of legitimacy and accessibility as being two elements that might determine the effectiveness of the rest of criteria. In particular, it is argued that the question of legitimacy and accessibility are the entry-level points of the specific instance procedure that deserve further attention.

As for the first criterion, legitimacy has been defined by the UNGPs as 'enabling trust from the stakeholder groups for whose use they are intended, and being accountable for the fair conduct of grievance processes'.[20] The main element to be considered is whether the procedure, its rules and its structure enable the trust from the stakeholders and potential applicants if they are opting for this mechanism, as well as ensuring that the parties to a grievance process cannot interfere with its fair conduct. The focus on rights holders' perspectives is essential as it has been emphasised by the UN Working Group indicating the centrality of rights holders in access to effective remedies and highlighting a number of relevant requirements attached to it, explicitly or implicitly linked to Guiding Principle 31.[21] For instance, the UN Working Group refers to the fact that rights holders cannot be merely seen as recipients of remedy but should be consulted meaningfully 'in creating, designing, reforming and operating such mechanisms' and the idea that 'the effectiveness of a remedy should be judged also from the perspective of affected rights holders'.[22] Therefore, the level of trust that rights holders and other relevant stakeholders have in this remedial procedure represents one key element to be considered and assessed.

---

[18] OECD (2020), *National Contact Points for Responsible Business Conduct. Providing access to remedy: 20 years and the road ahead*, https://mneguidelines.oecd.org/NCPs-for-RBC-providing-access-to-remedy-20-years-and-the-road-ahead.pdf (last accessed 15 May 2024), p. 33.

[19] See full project at OECD Watch, NCP Evaluations, https://www.oecdwatch.org/indicator/ (last accessed 15 May 2024).

[20] See Human Rights Council (2011), Guiding Principles on Business and Human Rights: Implementing the United Nations 'Protect, Respect and Remedy' Framework, A/HRC/17/31, adopted 21 March 2011, Principle 31 and its commentary.

[21] UN Working Group on the issue of human rights and transnational corporations and other business enterprises, *Report of the Working Group on the issue of human rights and transnational corporations and other business enterprises*, A/72/162, adopted 18 July 2017, pp. 8–16.

[22] UN Working Group on the issue of human rights and transnational corporations and other business enterprises, *Report of the Working Group on the issue of human rights and transnational corporations and other business enterprises*, A/72/162, adopted 18 July 2017, p. 8.

The legitimacy criterion is also directly connected with questions of impartiality, which is identified by the OECD Procedural Guidance as an additional requirement for the specific instances procedure. Being impartial means 'not prejudiced towards or against any particular side or party; fair; unbiased'.[23] Consequently, the composition and structure of the NCP, as well as the stakeholders' involvement would be of crucial relevance in order to ensure impartiality and independence, and therefore, ensure the trust by rights holders and other potential applicants. In fact, according to the Action Plan to Strengthen National Contact Points for Responsible Business Conduct 2022–2024, 'uneven visibility or stakeholder confidence in NCPs can lead for example to some NCPs receiving a higher number of specific instances than others'.[24] Among the strategic goals of this action plan, we can highlight improving stakeholder relations and confidence by implementing 'research and analysis on NCP structures that lead to visibility and confidence with stakeholders'.[25]

As regards the second criterion, accessibility is considered as 'being known to all stakeholder groups for whose use they are intended, and providing adequate assistance for those who may face particular barriers to access'.[26] In order to ensure accessibility a number of barriers should be removed, especially those related to lack of awareness of the mechanism, language, literacy, costs, physical location and fears of reprisal, as explained by the commentary to the Guiding Principle 31. In this aspect, the OECD Guidelines distinguish between 'visibility' and 'accessibility' and include them as the core criteria for functional equivalence.[27] Visibility refers to the question of raising awareness about the Guidelines and the NCP procedure by the adhering governments, whereas accessibility deals with removing obstacles and addressing complaints in an effective and timely manner.

In terms of visibility and accessibility, there seems to be two main difficulties. The first one is that many stakeholders and the public in general do not know NCPs well enough. The average of cases submitted between 2011 and 2023 ranges from 26 to

---

[23] 'Impartial', Collins Dictionary at https://www.collinsdictionary.com/dictionary/english/impartial#:~:text=(%C9%AAm'p%C9%91%CB%90%CA%83%C9%99l%20),Collins%20English%20Dictionary (last accessed 15 May 2024).

[24] OECD (2022), *Action Plan to Strengthen National Contact Points for Responsible Business Conduct 2022–2024*, OECD Paris, https://mneguidelines.oecd.org/action-plan-to-strengthen-national-contact-points-for-responsible-business-conduct%202022-2024.pdf (last accessed 15 May 2024), p. 5.

[25] OECD (2022), *Action Plan to Strengthen National Contact Points for Responsible Business Conduct 2022–2024*, OECD Paris, https://mneguidelines.oecd.org/action-plan-to-strengthen-national-contact-points-for-responsible-business-conduct%202022-2024.pdf (last accessed 15 May 2024), p. 5.

[26] See Human Rights Council (2011), Guiding Principles on Business and Human Rights: Implementing the United Nations 'Protect, Respect and Remedy' Framework, A/HRC/17/31, adopted 21 March 2011, Principle 31 and its commentary.

[27] OECD (2023), *OECD Guidelines for Multinational Enterprises on Responsible Business Conduct*, adopted 8 June 2023, https://www.oecd.org/publications/oecd-guidelines-for-multinational-enterprises-on-responsible-business-conduct-81f92357-en.htm (last accessed 15 May 2024), Commentary on the Implementation Procedures of the OECD Guidelines for Multinational Enterprises, p. 79.

42 cases per year, reaching a peak of 49 cases in 2018, which represents a relatively low figure.[28] As stated in the abovementioned Action Plan, improving visibility remains as one of the essential goals for the period 2022–2024.[29] The second issue relates to the difficulties in passing the initial assessment phase. In particular, between 2000 and 2018, 36% of all cases concluded by NCPs did not manage to pass initial assessment and continue to the good offices phase.[30] The unduly rejection of cases at the initial assessment stage have been raised by OECD Watch as a concerning factor that deserve further attention since this casts doubts on the accessibility of the NCP system.[31]

The next sections address the question of legitimacy and accessibility of the NCP procedures based on the available information provided the OECD Database of Specific Instances, the OECD annual reports on the NCP performance, and the assessment undertaken by OECD Watch in its project 'NCP Evaluations'.

3 Assessment of the Legitimacy of the NCP System

As explained above, legitimacy deals with the trust stakeholders and potential applicants have in the NCP system, together with questions of impartiality. Therefore, in order to assess the legitimacy of the NCP system, this chapter addresses three main elements, namely, the structure and institutional design of NCPs, the stakeholders' involvement in their bodies and the composition of the NCP based on the human resources attributed to them.

As for the structure and design of NCPs, the Guidelines give enough flexibility to governments to define the most suitable structure of the NCP depending on their political and administrative set ups.[32] In this regard, five types of organisational structure of NCPs can be identified: *monoagency* or *single agency*, where the NCP is composed of one or several representatives of a single ministry or an agency

---

[28] Data retrieved from the OECD Database of Specific Instances at https://mneguidelines.oecd.org/database/ (last accessed 15 May 2024).

[29] OECD (2022), *Action Plan to Strengthen National Contact Points for Responsible Business Conduct 2022–2024,* OECD Paris, https://mneguidelines.oecd.org/action-plan-to-strengthen-national-contact-points-for-responsible-business-conduct%202022-2024.pdf (last accessed 15 May 2024), p. 5.

[30] OECD (2020), *National Contact Points for Responsible Business Conduct. Providing access to remedy: 20 years and the road ahead*, https://mneguidelines.oecd.org/NCPs-for-RBC-providing-access-to-remedy-20-years-and-the-road-ahead.pdf (last accessed 15 May 2024), p. 30.

[31] See OECD Watch (2020), *State of Remedy under the OECD Guidelines* in 2019, published 17 June 2020, https://www.oecdwatch.org/the-state-of-remedy-under-the-oecd-guidelines-in-2019/ (last accessed 15 May 2024; OECD Watch (2022), *State of Remedy 2021,* published 27 June 2022, https://www.oecdwatch.org/state-of-remedy-2021/ (last accessed 15 May 2024).

[32] See OECD (2023), *OECD Guidelines for Multinational Enterprises on Responsible Business Conduct*, adopted 8 June 2023, https://www.oecd.org/publications/oecd-guidelines-for-multinational-enterprises-on-responsible-business-conduct-81f92357-en.htm (last accessed 15 May 2024), Procedural Guidance, p. 71.

Table 1 Institutional structure of NCPs

Single agency NCP	Inter-agency NCP	Multipartite NCP	Expert-based NCP	Hybrid structure NCP
Argentina	Brazil	Belgium	Denmark	Australia
Austria	Canada	Croatia	Lithuania	Korea
Chile	Costa Rica	Czech Republic	The Netherlands	
Colombia	Germany	Finland	Norway	
Estonia	Hungary	France		
Greece	Japan	Kazakhstan		
Iceland	Morocco	Latvia		
Ireland	New Zealand	Slovak Republic		
Israel	Portugal	Switzerland		
Italy	Romania	Sweden		
Luxembourg	Slovenia	Tunisia		
Mexico	Spain			
Peru	Uruguay			
Poland				
Turkey				
Ukraine				
UK				
USA				

Source Table compiled by the author based on information retrieved from the OECD Annual Report on the Activity of NCPs 2022[33]

within the same ministry; *inter-agency,* NCPs are composed of a group of representatives from several ministries or government agencies; *multipartite* NCPs are composed of representatives of the government, business and trade unions (tripartite), or also including representatives from civil society (quadripartite); *expert-based* or *independent* NCPs are composed of independent experts who are appointed by the government but do not represent particular interests; and finally those NCPs that follow a *hybrid structure* which could combine single-agency or inter-agency with expert-based (Table 1).

The different models have advantages and disadvantages, although some are preferred over others. For instance, NCPs that follow the single or inter-agency format face crucial challenges and limitations. While decision-making by single-agency NCP could limit 'the expertise immediately available to the NCP, especially when no advisory body is in place to provide support' and 'may also expose it to a

[33] There is no available information about Bulgaria, Jordan and Egypt.

perception of a lack of impartiality or disciplinary bias', inter-ministerial decision-making bodies 'may become unwieldy when they comprise many representatives'.[34] Therefore, as argued by different scholars, the preferred models would be the multi-partite or expert-based types, since these would increase the sense of trust by stakeholders and consequently the legitimacy of the procedure. In fact, Buhmann states that:

> It is likely that the more independent and/or multi-partite, the higher the likelihood that the NCP, the process, and the outcome will be perceived of by stakeholders to be legitimate. The less independent the institutional setup, the bigger the possibility that an NCP may be perceived by victims in host states as too closely linked to the national context of the home state of the transnational enterprise involved.[35]

Similarly, OECD Watch considers that the NCP structure should ensure broad expertise in its complaint handling and promotion functions 'through formally involving diverse relevant government departments, having a multipartite structure, or having an independent expert structure'.[36] On the contrary, some limitations of these preferred models could be related to the question of upholding policy coherence if the members are too isolated from the government, and other organizational challenges like the possible difficulties in respecting timeframes.

Consequently, only 5 NCPs, Australia, Denmark, Lithuania, Norway and the Netherlands would comply with this requirement. As it could be seen from Fig. 1, 60% of NCPs follow the single or inter-agency structure, meaning that the representatives in charge of dealing with the complaints belong to one or several ministries. Consequently, the trust by stakeholders could be relative considering these types of institutional structures. In this regard, peer reviews could serve to address the question of reorganization of the NCP design in order to incorporate the views of relevant stakeholders and increase the legitimacy of the system.

Another issue connected with the previous one relates to the level of stakeholders' involvement not only in the body of the NCP itself but in the advisory body. As regards the available data until 2021, 32 NCPs involved key stakeholders in their institutional arrangements, including 14 in their main body, 15 in their advisory body and 3 in both.[37] The existence of an advisory body that includes different stakeholders, among others, representatives from business, trade union, and civil society organisations, could serve to add certain level of legitimacy to the NCP, although the advisory body would not have decision-making powers. Still, it is advisable to have stakeholder's involvement at least in an advisory body. So far 19 out of 51 NCPs still do not count with any type of stakeholder involvement in their structures, something

[34] OECD (2019), *Guide for National Contact Points on Structures and Activities*, OECD Guidelines for Multinational Enterprises, pp. 8-9.

[35] Buhmann (2020), p. 47.

[36] OECD Watch, Indicators, NCP structure at https://www.oecdwatch.org/indicator/ncp-structure/ (last accessed 15 May 2024).

[37] OECD (2022), *Annual report on the Activity of National Contact Points for Responsible Business Conduct*, https://mneguidelines.oecd.org/ncps/annual-report-of-NCPs-for-RBC-2022.pdf (last accessed 15 May 2024), p. 39.

that should be improved in the upcoming years as advised by the abovementioned action plan.[38] A positive example of this trend could be seen in the Australian NCP which, after the independent review of the NCP in 2017, a number of reforms were conducted including the establishment of a new advisory body and the appointment of an independent expert for all specific instance work, so similar amendments could be potentially introduced in other NCPs in the future.[39]

As for the composition of the NCPs, it is noted that most NCPs do not count with sufficient human resources to fully comply with their task of promoting the Guidelines and handling complaints. In particular, as per 2021, only 4 NCPs reported having over 6 staff members, France (19), Japan (11), Latvia (17) and Uruguay (12), while the remaining staff at NCPs range between 2 and 6 members.[40] Moreover, only 22 NCPs reported having staff working full-time on NCP matters.[41] The main issue of having only part-time staff is the potential conflict of interest that can emerge, especially bearing in mind that most decisions are made by a group of representatives from one or several ministries, usually trade, industry and foreign affairs, that work on multiple topics with different parties involved. This could be considered as having a potential impact on possible conflicts of interest and consequently, could jeopardise the impartiality in decision-making. Finally, as regards the qualification of the staff who conduct substantial parts of the assessment of complaints, there are rising concerns as the staff tend to be 'generalist civil servants rather than experts on human rights or other substantive issues covered by the Guidelines'.[42] Consequently, the lack of expertise in relation to human rights and the environment is another element that should be tackled by Governments when assigning these tasks to civil servants or other members of their staff.

4 Assessment of the Accessibility of the NCP System

Accessibility to the NCP procedure means that making use of this non-judicial mechanism should be straightforward and not excessively onerous for the potential applicants. When examining the accessibility of specific instances, different elements could be subject of analysis. In fact, the level of accessibility of a grievance mechanism would depend on several external and internal factors or a combination of both. Having said that, this section will focus on inquiring the number of cases received by the NCP system and understanding what numbers said about accessibility; the

---

[38] OECD (2022), *Action Plan to Strengthen National Contact Points for Responsible Business Conduct 2022–2024*, p. 5.

[39] See the Australian NCP 2017 review at https://ausncp.gov.au/about/2017-review (last accessed 15 May 2024).

[40] OECD (2022), *Annual report on the Activity of National Contact Points for Responsible Business Conduct*, pp. 61–64.

[41] OECD (2022), *Annual report on the Activity of National Contact Points for Responsible Business Conduct*, pp. 40.

[42] Buhmann (2020), p. 48.

Table 2 Number of cases handled by individual NCPs

UK (59 cases)	Poland (8 cases)
USA (57 cases)	Colombia (7 cases)
Netherlands (54 cases)	Finland (7 cases)
Brazil (41 cases)	Spain (7 cases)
France (36 cases)	Turkey (7 cases)
Germany (34 cases)	Austria (6 cases)
Australia (28 cases)	Czech Republic (6 cases)
Canada (26 cases)	Kazakhstan (6 cases)
Switzerland (25 cases)	New Zealand (6 cases)
Italy (22 cases)	Mexico (5 cases)
Belgium (22 cases)	Peru (5 cases)
Denmark (21 cases)	Luxembourg (4 cases)
Korea 20 cases)	Morocco (4 cases)
Norway (20 cases)	Hungary (3 cases)
Chile (19 cases)	Israel (2 cases)
Argentina (15 cases)	Latvia (2 cases)
Japan (11 cases)	Portugal (1 case)
Ireland (10 cases)	
Sweden (9 cases)	

Source Table compiled by the author based on data retrieved from OECD Database of Specific Instances until December 2022

extent to which cases have passed the initial assessment phase as a crucial moment of the complaint; and the efforts made by NCPs in awareness raising campaigns.

Between 2000 and 2022, NCPs have handled over 650 cases relating to company operations in over 100 countries and territories in all five continents.[43] We need to remind here that cases related to the human rights chapter could only be filed after 2011 with the revisions of the Guidelines. In fact, the number of filed cases substantively increased after that period. Moreover, only the NCPs who have received a specific instance are listed in the OECD database. This means that only 36 out of 51 NCPs have dealt with at least one case, with 10 NCPs dealing with more than half of all submissions (Table 2).[44]

Overall, these figures represent an asymmetrical distribution of cases among NCPs, with only a few of them having handled a substantive number of cases, while

[43] OECD (2022), *Cases handled by the National Contacts Points on Responsible Business Conduct,* https://mneguidelines.oecd.org/Flyer-OECD-National-Contact-Points.pdf (last accessed 15 May 2024).

[44] The numbers included in this analysis are the ones provided by the OECD database. However, this data has to be updated with the information sent directly by each NCP. There are some NCPs that have not provided this information to date or has not been updated by the NCP regularly. For instance, the information included for each NCP might vary as some only covers cases handled until 2020 and/or 2021 which needs to be updated annually.

64% of NCPs having dealt with less than 10 cases and even some of them not having received any submissions yet. Moreover, these numbers refer to all cases including those that were concluded after a mediation process, those that led to the final statement, and those that have been rejected. If we look at the outcomes achieved by NCPs between 2011 and 2019, the numbers are not very promising as only 40% of concluded cases resulted in an agreement.[45] Nevertheless, it is difficult to compare NCPs against each other without considering differences in sectors and industries, the regulatory environment, size of companies, whether the complaint refers to a country as a host or home country, or the type of breaches being raised at the NCPs. In terms of geographical regions, as it will be addressed later, NCPs in Southern Europe are having a low performance in terms of the number of submissions and concluded cases, with the exception of Italy.

As stated before, the accessibility of NCPs as grievance mechanisms 'does not only mean that filing a case should be easy, but also that barriers to accessing good offices should be low'.[46] Therefore, in relation to the different phases of the mediation process, the initial assessment phase represents a crucial moment of the complaint that would determine whether the dispute progress to the good office phase or not. In this regard, the available data has shown that until 2018 '36% of all cases concluded by NCPs failed to pass initial assessment and progress to good offices', with many cases being only partially accepted.[47] As indicated by the OECD Secretariat, '[a] recurrent criticism by submitters has been that there is much variation across the network regarding requirements for acceptance, which is in part due to the broad scope of the initial assessment criteria listed in the Guidelines'.[48] In particular, there are divergences as to what is required to accept a case, some NCPs only require submitters to demonstrate the 'plausibility' of the issues, others request a significant level of evidence. The comparative analysis undertaken by Olsen and Sørensen in 2013 examining the Danish, Norwegian and UK NCPs, also showed variations in relation to who could bring a complaint and against whom a complaint could be filed.[49]

More importantly, it is essential to understand the reasons why cases have been rejected by NCPs at the initial assessment. After analysing the rejected cases since 2020 onwards, there are several common reasons that could be identified as being alleged by different NCPs: insufficient substantiation of allegations or lack of significant evidence; existence of parallel proceedings that could negatively prejudice the existing proceedings; the fact that the good offices would not contribute to the resolution of the issues raised; the lack of evidence of the business relationship between

[45] OECD (2020), *National Contact Points for Responsible Business Conduct. Providing access to remedy: 20 years and the road ahead*, p. 22.

[46] OECD (2020), *National Contact Points for Responsible Business Conduct. Providing access to remedy: 20 years and the road ahead*, p. 29.

[47] OECD (2020), *National Contact Points for Responsible Business Conduct. Providing access to remedy: 20 years and the road ahead*, p.30.

[48] OECD (2020), *National Contact Points for Responsible Business Conduct. Providing access to remedy: 20 years and the road ahead*, p. 31.

[49] Sørensen and Egelund Olsen (2013).

the multinational enterprise and the issues being addressed; and the refusal to apply the Guidelines to certain financial services.[50] When examining these reasons, one might wonder how the NCP could facilitate mediation and provide effective remedies without placing an overly high burden of proof on the complainants' allegations. In particular, the *OECD's Guide for National Contacts Points on the Initial Assessment of Specific Instances* indicates that 'the initial assessment should not be unnecessarily onerous and should not reflect the level of examination required in later stages of the process'.[51] Moreover, also during the initial assessment phase the 'evidentiary requirements need not be analogous to those required in legal proceedings'.[52] If something characterises an extrajudicial mechanism would be its flexibility in terms of time-limits, simplicity of procedure, its affordability as for the lack of costs. However, requiring the same or similar evidentiary requirements in the initial assessment phase endangers the accessibility of the mechanism and puts into question its overall effectiveness.

Finally, as regards accessibility in the form of visibility of the mechanism, NCPs have a duty to promote the Guidelines and the attached grievance mechanism through the organisation and participation in events. The last annual report of activities of the NCPs shows that promotional activities that increase the visibility of NCPs should be highly expanded. In 2021, 31 NCPs organised or co-organised 138 events, which represents a decrease in the number of NCPs organising and co-organising events in comparison to the figures from 2020.[53] On the other side of the coin, 17 NCPs did not organise or co-organise any promotional events in 2021, including the Spanish and the Portuguese NCP as will be analysed in the following section.

5 Case Studies: NCPs in Spain and Portugal

As indicated in the introduction, this chapter places particular emphasis on the performance of the Spanish and Portuguese NCPs, since there is no comprehensive research undertaken on the Southern European NCPs so far. In particular, the analysis will examine how these NCP comply with the legitimacy and accessibility requirements explained above.

---

[50] These reasons have been identified by examining 60 cases rejected from 2020 until 2023 according to the available data retrieved from the OEC Database on Specific Instance. See also OECD Watch (2020), *State of Remedy under the OECD Guidelines* in 2019, published 17 June 2020, https://www.oecdwatch.org/the-state-of-remedy-under-the-oecd-guidelines-in-2019/ (last accessed 15 May 2024; OECD Watch (2022), *State of Remedy 2021*, published 27 June 2022, https://www.oecdwatch.org/state-of-remedy-2021/ (last accessed 15 May 2024).

[51] OECD (2019), *Guide for National Contacts Points on the Initial Assessment of Specific Instances*, OECD Guidelines for Multinational Enterprises, p. 7.

[52] OECD (2019), *Guide for National Contacts Points on the Initial Assessment of Specific Instances*, OECD Guidelines for Multinational Enterprises, p.8.

[53] See OECD (2022), *Annual report on the Activity of National Contact Points for Responsible Business Conduct*, pp. 43–46.

5.1 The Spanish NCP

The Spanish NCP was established in 2001 to ensure the dissemination and promotion of the Guidelines as well as their effective implementation.[54] In 2014, its composition and operation were defined through the Ministerial Order of 11 November 2014.[55] The NCP is attached to the Secretary of State for Trade, within the Ministry of Industry, Trade and Tourism. The NCP is configured as an inter-ministerial collegiate body which includes representatives of the Ministry of Economy and Competitiveness, Ministry of Employment and Social Security, Ministry of Industry, Energy and Tourism, and Ministry of Foreign Affairs and Cooperation. Therefore, it follows the inter-agency model. Moreover, it counts with an advisory body composed of two representatives of the business sector (one from the Spanish Confederation of Business Organizations and another from the Superior Council of Chambers of Commerce, Industry and Navigation of Spain), one representative for each of the member unions of the Consultative Union Committee of the OECD (TUAC) and with representation at the state level (General Union of Workers (UGT), Union Confederation of Workers Commissions (CC.OO.) and Union Sindical Obrera (USO), and two representatives of non-governmental organizations (a representative of the Observatory on Corporate Social Responsibility and a representative of Transparency International). Although not following a multipartite or expert-based model, it has nevertheless stakeholders' involvement in its advisory body, without decision-making power. In terms of the staff, according to the available data, it has only three staff members, one working full-time and two other part-time.

As for the role of the NCP in handling specific instances, its website shows that the Spanish NCP has been involved in 13 cases as lead NCP (as opposed to the information included in the OECD database that only shows 7 cases).[56] From these 13 cases, there was only one agreement achieved in a case from 2004 and the NCP issued final statements in 6 cases including recommendations to the respective enterprises. Nevertheless, there was no determination as to whether a breach of the Guidelines occurred in any of the cases mentioned. The rest of the cases were either rejected by the NCP (issue not covered by the Guidelines; lack of substantiation; or parallel proceedings) or closed for the lack of willingness of the company to participate in the mediation process. There has not been any follow-up of the cases. Most cases relate to questions of employment and industrial relations.

---

[54] Website of the Spanish NCP:
https://comercio.gob.es/InversionesExteriores/PNCLD/Punto_Nacional_Contacto_España/Paginas/default.aspx.

[55] See Ministerial Order of 11 November 2014 at:
https://comercio.gob.es/InversionesExteriores/PNCLD/Punto_Nacional_Contacto_España/Documents/Orden-PRE_2167_2014-creacion-regulacion-PNC-directrices-OCDE-1.pdf.

[56] See list of cases: https://comercio.gob.es/InversionesExteriores/PNCLD/Casos_tratados_PNCs/Paginas/default.aspx.

There is one case that deserves consideration which is *Alianza por la Solidaridad vs. Grupo ACS Cobra* submitted in November 2017.[57] The NGO Alianza por la Solidaridad filed a complaint with the Spanish NCP in connection with the activities of a Spanish company as a contractor in the RENACE hydroelectric project in Alta Verapaz, Guatemala. The complaint alleged that the hydroelectric project had caused negative environmental and human rights impacts affecting indigenous people. The case concluded without agreement, but the NCP issued a final statement with a number of recommendations.[58] Among these recommendations the NCP emphasized that the position of contractor does not exempt the Spanish company from compliance with the highest international standards, including the OECD Guidelines, which include the duty to require and urge the local partner to comply with them in the event of non-compliance. In addition, the NCP also recommended the Spanish company to collaborate with the Guatemalan judicial authorities for mitigation and remediation of the damages. Even though this case did not end up in an agreement, the role of the NCP in enforcing the Guidelines and recommending mitigation and remediation measures is to be highlighted as a positive outcome.

With regards to the NCP's duty of promoting the Guidelines and organising awareness raising events, the role of the Spanish NCP has been quite limited. According to the information available in its website, the NCP organised or participated in 4 events in the period 2017 to 2018, with no reported activities in 2019, 2020, and 2021. The rest of information available in its website is incomplete as there are only 3 published reports of the OECD and it has no social media presence. A peer review process of the Spanish NCP was conducted in April 2022 with the participation of the OECD Secretariat, the Slovenian and the Dutch NCP, as well as relevant stakeholders from the business sector, trade unions, and very few representatives from civil society. The report containing the assessment and recommendations was also published that year.[59]

Therefore, it seems the activity of the NCP in Spain has been very limited, with certain promotional activities since 2022 and an increase of NCP submissions since 2021. However, the main issues continue to be the lack of visibility of the mechanism, an institutional design exclusively based on representatives of Ministries with very limited human resources and the refusal of the NCP to issue determinations as to whether a breach has occurred. As for the peer review processes conducted in 2022, it is to be noted that only a few civil society organisations participated providing feedback and no members of academia joined the process.

---

[57] See a summary of the case produced by OECD Watch at OECD Watch Complaints Database, *Alianza por la Solaridad v. Grupo ACS-COBRA*, https://www.oecdwatch.org/complaint/alianza-por-la-solidaridad-v-grupo-acs-cobra/ (last accessed 15 May 2024).

[58] Final Statement by the Spanish NCP issued 19 December 2019 available in Spanish at https://comercio.gob.es/InversionesExteriores/PNCLD/Casos_tratados_PNCs/Documents/Informe-Final-caso-E-00007.pdf.

[59] OECD (2022), *OECD Guidelines for Multinational Enterprises National Contact Point Peer Reviews: Spain*, at https://mneguidelines.oecd.org/national-contact-point-peer-reviews-spain.pdf (last accessed 15 May 2024).

5.2 The Portuguese NCP

The Portuguese NCP is a body composed of the Directorate-General for Economic Activities (DGAE) and the Portuguese Agency for Investment and Foreign Trade, E.P.E. (AICEP).[60] The advantage of this structure is that is easy to identify who the representatives in charge are and it includes the Ministries that are more directly related to issues of responsible business conduct. However, the main disadvantage is that there is no broad expertise or participation of different stakeholders which endangers the principles of accountability and impartiality. The NCP does not have an advisory body. Another disadvantage relates to the resources of the NCP. The staff at the NCP works only part-time on NCP matters. Not only is this a resource issue, but it could also potentially question impartiality if the staff works on potentially conflicting issues during the rest of their working time. Finally, there is no available information on who the staff members of the NCP are and what their expertise is.

As for the submission of cases, the NCP has participated as lead NCP in one case from 3rd May 2004, and as indicated by Beatriz Albuquerque, it has intervened in 4 other cases led by the Danish NCP in 2013, the Polish NCP in 2013, the French NCP in 2020 and the Chilean NCP in 2020.[61] Yet, no information about these other cases is available on the NCP's website. Therefore, the role of the Portuguese NCP as a non-judicial mechanism on responsible business conduct should be reinforced and promoted at different levels. The lack of visibility and transparency seem to be the core elements that will need to be improved as most stakeholders in Portugal are not aware of the existence of this non-judicial procedure to solve potential disputes in areas related to the OECD Guidelines. A broader element of concern is the fact that Portugal has yet to adopt its National Action Plan on Business and Human Rights that has been under negotiation during last years.[62]

In terms of promotional activities, the Portuguese NCP did not organise, co-organise, nor participate in any promotional event during 2020 nor 2021.[63] During 2022 and 2023 the NCP participated and organised some events both online and in person.[64] These events show a recent effort to perform better, but remain limited. The NCP has no social media presence expect for a recent YouTube Channel that was

---

[60] Website of the Portuguese NCP at https://www.dgae.gov.pt/wwwbase/raiz/Erro.aspx?aspxerrorpath=/servicos/sustentabilidade-empresarial/ponto-de-contacto-nacional-para-as-diretrizes-da-ocde-para-as-empresas-multinacionais.aspx.

[61] See Albuquerque (2022).

[62] A current study about the proposals with recommendations for a Portuguese NAP has been published in 2023 by the NOVA BHRE and ELSA Portugal, available at https://novabhre.novalaw.unl.pt/projects/recommendations-for-the-upcoming-portuguese-national-action-plan-on-business-and-human-rights/ (last accessed 15 May 2024).

[63] OECD (2022), *Annual report on the Activity of National Contact Points for Responsible Business Conduct*, p. 46.

[64] See the list of activities at https://www.dgae.gov.pt/wwwbase/raiz/Erro.aspx?aspxerrorpath=/servicos/sustentabilidade-empresarial/ponto-de-contacto-nacional-para-as-diretrizes-da-ocde-para-as-empresas-multinacionais.aspx.

created at the beginning of 2023.[65] Therefore, there is much room for improvement in the task of promoting the Guidelines by the Portuguese NCP. Nevertheless, the NCP conducted a peer review process in 2023 which counted with the support of the OECD Secretariat, the Spanish and the Chilean NCP, as well as relevant stakeholders from the business sector, trade unions, civil society and academia. The results of this peer-review process were published in December 2023.[66]

Similarly to the Spanish NCP, there are many substantive issues that need to be improved in terms of visibility, accessibility and legitimacy. In particular, its structure would benefit from having an advisory body with the participation of relevant stakeholders. More promotional activities are expected to be developed in order to increase its visibility and awareness raising campaigns. It remains to be seen whether the recommendations included in the peer review process are fully implemented afterwards.

6 Concluding Remarks

Visibility, accessibility and legitimacy remain key challenges of both the NCP system and individual NCPs. In line with the strategic goals of the OECD Action Plan for 2022–2024, improving visibility, stakeholders' relations and confidence should be further emphasized by the different NCPs. As stated in the Action Plan, 'stakeholder engagement efforts will de facto increase the visibility of NCPs and, if done well, foster confidence in the process'.[67] In order to do so, building partnerships with relevant stakeholders at the national and regional level, including business, trade union, civil society and academia should be fostered, as well as peer learning about NCP structures, although tailored to the specific institutional and administrative characteristics of states. As indicated by the UN Working Group, the accessibility of non-judicial grievance mechanisms should be considered from the perspective of affected rights holders seeking remedies. Therefore, 'rights holders would consider a remedy to be accessible only if they know about its existence and could gain access to it without too much expense, inconvenience or the help of technical experts'.[68]

In terms of legitimacy, the structure of NCPs should be reassessed especially during peer review processes. In particular, future research lines might consider the correlation between the type of NCP structure, the number of complaints received, the outcomes of the mediation, as well as the content of the recommendations in the

---

65 See PCN OCDE Portugal at https://www.youtube.com/@pcnocdeportugal9012.

66 OECD (2023), *OECD Guidelines for Multinational Enterprises National Contact Point Peer Reviews: Portugal*, https://mneguidelines.oecd.org/ncps/national-contact-point-peer-reviews-portugal.pdf (last accessed 15 May 2024).

67 OECD (2022), *Action Plan to Strengthen National Contact Points for Responsible Business Conduct 2022–2024*, p. 5.

68 UN Working Group on the issue of human rights and transnational corporations and other business enterprises, *Report of the Working Group on the issue of human rights and transnational corporations and other business enterprises*, A/72/162, adopted 18 July 2017, p. 11, para. 32.

NCP's final statement, in order to learn from the different NCP practices and experiences. Governments must also reflect about the required expertise needed to fulfil their mandate across all possible issues that may come up in promotion or specific instances. In this line, objective number 4 of the Action Plan rests on increasing expertise within the Network.[69] In this sense, list of experts could be shared among NCPs and compendium or handbooks on thematic issues reflected by the NCP jurisprudence could be developed and disseminated among NCPs.

In relation to the NCPs in Southern Europe, it would be key to share expertise and good practices as Spain and Portugal have similar characteristics in terms of industries, socio-economic factors and legal culture. Joint events could potentially be organised by both NCPs. Moreover, a network of Southern European NCPs, possibly including Italy and Greece, could be encouraged similarly to the work of the NCPs in the Benelux area in order to develop capacity-building initiatives regarding both promotional activities and mediation work. Both NCPs need to work in improving their accessibility and visibility as many civil society organisations and NGOs are not aware of the existence of this mechanism. As mentioned in the introduction, specific instance procedures as non-judicial mechanisms serve to complement judicial mechanisms and NCPs could offer certain level of redress when judicial remedies might not be able to deliver them due to challenges related to jurisdictional, territorial or time limitations. At the same time, companies should consider the reputational damage in case of being found in breach of the OECD Guidelines and the potential impact of final statements issued by NCPs.

References

Albuquerque B (2022) The Portuguese National Contact Point: challenges and opportunities, Nova Centre on Business, Human Rights and the Environment Blog, 25 January 2022. https://novabhre.novalaw.unl.pt/the-portuguese-national-contact-point-challenges-and-opportunities/

Bhatt K, Türkelli GE (2021) OECD national contact points as sites of effective remedy: new expressions of the role and rule of law within market globalization? Bus Human Rights J 6(3):423-448

Buhmann K (2020) National contact points under OECD's guidelines for multinational enterprises: institutional diversity affecting assessments of the delivery of access to remedy. In: Enneking L, Giesen I, Schaap AJ, Ryngaert C, Kristen F, Roorda L (eds) Accountability, international business operations and the law: providing justice for corporate human rights violations in global value Chains. Routledge, London, pp 38–59

O'Brien CM (2018) Business and human rights. A handbook for legal practitioners, Council of Europe

Otteburn O, Marx A (2022) Seeking remedies for corporate human rights abuses: what is the contribution of OECD national contact points? In: Marx A, Van Calster G, Wouters J (eds) Research handbook on global governance. Business and Human Rights, Edward Elgar Publishing, Cheltenham and Northampton, pp 229–253

[69] OECD (2022), Action Plan to Strengthen National Contact Points for Responsible Business Conduct 2022–2024, p. 7.

Sørensen KE, Egelund Olsen B (2013) Strengthening the enforcement of CSR through mediation and conflict resolution by national contact points: finding a new balance between hard law and soft law, Nordic & European Company Law Working Paper No. 10–38. https://papers.ssrn.com/sol3/papers.cfm?abstract_id=2269555

Business and Human Rights Dispute Settlement: The OECD NCPs as Grievance Mechanism

Tamar Meshel

Abstract This chapter presents a qualitative and quantitative study of 225 specific instances concluded by OECD National Contact Points (NCPs) between 2001 and 2022. The grievances in these cases were accepted and the relevant NCPs offered to the parties one or more of the following dispute resolution services: good office, mediation, and conciliation. The study first provides aggregated statistical data on variables such as the processes used by NCPs in these cases, the participation of the parties, and the outcome. The study then delves more deeply into some of these statistics, for instance examining which NCPs saw the most agreements reached and which mechanisms were offered by each NCP. Logistic regression analysis follows, to see if any meaningful cross-observation relationships can be found. In addition, the study undertakes a comparative qualitative analysis of the dispute resolution mechanisms used by different NCPs and the manner in which they are used. The goals of this study are to uncover trends as well as inconsistencies in the dispute resolution practices of different NCPs and to identify those mechanisms, or combinations of mechanisms, that have proven effective in the resolution of grievances.

1 Introduction

A central purpose of the OECD National Contact Points (NCPs) is to resolve specific instances, also known as grievances or complaints, brought against companies for alleged violations of the OECD Guidelines for Multinational Enterprises (Guidelines).[1] Broadly speaking, NCPs use three main processes to resolve grievances. These processes, placed on a spectrum from the most structured and formal to the least, are "conciliation", "mediation", and "good offices".

[1] OECD (2023), OECD Guidelines for Multinational Enterprises on Responsible Business Conduct, OECD Publishing, Paris, https://doi.org/10.1787/81f92357-en (last accessed 13 April 2024), p. 56.

T. Meshel (✉)
University of Alberta, Alberta, Canada
e-mail: meshel@ualberta.ca

O. Davaanyam and M. Krajewski (eds.), *Exploring Corporate Human Rights Responsibilities in OECD Case Law*, Interdisciplinary Studies in Human Rights 14,
https://doi.org/10.1007/978-3-031-75717-4_8

Generally, in conciliation "[a]n impartial third party conciliator investigates the entire dispute, including the facts and the applicable law, and provides the disputants with formal recommendations for the settlement of a dispute".[2]

Mediation is generally considered to be less structured than conciliation. In mediation, "[t]he mediator acts as a conduit for disputant proposals, although the mediator can provide her own proposals albeit 'informally and on the basis of information supplied by the parties, rather than independent investigations'".[3] The Guidelines provide that "NCPs may choose to carry out the mediation themselves or engage external mediators in consultation with the parties to conduct or support mediation".[4]

Finally, "[t]hrough good offices, NCPs will offer a platform for dialogue between the parties to assist with the resolution of the issues raised".[5]

While all of these mechanisms can be effective,[6] NCPs have long been criticized for offering them in an ineffective manner.[7] At the same time, few studies have undertaken an in-depth examination of NCPs' dispute resolution processes with a view to drawing lessons for their future development and improvement.[8]

While several studies have focused on NCPs' dispute resolution processes, they are older and not comprehensive in their coverage. For instance, one study was undertaken over a decade ago and examined 57 final statements published by NCPs, out of which only 23 addressed dispute resolution procedures applied in specific instances.[9] A newer study was conducted in 2016, but included only 18 cases.[10] Two additional studies focused on a comparison between a limited number of NCPs, such as the United States, the Netherlands, France, Norway, and the United Kingdom[11] Another study analysed 403 specific instances filed with NCPs, both resolved and unresolved, but did not address the details of the dispute resolution methods offered or used.[12]

This chapter presents a quantitative and qualitative study of the dispute resolution processes used by NCPs in 225 concluded specific instances that were filed around the

---

[2] Reif (2007), pp. 20, 22.

[3] Reif (2007), pp. 20, 21–22; Merrills (2005), pp. 28–29.

[4] OECD (2023), OECD (2023), OECD Guidelines for Multinational Enterprises on Responsible Business Conduct, OECD Publishing, Paris, https://doi.org/10.1787/81f92357-en (last accessed 13 April 2024), p. 71.

[5] OECD (2023), OECD (2023), OECD Guidelines for Multinational Enterprises on Responsible Business Conduct, OECD Publishing, Paris, https://doi.org/10.1787/81f92357-en (last accessed 13 April 2024), p. 70.

[6] Hill (1998), p. 173.

[7] OECD Watch (2022), State of Remedy 2021, https://www.oecdwatch.org/state-of-remedy-2021/ (last accessed 13 April 2024).

[8] Buhmann (2020), p. 54 (calling for further research in order to obtain "[a]n understanding of the types of NCP procedures that offer the highest extent of justice... can serve as inspiration for reforms of existing NCPs and the establishment of new NCPs").

[9] Davarnejad (2011), p. 351.

[10] Karin, et al. (2016), p. 30.

[11] Franciose (2007), p. 223; Olsen and Sørensen (2014), p. 9.

[12] Khoury and Whyte (2019), p. 363.

world between 2001 and 2022. The chapter is structured as follows. Section 2 summarizes the results of a two-stage quantitative analysis of the 225 specific instances. In the first stage, the frequencies of eight variables—related to the NCP, the dispute resolution mechanism, the specific instances, and the outcome of the process—were analysed. In the second stage, multinomial logistic regressions were used in order to obtain a more accurate picture of which variables appear most salient to reaching a full or partial agreement within the NCP process. Section 3 of the chapter presents the results of a qualitative study of the dispute resolution mechanisms used by NCPs in these specific instances. The goals of this part of the study are to identify trends as well as inconsistencies in the dispute resolution practices of different NCPs and to uncover possible explanations for some of the quantitative outcomes identified in Sect. 2. The chapter concludes with recommendations for improving the future resolution of specific instances by NCPs.

2 A Quantitative Analysis of NCPs' Dispute Resolution Processes

This Section presents the results of frequencies and logistic regressions analysis of an original dataset of 225[13] concluded specific instances filed with NCPs around the world between 2001 and 2022. The specific instances were collected from the OECD database of specific instances[14] and cross-referenced with the OECD Watch database.[15] "Concluded" specific instances are defined in the OECD database as those that were "determined to merit further examination and have been closed following an offer of good offices".[16] As of February 1, 2023, the OECD database contained 340 "concluded" cases. However, a review of these cases revealed that 115 of them were actually not accepted by the NCP or no dispute resolution service was offered. These cases were therefore excluded from the analysis. The specific instances included in the dataset were then coded on the basis of summaries provided in the OECD database as well as statements issued by NCPs, where available.

---

[13] The final number of specific instances that were coded for statistical analysis was 227, because two specific instances involved two dispute resolution mechanisms that had to be coded differently due to the parties' participation in one and their lack of participation in the other. In one of these cases the outcome was also different for each dispute resolution mechanism used.

[14] OECD Database for Specific Instances, https://mneguidelines.oecd.org/database/ (last accessed 14 April 2024).

[15] OECD Watch Complaints Database, https://www.oecdwatch.org/complaints-database/ (last accessed 14 April 2024).

[16] OECD NCP Database of Specific Instances, https://mneguidelines.oecd.org/specificinstances.htm (last accessed 14 April 2024). Specific instances that were labelled as "in progress" in the OECD database were excluded from the analysis.

2.1 Frequencies Analysis

The frequencies analysis examined the following 8 variables[17]:

Variable	Description
Outcome	A partial agreement, full agreement, or no agreement within the NCP process, or a partial/full agreement outside the NCP process
All parties participated	Whether both the complainant(s) and the company(ies) participated in the NCP dispute resolution process
NCP	The lead NCP that processed the specific instance
Dispute resolution mechanism(s)	Any combination of three mechanisms offered by NCPs: conciliation,[18] mediation,[19] and good offices[20]
External facilitator	Whether the NCP engaged an external facilitator in the dispute resolution process[21]
Theme(s)	As defined in the OECD database[22]
Source(s)	As defined in the OECD database[23]
Industry(ies)	As defined in the OECD database[24]

[17] Additional potentially relevant variables that were not tested include the institutional structure of the NCP and the duration of the NCP process in specific instances.

[18] Includes all cases where the NCP labelled the process as "conciliation".

[19] Includes all cases where the NCP labelled the process as "mediation".

[20] Includes all cases where the NCP labelled the process as "good offices", "dialogue", "consultations", or "negotiations". The author recognizes that some treat "mediation" and "conciliation" as part of the "good offices" offered by NCPs. However, for the purpose of this study these two mechanisms are treated separately.

[21] An external facilitator (mediator or conciliator) was considered to be engaged in the process only if they were appointed and led at least some of the process, rather than merely being proposed to the parties.

[22] The OECD database of specific instances contains 11 "themes": combating bribery, bribe solicitation and extortion; competition; concepts and principles; consumer interests; disclosure; employment and industrial relations; environment; general policies; human rights; science and technology; taxation, see OECD Database for Specific Instances, https://mneguidelines.oecd.org/database/ (last accessed 14 April 2024).

[23] The OECD database of specific instances contains 5 "sources": business, individuals, NGO, other interested parties, and trade union, see OECD Database for Specific Instances, https://mneguidelines.oecd.org/database/ (last accessed 14 April 2024).

[24] The OECD database of specific instances contains 21 "industries": accommodation and food service; activities of extraterritorial organisations and bodies; activities of households as employers; administrative and support service activities; agriculture, forestry and fishing; arts, entertainment and recreation; construction; education; electricity, gas, steam and air conditioning supply; financial and insurance activities; human health and social work activities; information and communication; manufacturing; mining and quarrying; other service activities; professional, scientific and technical activities; public administration and defence; real estate activities; transportation and storage; water supply, sewerage, waste management and remediation activities; wholesale and retail trade, see OECD Database for Specific Instances, https://mneguidelines.oecd.org/database/ (last accessed 14 April 2024).

2.1.1 Outcome and Party Participation

A full agreement between the parties was reached in 30% of specific instances included in the dataset. A partial agreement between the parties was reached in 4% of specific instances. A full/partial agreement between the parties was reached outside the NCP process in 6% of specific instances.[25]

Not surprisingly, in all of the specific instances where a partial or full agreement was reached between the parties in the NCP process, the parties all participated in the process. However, participation is a necessary but not sufficient condition for reaching an agreement. Even though all of the parties participated in 68% of the specific instances, an agreement was reached within the NCP process only in 49% of those instances. In the specific instances where an external facilitator was appointed, a full or partial agreement was reached more frequently—57% of the time.[26]

2.1.2 NCPs

There are a total of 51 NCPs around the world.[27] Out of those, 31 NCPs concluded at least one specific instance that was included in the dataset. The NCPs that concluded the most specific instances were the United Kingdom (13%), Switzerland and the Netherlands (9% each), France (8%), the United States (7%), and Germany (6%) (Table 1).[28]

The NCPs that offered mediation most frequently out of all specific instances in which mediation was offered were the United Kingdom (16%), Switzerland (12%), the United States (11%), Norway and Germany (7% each), and France, the Netherlands, and South Korea (6% each) (Table 2).[29]

The NCPs that offered good offices most frequently out of all specific instances in which good offices was offered were the Netherlands (14%), France (12%), Germany (7%), Canada (6%), and Argentina and Norway (5% each) (Table 3).[30]

---

[25] This information was derived by the author from the specific instances contained in the dataset.

[26] This information was derived by the author from the specific instances contained in the dataset.

[27] OECD, What are the National Contact Points for RBC?, http://mneguidelines.oecd.org/ncps/ (last accessed 14 April 2024).

[28] The information presented in this table was derived by the author from the specific instances contained in the dataset.

[29] The information presented in this table was derived by the author from the specific instances contained in the dataset. Among the NCPs that concluded at least two specific instances, those that offered mediation most frequently in the specific instances submitted to them were South Korea (100%), the United States (93%), Norway (80%), Switzerland (75%), Denmark (67%), the United Kingdom (63%), Australia (62.5%), Germany (62%), Brazil (60%), Belgium (56%), and Turkey and Japan (50% each). These results were derived by the author from the information contained in Table 2.

[30] The information presented in this table was derived by the author from the specific instances contained in the dataset. Among the NCPs that concluded at least two specific instances, those that offered good offices most frequently in the specific instances submitted to them were Turkey, Poland, Argentina, the Czech Republic, Peru, and Sweden (100%), the Netherlands (80%), France,

Table 1 Concluded specific instances by NCP

NCP	Freq	Percent
Argentina	6	2.67
Australia	8	3.56
Austria	1	0.44
Belgium	9	4.00
Brazil	10	4.44
Canada	10	4.44
Chile	9	4.00
Czech Republic	4	1.78
Denmark	3	1.33
Finland	2	0.89
France	18	8.00
Germany	13	5.78
Hungary	1	0.44
Ireland	1	0.44
Italy	3	1.33
Japan	8	3.56
Luxembourg	1	0.44
Mexico	1	0.44
Morocco	1	0.44
Netherlands	20	8.89
New Zealand	1	0.44
Norway	10	4.44
Peru	3	1.33
Poland	2	0.89
South Korea	7	3.11
Spain	2	0.89
Sweden	4	1.78
Switzerland	20	8.89
Turkey	2	0.89
United Kingdom	30	13.33
United States	15	6.67
Total	225	100.00

Conciliation was offered in only 20 cases by four NCPs. Finland and Italy offered conciliation in 100% of the specific instances submitted to them, which accounted

(74%), Canada (70%), Spain (67%), Australia and Japan (62.5%), Germany (62%), Norway (60%), Belgium and Chile (56% each). These results were derived by the author from the information contained in Table 3.

Table 2 Mediation offered by NCP

NCP	Mediation offered		
	N	Y	Total
Argentina	6	0	6
	5.71	0.00	2.64
Australia	3	5	8
	2.86	4.10	3.52
Austria	0	1	1
	0.00	0.82	0.44
Belgium	4	5	9
	3.81	4.10	3.96
Brazil	4	6	10
	3.81	4.92	4.41
Canada	7	3	10
	6.67	2.46	4.41
Chile	5	4	9
	4.76	3.28	3.96
Czech Republic	4	0	4
	3.81	0.00	1.76
Denmark	1	2	3
	0.95	1.64	1.32
Finland	2	0	2
	1.90	0.00	0.88
France	12	7	19
	11.43	5.74	8.37
Germany	5	8	13
	4.76	6.56	5.73
Hungary	0	1	1
	0.00	0.82	0.44
Ireland	0	1	1
	0.00	0.82	0.44
Italy	3	0	3
	2.86	0.00	1.32
Japan	4	4	8
	3.81	3.28	3.52
Luxembourg	0	1	1
	0.00	0.82	0.44
Mexico	1	0	1
	0.95	0.00	0.44
Morocco	1	0	1

(continued)

Table 2 (continued)

NCP	Mediation offered		
	N	Y	Total
	0.95	0.00	0.44
Netherlands	13	7	20
	12.38	5.74	8.81
New Zealand	0	1	1
	0.00	0.82	0.44
Norway	2	8	10
	1.90	6.56	4.41
Peru	3	0	3
	2.86	0.00	1.32
Poland	2	0	2
	1.90	0.00	0.88
South Korea	0	7	7
	0.00	5.74	3.08
Spain	2	1	3
	1.90	0.82	1.32
Sweden	3	1	4
	2.86	0.82	1.76
Switzerland	5	15	20
	4.76	12.30	8.81
Turkey	1	1	2
	0.95	0.82	0.88
United Kingdom	11	19	30
	10.48	15.57	13.22
United States	1	14	15
	0.95	11.48	6.61
Total	105	122	227
	100.00	100.00	100.00

First row has *frequencies* and second row has *column percentages*

for 10% and 15% of all cases in which conciliation was used, respectively. The United Kingdom offered conciliation in 47% of the specific instances submitted to it, which accounted for 70% of all cases in which conciliation was used. Belgium offered conciliation in 11% of its cases, which account for 5% of all cases in which conciliation was used (Tables 4 and 5).[31]

[31] The information presented in these tables was derived by the author from the specific instances contained in the dataset.

Table 3 Good offices offered by NCP

	Good offices offered				Good offices offered		
NCP	N	Y	Total	NCP	N	Y	Total
Argentina	0	6	6	Mexico	0	1	1
	0.00	5.31	2.64		0.00	0.88	0.44
Australia	3	5	8	Morocco	0	1	1
	2.63	4.42	3.52		0.00	0.88	0.44
Austria	1	0	1	Netherlands	4	16	20
	0.88	0.00	0.44		3.51	14.16	8.81
Belgium	4	5	9	New Zealand	1	0	1
	3.51	4.42	3.96		0.88	0.00	0.44
Brazil	6	4	10	Norway	4	6	10
	5.26	3.54	4.41		3.51	5.31	4.41
Canada	3	7	10	Peru	0	3	3
	2.63	6.19	4.41		0.00	2.65	1.32
Chile	4	5	9	Poland	0	2	2
	3.51	4.42	3.96		0.00	1.77	0.88
Czech Republic	0	4	4	South Korea	7	0	7
	0.00	3.54	1.76		6.14	0.00	3.08
Denmark	2	1	3	Spain	1	2	3
	1.75	0.88	1.32		0.88	1.77	1.32
Finland	2	0	2	Sweden	0	4	4
	1.75	0.00	0.88		0.00	3.54	1.76
France	5	14	19	Switzerland	15	5	20
	4.39	12.39	8.37		13.16	4.42	8.81
Germany	5	8	13	Turkey	0	2	2
	4.39	7.08	5.73		0.00	1.77	0.88
Hungary	0	1	1	United Kingdom	26	4	30
	0.00	0.88	0.44		22.81	3.54	13.22
Ireland	1	0	1	United States	14	1	15
	0.88	0.00	0.44		12.28	0.88	6.61
Italy	3	0	3				
	2.63	0.00	1.32				
Japan	3	5	8				
	2.63	4.42	3.52				
Luxembourg	0	1	1				
	0.00	0.88	0.44				
				Total	114	113	227
					100.00	100.00	100.00

First row has *frequencies* and second row has *column percentages*

Table 4 Conciliation offered by NCPs as a percentage of NCP cases

NCP	Conciliation offered		
	N	Y	Total
Belgium	8	1	9
	88.89	11.11	100.00
Finland	0	2	2
	0.00	100.00	100.00
Italy	0	3	3
	0.00	100.00	100.00
United Kingdom	16	14	30
	53.33	46.67	100.00

First row has *frequencies* and second row has *column percentages*

Table 5 Conciliation offered by NCPs as a percentage of all conciliation cases

NCP	Conciliation offered
Belgium	1
	5.00
Finland	2
	10.00
Italy	3
	15.00
United Kingdom	14
	70.00
Total	20
	100.00

First row has *frequencies* and second row has *column percentages*

The NCPs that achieved the most full or partial party agreements out of all specific instances in which such an agreement was reached were the United Kingdom and the Netherlands (16% each), Switzerland (14%), Germany (9%), and the Czech Republic, France, and Norway (5% each) (Table 6).[32]

The NCPs that had the highest party participation out of all specific instances in which the parties participated were the United Kingdom (13%), Switzerland (11%), the Netherlands (10%), France (8%), and Germany (7%) (Table 7).[33]

[32] The information presented in this table was derived by the author from the specific instances contained in the dataset. Among the NCPs that concluded at least two specific instances, those that achieved the most full or partial party agreements in the specific instances submitted to them were the Czech Republic and Poland (100%), the Netherlands (60%), Switzerland (55%), and Germany (54%). These results were derived by the author from the information contained in Table 5.

[33] The information presented in this table was derived by the author from the specific instances contained in the dataset. Among the NCPs that concluded at least two specific instances, those that had the highest party participation in the specific instances submitted to them were Sweden

Table 6 Full/partial agreement by NCP

NCP	Full/Partial Agreement				Full/Partial Agreement		
	N	Y	Total	NCP	N	Y	Total
Argentina	6	0	6	Peru	3	0	3
	3.97	0.00	2.64		1.99	0.00	1.32
Australia	6	2	8	Poland	0	2	2
	3.97	2.63	3.52		0.00	2.63	0.88
Austria	0	1	1	South Korea	5	2	7
	0.00	1.32	0.44		3.31	2.63	3.08
Belgium	7	2	9	Spain	2	1	3
	4.64	2.63	3.96		1.32	1.32	1.32
Brazil	9	1	10	Sweden	4	0	4
	5.96	1.32	4.41		2.65	0.00	1.76
Canada	8	2	10	Switzerland	9	11	20
	5.30	2.63	4.41		5.96	14.47	8.81
Chile	7	2	9	Turkey	2	0	2
	4.64	2.63	3.96		1.32	0.00	0.88
Czech Republic	0	4	4	United Kingdom	18	12	30
	0.00	5.26	1.76		11.92	15.79	13.22
Denmark	3	0	3	United States	13	2	15
	1.99	0.00	1.32		8.61	2.63	6.61
Finland	2	0	2				
	1.32	0.00	0.88				
France	15	4	19				
	9.93	5.26	8.37				
Germany	6	7	13				
	3.97	9.21	5.73				
Hungary	1	0	1				
	0.66	0.00	0.44				
Ireland	1	0	1				
	0.66	0.00	0.44				
Italy	2	1	3				
	1.32	1.32	1.32				
Japan	7	1	8				
	4.64	1.32	3.52				
Luxembourg	0	1	1				
	0.00	1.32	0.44				
Mexico	0	1	1				

(continued)

Table 6 (continued)

NCP	Full/Partial Agreement			NCP	Full/Partial Agreement		
	N	Y	Total	NCP	N	Y	Total
	0.00	1.32	0.44				
Morocco	1	0	1				
	0.66	0.00	0.44				
Netherlands	8	12	20				
	5.30	15.79	8.81				
New Zealand	0	1	1				
	0.00	1.32	0.44				
Norway	6	4	10				
	3.97	5.26	4.41				
				Total	151	76	227
					100.00	100.00	100.00

First row has *frequencies* and second row has *column percentages*

The NCPs that engaged an external facilitator most often out of all specific instances in which an external facilitator was engaged were the United Kingdom (30%) and Switzerland (24%).[34]

2.1.3 Dispute Resolution Mechanism

The NCP Mediation Manual (Mediation Manual)[35] defines "mediation" and "conciliation" as follows[36]:

(100%), Belgium (89%), Switzerland and Germany (85%), the Netherlands and Norway (80% each), France (68%), and South Korea (71%). These results were derived by the author from the information contained in Table 6.

[34] Next was the United States with 11%, and Canada and South Korea with 6% each. Among the NCPs that concluded at least 2 specific instances, those that engaged an external facilitator most frequently in the specific instances submitted to them were Italy (67%), Switzerland (65%), and the United Kingdom (53%). These results were derived by the author from the specific instances contained in the dataset.

[35] The Consensus Building Institute (2012), NCP Mediation Manual, https://files.nettsteder.regjeringen.no/wpuploads01/blogs.dir/263/files/2015/10/NCP_mediation_manual.pdf (last accessed 14 April 2024), p. 20.

[36] The Manual does not define "good office". It is worth noting that not all NCPs used these mechanisms in the way described in these definitions. This is discussed further in the qualitative analysis below.

Table 7 Party participation by NCP

NCP	All parties participated				All parties participated		
	N	Y	Total	NCP	N	Y	Total
Argentina	5	1	6	Mexico	0	1	1
	6.94	0.65	2.64		0.00	0.65	0.44
Australia	3	5	8	Morocco	0	1	1
	4.17	3.23	3.52		0.00	0.65	0.44
Austria	0	1	1	Netherlands	4	16	20
	0.00	0.65	0.44		5.56	10.32	8.81
Belgium	1	8	9	New Zealand	0	1	1
	1.39	5.16	3.96		0.00	0.65	0.44
Brazil	4	6	10	Norway	2	8	10
	5.56	3.87	4.41		2.78	5.16	4.41
Canada	4	6	10	Peru	0	3	3
	5.56	3.87	4.41		0.00	1.94	1.32
Chile	3	6	9	Poland	0	2	2
	4.17	3.87	3.96		0.00	1.29	0.88
Czech Republic	0	4	4	South Korea	2	5	7
	0.00	2.58	1.76		2.78	3.23	3.08
Denmark	1	2	3	Spain	1	2	3
	1.39	1.29	1.32		1.39	1.29	1.32
Finland	2	0	2	Sweden	0	4	4
	2.78	0.00	0.88		0.00	2.58	1.76
France	6	13	19	Switzerland	3	17	20
	8.33	8.39	8.37		4.17	10.97	8.81
Germany	2	11	13	Turkey	2	0	2
	2.78	7.10	5.73		2.78	0.00	0.88
Hungary	1	0	1	United Kingdom	10	20	30
	1.39	0.00	0.44		13.89	12.90	13.22
Ireland	0	1	1	United States	10	5	15
	0.00	0.65	0.44		13.89	3.23	6.61
Italy	1	2	3				
	1.39	1.29	1.32				
Japan	5	3	8				
	6.94	1.94	3.52				
Luxembourg	0	1	1				
	0.00	0.65	0.44				
				Total	72	155	227
					100.00	100.00	100.00

First row has *frequencies* and second row has *column percentages*

> "Mediation": "a voluntary and guided process in which a skilled mediator helps the parties to negotiate the settlement of a dispute. The process is not binding unless or until the parties reach agreement".[37]
>
> "Conciliation": "a non-binding dispute resolution procedure in which a conciliator 'plays a relatively direct role in the actual resolution of a dispute and even advises the parties on certain solutions by making proposals for settlement. In conciliation, the neutral is usually seen as an authority figure who is responsible for the figuring out the best solution for the parties'".[38]

The Mediation Manual uses the term "good offices" to refer to either mediation or conciliation. In contrast, in some of the specific instances included in the dataset, the NCPs referred to "good offices" as a distinct dispute resolution process rather than as an umbrella term. The results reported below reflect this inconsistency.[39]

In 88% of specific instances, the NCP offered only one dispute resolution mechanism (good offices, mediation, or conciliation) to the parties, and in 12% the NCP offered two of these mechanisms. In 24% of specific instances, an external facilitator was appointed, and out of those cases the parties fully participated in the process led by the external facilitator 91% of the time.

NCPs offered what they termed as "mediation" in 54% of all specific instances. In 65% of the specific instances in which mediation was offered, all parties participated in the process but a full or partial agreement was reached only 34% of the time.[40] In 32% of the specific instances in which mediation was offered, an external mediator was appointed and the parties participated in the mediation. Out of those, in 56% of cases the parties reached an agreement. In 78% of the specific instances in which mediation was offered, it was the only dispute resolution mechanism offered by the NCP, in 16% of these instances mediation was offered together with good offices, and in 6% both mediation and conciliation were offered.

NCPs offered what they termed as "good offices" in 50% of all specific instances. In 70% of specific instances in which good offices was offered, all parties participated in the process but a full or partial agreement was reached only 28% of the time.[41] In 81% of the specific instances in which good offices was offered, this was the only dispute resolution mechanism offered by the NCP, in 18% good offices was offered together with mediation, and in 1% (one specific instance) both good offices and conciliation were offered.

NCPs offered what they termed as "conciliation" in 9% of all specific instances. In 55% of the specific instances in which conciliation was offered, all parties participated

---

[37] The Consensus Building Institute (2012), NCP Mediation Manual, https://files.nettsteder.regjeringen.no/wpuploads01/blogs.dir/263/files/2015/10/NCP_mediation_manual.pdf (last accessed 14 April 2024), p. 21.

[38] The Consensus Building Institute (2012), NCP Mediation Manual, https://files.nettsteder.regjeringen.no/wpuploads01/blogs.dir/263/files/2015/10/NCP_mediation_manual.pdf (last accessed 14 April 2024), p. 21.

[39] These results were derived by the author from the specific instances contained in the dataset.

[40] A full agreement was concluded in 30% of these specific instances and a partial agreement was concluded in 4% of specific instances.

[41] An external facilitator was engaged only in one "good offices" process.

Table 8 Concluded specific instances by Theme

Theme(s)	Freq	Percent
Combating bribery, bribe solicitation and extortion	10	1.86
Competition	6	1.12
Concepts and principles	25	4.66
Consumer interests	11	2.05
Disclosure	46	8.57
Employment and industrial relations	116	21.60
Environment	61	11.36
General policies	144	26.82
Human rights	109	20.30
Science and technology	2	0.37
Taxation	7	1.30
Total	537	100.00

in the process and a full agreement was reached 45% of the time.[42] In 50% of the specific instances in which conciliation was offered, an external conciliator was appointed and the parties participated in the process.[43] Out of those, in 90% of cases the parties reached an agreement. In 60% of the specific instances in which conciliation was offered, it was the only dispute resolution mechanism offered by the NCP, in 35% of instances both conciliation and mediation were offered, and in 5% (one specific instance) conciliation was offered together with good offices.

2.1.4 Theme

The most common themes of specific instances were general policies (27%), employment and industrial relations (22%), human rights (20%), environment (11%), and disclosure (9%) (Table 8).[44]

Table 9 presents the frequency of reaching a full or partial agreement in specific instances involving each of the above themes, as well as the most commonly used dispute resolution mechanism in each theme and the rate of party participation.[45]

---

[42] These were only full agreements, no partial agreements were concluded through conciliation.

[43] In the remaining 50% of conciliation cases an external conciliator was not appointed and in 90% of those cases the parties did not participate in the process. In none of these cases was an agreement reached.

[44] The information presented in this table was derived by the author from the specific instances contained in the dataset. The number of specific instances in this table is 537, because some specific instances concerned multiple themes and therefore had to be duplicated in the coding process.

[45] The information presented in this table was derived by the author from the specific instances contained in the dataset.

Table 9 Features of specific instances by theme

Theme	Frequency of reaching full/partial agreement (%)	Most commonly used mechanism	Party participation (%)
General policies	36	Mediation (56%)	70
Employment and industrial relations	37	Mediation (53%)	71
Human rights	29	Mediation (68%)	63
Environment	30	Good offices (57%)	64
Disclosure	17	Good offices (61%)	65

Table 10 Concluded specific instances by source

Source	Freq	Percent
Business	4	1.62
Individuals	15	6.07
Multi-stakeholder	7	2.83
NGO	118	47.77
Other interested parties	9	3.64
Trade Union	94	38.06
Total	247	100.00

2.1.5 Source

The most common sources of specific instances were NGOs (48%) and trade unions (38%) (Table 10).[46]

In specific instances filed by NGOs, mediation was used in most cases (55%). In specific instances filed by trade unions, mediation and good offices were used with equal frequency (51% each). In 69% of specific instances filed by NGOs and in 68% of specific instances filed by trade unions, all of the parties participated in the NCP dispute resolution process. NGOs reached a full or partial agreement in 34% of the specific instances they filed and trade unions reached a full or partial agreement in 32% of the specific instances they filed.[47]

[46] The information presented in this table was derived by the author from the specific instances contained in the dataset. The number of specific instances in this table is 247, because some specific instances were relevant to multiple industries and therefore had to be duplicated in the coding process.

[47] These results were derived by the author from the specific instances contained in the dataset.

Table 11 Concluded specific instances by industry

Industry sector	Freq	Percent
Accommodation and food service	8	3.21
Activities of extraterritorial organisations and bodies	1	0.40
Administrative and support service activities	3	1.20
Agriculture, forestry and fishing	22	8.84
Arts, entertainment and recreation	3	1.20
Construction	18	7.23
Electricity, gas, steam and air conditioning supply	13	5.22
Financial and insurance activities	22	8.84
Human health and social work activities	1	0.40
Information and communication	11	4.42
Manufacturing	68	27.31
Mining and quarrying	41	16.47
Other service activities	9	3.61
Professional, scientific and technical activities	3	1.20
Public administration and defence	4	1.61
Real estate activities	2	0.80
Transportation and storage	6	2.41
Water supply; sewerage, waste management and remediation activities	3	1.20
Wholesale and retail trade	11	4.42
Total	249	100.00

2.1.6 Industry

The most common industries of specific instances were manufacturing (27%); mining and quarrying (16%); financial and insurance activities (9%); agriculture, forestry and fishing (9%); and construction (7%) (Table 11).[48]

Table 12 presents the frequency of reaching a full or partial agreement in specific instances involving each of the above industries, as well as the most commonly used dispute resolution mechanism in each industry and the rate of party participation.[49]

The results of these frequencies analyses will be summarized following the logistic regression section.

---

[48] The information presented in this table was derived by the author from the specific instances contained in the dataset. The number of specific instances in this table is 249, because some specific instances were relevant to multiple industries and therefore had to be duplicated in the coding process.

[49] The information presented in this table was derived by the author from the specific instances contained in the dataset.

Table 12 Features of specific instances by industry

Industry	Frequency of reaching full/partial agreement (%)	Most commonly used mechanism	Party participation (%)
Manufacturing	35	Mediation (59%)	69
Mining and quarrying	20	Good offices (66%)	61
Financial and insurance	55	Mediation (59%)	95
Agriculture, forestry and fishing	50	Mediation (64%)	68
Construction	28	Mediation (67%)	67

2.2 Logistic Regression Analysis

I used multinomial logistic regression analysis to gain a better understanding of which variables contributed in a statistically significant manner to reaching a full or partial agreement between the parties within the NCP process. Multinomial regressions examine the impact of many variables, known as independent variables, on the occurrence or lack of occurrence of a specific variable, known as the dependent variable. The question that regression analysis seeks to answer is what is the expected value of the dependent variable conditional on knowing the values of the various independent variables. In addition to measuring the impact of the presence of specific variables on the outcome variable, the analysis can also inform us about which specific variables have a statistically significant impact on the outcome, given the presence of all the other independent variables in the analysis.

Out of numerous model specifications examined in the study, reported in this Section are those that provided the most insights. All of the models presented below explain approximately 30% of the variation in the outcome of reaching a full or partial agreement within the NCP process (measured by an adjusted R^2).[50]

[50] However, it should also be noted that when the variable "all parties participated" was removed from the regression, the R^2 dropped to approximately 7%. This makes sense, given that the participation of all parties in the NCP dispute resolution process was a necessary condition for reaching a partial or full agreement. This is also the reason why this variable was kept in all regression models, notwithstanding it not being statistically significant in itself to reaching an agreement. I further note that all of the regression results remained the same, other than the reduction in the R^2, regardless of whether this variable was included or not.

Table 13 Regression model I(A)

Full/partial agreement	Coef	St. Err	t-value	p-value	[95% Conf. Interval]		Sigm
NCP	0.734	0.343	2.14	0.032	0.062	1.406	**
Mediation	−0.135	0.626	−0.22	0.829	−1.363	1.092	
Conciliation	1.097	0.986	1.11	0.266	−0.835	3.029	
Good offices	−0.56	0.652	−0.86	0.391	−1.837	0.718	
All parties participated	19.219	1560.993	0.01	0.99	−3040.271	3078.71	
External facilitator	0.244	0.475	0.51	0.607	−0.686	1.175	
Constant	−19.432	1560.993	−0.01	0.99	−3078.923	3040.059	
Mean dependent var			1.335	SD dependent var			0.473
Pseudo r-squared			0.306	Number of obs			227.000
Chi-square			88.575	Prob > chi2			0.000
Akaike crit. (AIC)			214.862	Bayesian crit. (BIC)			238.837

*** $p < 0.01$, ** $p < 0.05$, * $p < 0.1$

2.2.1 Model I(A)—Basic

Model I(A) includes the following combination of variables:

(1) The NCPs that handled more than 5% of all specific instances as a single variable (the United States, the United Kingdom, Switzerland, the Netherlands, France, and Germany)
(2) Mediation was offered
(3) Conciliation was offered
(4) Good offices was offered
(5) All of the parties participated in the NCP process
(6) An external facilitator was engaged in the NCP process

The NCPs variable was the only variable related to reaching an agreement in a statistically significant way. In other words, in the presence of the variables included in Model I(A), submitting a specific instance to one of these six NCPs is the only variable that explains the outcome of reaching an agreement (Table 13).[51]

In light of this outcome, each of the six NCPs was tested separately. The only NCP that proved statistically significant on its own to reaching an agreement was the Netherlands NCP. This led to Model I(B) below.

[51] The information presented in this table was derived by the author from the specific instances contained in the dataset.

Table 14 Regression model I(B)

Full/partial agreement	Coef	St.Err	t-value	p-value	[95% Conf. Interval]		Sig.
Netherlands NCP	1.653	0.626	2.64	0.008	0.426	2.879	***
Mediation	–0.033	0.639	–0.05	0.958	–1.286	1.22	
Conciliation	1.293	0.987	1.31	0.19	–0.641	3.228	
Good offices	–0.582	0.656	–0.89	0.376	–1.868	0.705	
All parties participated	19.125	1557.661	0.01	0.99	–3033.835	3072.085	
External facilitator	0.44	0.467	0.94	0.346	–0.476	1.356	
Constant	–19.231	1557.662	–0.01	0.99	–3072.192	3033.729	
Mean dependent var	1.335		SD dependent var			0.473	
Pseudo r-squared	0.318		Number of obs			227.000	
Chi-square	92.047		Prob > chi2			0.000	
Akaike crit. (AIC)	211.391		Bayesian crit. (BIC)			235.365	

*** $p < 0.01$, ** $p < 0.05$, * $p < 0.1$

2.2.2 Model I(B)-Basic

Model I(B) includes the following combination of variables:

(1) The Netherlands NCP
(2) Mediation was offered
(3) Conciliation was offered
(4) Good offices was offered
(5) All of the parties participated in the NCP process
(6) An external facilitator was engaged in the NCP process

The Netherlands NCP variable remained the only variable related to reaching an agreement in a statistically significant way. In other words, in the presence of the variables included in Model I(B), submitting a specific instance to the Netherlands NCP is the only variable that explains the outcome of reaching an agreement (Table 14).[52]

Given the statistical significance of the Netherlands NCP, the remaining models below were run separately with the six NCPs and with the Netherlands NCP.

[52] The information presented in this table was derived by the author from the specific instances contained in the dataset.

Table 15 Regression model II(A)

Full/partial agreement	Coef.	St.Err.	t-value	p-value	[95% Conf. Interval]		Sig.
NCP	0.707	0.337	2.10	0.036	0.047	1.367	**
One/two mechanisms	–0.184	0.579	–0.32	0.75	–1.32	0.951	
All parties participated	17.627	860.151	0.02	0.984	–1668.237	1703.491	
External facilitator	0.713	0.365	1.95	0.051	–0.002	1.429	*
Constant	–18.248	860.151	–0.02	0.983	–1704.112	1667.617	
Mean dependent var		1.335	SD dependent var			0.473	
Pseudo r-squared		0.294	Number of obs			227.000	
Chi-square		85.038	Prob > chi2			0.000	
Akaike crit. (AIC)		214.399	Bayesian crit. (BIC)			231.524	

*** $p < 0.01$, ** $p < 0.05$, * $p < 0.1$

2.2.3 Model II—Number of Mechanisms Offered

Model II(A) includes the following combination of variables:

(1) The NCPs that handled more than 5% of all specific instances as a single variable (the United States, the United Kingdom, Switzerland, the Netherlands, France, and Germany)
(2) Whether one or two dispute resolution mechanisms were offered by an NCP
(3) All of the parties participated in the NCP process
(4) An external facilitator was engaged in the NCP process

The NCPs and external facilitator variables were related to reaching an agreement in a statistically significant way. In other words, in the presence of the variables included in Model II(A), submitting a specific instance to one of these six NCPs and engaging an external facilitator explain the outcome of reaching an agreement (Table 15).[53]

Model II(B) includes the following combination of variables:

(1) The Netherlands NCP
(2) Whether one or two dispute resolution mechanisms were offered by an NCP
(3) All of the parties participated in the NCP process
(4) An external facilitator was engaged in the NCP process

The Netherlands NCP and external facilitator variables were related to reaching an agreement in a statistically significant way. In other words, in the presence of

[53] The information presented in this table was derived by the author from the specific instances contained in the dataset.

Table 16 Regression model II(B)

Full/partial agreement	Coef.	St.Err.	t-value	p-value	[95% Conf. Interval]		Sig.
Netherlands NCP	1.496	0.615	2.43	0.015	0.29	2.701	**
One/two mechanisms	–0.129	0.587	–0.22	0.826	–1.278	1.021	
All parties participated	17.54	856.351	0.02	0.984	–1660.877	1695.958	
External facilitator	0.992	0.366	2.71	0.007	0.275	1.709	***
Constant	–18.025	856.351	–0.02	0.983	–1696.443	1660.393	
Mean dependent var		1.335	SD dependent var			0.473	
Pseudo r-squared		0.302	Number of obs			227.000	
Chi-square		87.413	Prob > chi2			0.000	
Akaike crit. (AIC)		212.024	Bayesian crit. (BIC)			229.149	

*** $p < 0.01$, ** $p < 0.05$, * $p < 0.1$

the variables included in Model II(B), submitting a specific instance to the Netherlands NCP and engaging an external facilitator explain the outcome of reaching an agreement (Table 16).[54]

2.2.4 Model III—Themes

Model III(A) includes the following combination of variables:

(1) The NCPs that handled more than 5% of all specific instances as a single variable (the United States, the United Kingdom, Switzerland, the Netherlands, France, and Germany)
(2) The most common themes of specific instances (general policies, employment and industrial relations, human rights, environment, and disclosure)
(3) Whether one or two dispute resolution mechanisms were offered by an NCP
(4) All of the parties participated in the NCP process
(5) An external facilitator was engaged in the NCP process

The NCPs, external facilitator, and themes variables were related to reaching an agreement in a statistically significant way. In other words, in the presence of the variables included in Model III(A), having a specific instance that concerns one of

[54] The information presented in this table was derived by the author from the specific instances contained in the dataset.

Table 17 Regression model III(A)

Full/partial agreement	Coef.	St.Err.	t-value	p-value	[95% Conf. Interval]		Sig.
NCP	0.721	0.223	3.24	0.001	0.285	1.157	***
Theme	0.454	0.243	1.87	0.062	−0.022	0.931	*
One/two mechanisms	−0.148	0.344	−0.43	0.667	−0.822	0.526	
All parties participated	17.145	461.145	0.04	0.97	−886.683	920.973	
External facilitator	0.587	0.241	2.44	0.015	0.116	1.059	**
Constant	−18.205	461.145	−0.04	0.969	−922.033	885.624	
Mean dependent var		1.302	SD dependent var			0.459	
Pseudo r-squared		0.284	Number of obs			537.000	
Chi-square		186.854	Prob > chi2			0.000	
Akaike crit. (AIC)		482.732	Bayesian crit. (BIC)			508.448	

*** $p < 0.01$, ** $p < 0.05$, * $p < 0.1$

these five themes, submitting it to one of these six NCPs, and engaging an external facilitator explain the outcome of reaching an agreement (Table 17).[55]

Model III(B) includes the following combination of variables:

(1) The Netherlands NCP
(2) The most common themes of specific instances (general policies, employment and industrial relations, human rights, environment, and disclosure)
(3) Whether one or two dispute resolution mechanisms were offered by an NCP
(4) All of the parties participated in the NCP process
(5) An external facilitator was engaged in the NCP process

The Netherlands NCP, external facilitator, and themes variables were related to reaching an agreement in a statistically significant way. In other words, in the presence of the variables included in Model III(B), having a specific instance that concerns one of these five themes, submitting it to the Netherlands NCP, and engaging an external facilitator explain the outcome of reaching an agreement (Table 18).[56]

[55] The information presented in this table was derived by the author from the specific instances contained in the dataset.

[56] The information presented in this table was derived by the author from the specific instances contained in the dataset.

Table 18 Regression model III(B)

Full/partial agreement	Coef.	St.Err.	t-value	p-value	[95% Conf. Interval]		Sig.
Netherlands NCP	1.539	0.394	3.90	0	0.766	2.312	***
Theme	0.473	0.246	1.92	0.055	–0.01	0.955	*
One/two mechanisms	–0.066	0.349	–0.19	0.85	–0.75	0.619	
All parties participated	17.112	456.607	0.04	0.97	–877.821	912.046	
External facilitator	0.844	0.24	3.51	0	0.372	1.315	***
Constant	--18.06	456.607	–0.04	0.968	–912.993	876.874	
Mean dependent var		1.302	SD dependent var			0.459	
Pseudo r–squared		0.295	Number of obs			537.000	
Chi-square		193.684	Prob > chi2			0.000	
Akaike crit. (AIC)		475.902	Bayesian crit. (BIC)			501.618	

*** $p < 0.01$, ** $p < 0.05$, * $p < 0.1$

2.2.5 Model IV—Sources

Model IV(A) includes the following combination of variables:

(1) The NCPs that handled more than 5% of all specific instances as a single variable (the United States, the United Kingdom, Switzerland, the Netherlands, France, and Germany)
(2) The most common sources of specific instances (NGOs and trade unions)
(3) Whether one or two dispute resolution mechanisms were offered by an NCP
(4) All of the parties participated in the NCP process
(5) An external facilitator was engaged in the NCP process

The NCPs variable was related to reaching an agreement in a statistically significant way. In other words, in the presence of the variables included in Model IV(A), submitting a specific instance to one of these six NCPs explains the outcome of reaching an agreement (Table 19).[57]

Model IV(B) includes the following combination of variables:

(1) The Netherlands NCP
(2) The most common sources of specific instances (NGOs and trade unions)
(3) Whether one or two dispute resolution mechanisms were offered by an NCP
(4) All of the parties participated in the NCP process
(5) An external facilitator was engaged in the NCP process

[57] The information presented in this table was derived by the author from the specific instances contained in the dataset.

Table 19 Regression model IV(A)

Full/partial agreement	Coef.	St.Err.	t-value	p-value	[95% Conf. Interval]		Sig.
NCP	0.792	0.328	2.41	0.016	0.149	1.435	**
Source	0.268	0.533	0.50	0.616	−0.777	1.312	
One/two mechanisms	−0.001	0.594	−0.00	0.998	−1.166	1.164	
All parties participated	17.871	909.637	0.02	0.984	−1764.985	1800.728	
External facilitator	0.546	0.35	1.56	0.118	−0.139	1.232	
Constant	−18.809	909.637	−0.02	0.984	−1801.665	1764.048	
Mean dependent var		1.312	SD dependent var			0.464	
Pseudo r-squared		0.302	Number of obs			247.000	
Chi-square		92.419	Prob > chi2			0.000	
Akaike crit. (AIC)		226.102	Bayesian crit. (BIC)			247.158	

*** $p < 0.01$, ** $p < 0.05$, * $p < 0.1$

The Netherlands NCP and external facilitator variables were related to reaching an agreement in a statistically significant way. In other words, in the presence of the variables included in Model IV(B), submitting a specific instance to the Netherlands NCP and engaging an external facilitator explain the outcome of reaching an agreement (Table 20).[58]

2.2.6 Model V—Industries

Model V(A) includes the following combination of variables:

(1) The NCPs that handled more than 5% of all specific instances as a single variable (the United States, the United Kingdom, Switzerland, the Netherlands, France, and Germany)
(2) The most common industry for specific instances (manufacturing; mining and quarrying; financial and insurance activities; agriculture, forestry and fishing; and construction)
(3) Whether one or two dispute resolution mechanisms were offered by an NCP
(4) All of the parties participated in the NCP process
(5) An external facilitator was engaged in the NCP process

The NCPs and external facilitator were related to reaching an agreement in a statistically significant way. In other words, in the presence of the variables included

[58] The information presented in this table was derived by the author from the specific instances contained in the dataset.

Table 20 Regression model IV(B)

Full/partial agreement	Coef.	St.Err.	t-value	p-value	[95% Conf. Interval]		Sig.
Netherlands NCP	1.742	0.622	2.80	0.005	0.523	2.962	***
Source	0.607	0.569	1.07	0.286	–0.507	1.722	
One/two mechanisms	0.114	0.604	0.19	0.85	–1.07	1.298	
All parties participated	17.366	696.402	0.02	0.98	–1347.557	1382.29	
External facilitator	0.853	0.353	2.42	0.016	0.162	1.545	**
Constant	–18.473	696.403	–0.03	0.979	–1383.397	1346.451	
Mean dependent var		1.312	SD dependent var			0.464	
Pseudo r-squared		0.313	Number of obs			247.000	
Chi-square		95.890	Prob > chi2			0.000	
Akaike crit. (AIC)		222.630	Bayesian crit. (BIC)			243.686	

*** *p < 0.01*, ** *p < 0.05*, * *p < 0.1*

Table 21 Regression model V(A)

Full/partial agreement	Coef.	St.Err.	t-value	p-value	[95% Conf. Interval]		Sig.
NCP	0.718	0.324	2.21	0.027	0.082	1.354	**
Industry	0.252	0.352	0.71	0.475	–0.439	0.942	
One/two mechanisms	–0.149	0.576	–0.26	0.796	–1.278	0.981	
All parties participated	17.64	823.954	0.02	0.983	–1597.28	1632.56	
External facilitator	0.628	0.354	1.78	0.076	–0.065	1.322	*
Constant	–18.426	823.954	–0.02	0.982	–1633.346	1596.494	
Mean dependent var		1.333	SD dependent var			0.472	
Pseudo r-squared		0.289	Number of obs			249.000	
Chi-square		91.622	Prob > chi2			0.000	
Akaike crit. (AIC)		237.362	Bayesian crit. (BIC)			258.467	

*** *p < 0.01*, ** *p < 0.05*, * *p < 0.1*

in Model V(A), submitting a specific instance to one of these six NCPs and engaging an external facilitator explain the outcome of reaching an agreement (Table 21).[59]

[59] The information presented in this table was derived by the author from the specific instances contained in the dataset.

Table 22 Regression model V(B)

Full/partial agreement	Coef.	St.Err.	t-value	p-value	[95% Conf. Interval]		Sig.
Netherlands NCP	1.41	0.506	2.79	0.005	0.419	2.401	***
Industry	0.321	0.36	0.89	0.373	−0.385	1.028	
One/two mechanisms	−0.038	0.587	−0.06	0.948	−1.189	1.113	
All parties participated	17.557	814.098	0.02	0.983	−1578.045	1613.16	
External facilitator	0.971	0.359	2.70	0.007	0.266	1.675	***
Constant	−18.306	814.098	−0.02	0.982	−1613.909	1577.296	
Mean dependent var		1.333	SD dependent var			0.472	
Pseudo r-squared		0.301	Number of obs			249.000	
Chi-square		95.277	Prob > chi2			0.000	
Akaike crit. (AIC)		233.707	Bayesian crit. (BIC)			254.811	

*** $p < 0.01$, ** $p < 0.05$, * $p < 0.1$

Model V(B) includes the following combination of variables:

(1) The Netherlands NCP
(2) The most common industry for specific instances (manufacturing; mining and quarrying; financial and insurance activities; agriculture, forestry and fishing; and construction)
(3) Whether one or two dispute resolution mechanisms were offered by an NCP
(4) All of the parties participated in the NCP process
(5) An external facilitator was engaged in the NCP process

The Netherlands NCP and external facilitator were related to reaching an agreement in a statistically significant way. In other words, in the presence of the variables included in Model V(B), submitting a specific instance to the Netherlands NCP and engaging an external facilitator explain the outcome of reaching an agreement (Table 22).[60]

2.3 *Summary of Quantitative Findings*

First, it is important to note that any statistical information derived from the data used in this study is limited given the vast differences in quality, style, and depth of

[60] The information presented in this table was derived by the author from the specific instances contained in the dataset.

reporting among the different NCPs regarding their use of dispute resolution mechanisms. While consistent coding was used, this coding was applied to inconsistent data. Moreover, the lack of nuanced reporting by NCPs, coupled with the lack of variety in the dispute resolution mechanisms used, means that many specific instances in the dataset were quite similar across variables, making meaningful statistical testing challenging.

Overall, a partial or final agreement was reached by the parties within the NCP process only in 34% of all specific instances, in 49% of specific instances in which all of the parties participated (no agreement was reached without such participation), and in 57% of specific instances in which an external facilitator was engaged. The engagement of an external facilitator was also related to reaching an agreement in a statistically significant way in most of the regression models.

What was termed by NCPs as "mediation" was the most frequently offered dispute resolution process, followed closely by "good offices", and "conciliation" was a distant third. In 12% of specific instances the NCP offered two of these three mechanisms. Party participation varied across mechanisms, with the highest participation observed with good offices and the lowest with conciliation. The rate at which agreements were reached when mediation was offered was relatively low but increased when an external mediator was involved, while the least agreements were reached when good offices was offered. An agreement was reached more frequently when conciliation was offered, and most frequently in conciliations involving an external facilitator. However, there were relatively few cases in which conciliation was used overall. "General policies" was the most frequent theme of specific instances, the most frequent source of specific instances was NGOs, and the most frequent industry was "manufacturing". Out of these latter three variables, only the themes variable was related to the outcome of reaching a full or partial agreement in a statistically significant way.

The single variable that was consistently related to reaching an agreement in a statistically significant way across regression models was submitting specific instances to the top six NCPs, and in particular to the Netherlands NCP. The top six NCPs being statistically significant to reaching an agreement may be explained by the fact that they collectively handled the vast majority of specific instances. However, the effect of the Netherlands NCP is more curious.

The United Kingdom NCP, rather than the Netherlands NCP, concluded the most specific instances. While the Netherland NCP offered "good offices" most frequently, this was the least effective mechanism overall, and the Netherland NCP did not offer "conciliation" at all, which was the most successful mechanism overall (in relative terms). The Netherlands NCP also did not stand out in terms of party participation or engaging external facilitators. And while the United Kingdom and the Netherlands NCPs were tied for the most partial or final agreements reached, only the Netherlands NCP proved to be related to this outcome in a statistically significant way.

One possible explanation for this result might be that the United Kingdom NCP frequently engaged an external facilitator, which was in itself a statistically significant variable in most regression models. Therefore, it is possible that any effect that the United Kingdom NCP may have had on reaching an agreement was already subsumed within the variable of engaging an external facilitator. In contrast, the Netherlands NCP only engaged an external facilitator in two specific instances. Therefore, its effect on the outcome of reaching an agreement likely lies elsewhere. For instance, the Netherlands NCP may have used a procedure or process that has not been captured in the variables tested in this study and that sets it apart from the other NCPs, or it might operate in a legal and political environment that is conducive to reaching agreements in the NCP process.[61] Cultural and social factors may also play a role in the relative success of the Netherlands NCP.[62] Some of the internal practices of the Netherlands NCP, as well as other NCPs, are discussed in the next Section.

3 A Qualitative Analysis of NCPs' Dispute Resolution Processes

This Section presents the results of a qualitative analysis of the dispute resolution mechanisms used by NCPs. This analysis is based on summaries provided in the OECD database of specific instances as well as on statements issued by NCPs, where available. The goals of this analysis are to reveal trends as well as inconsistencies in the dispute resolution practices of different NCPs and to identify possible reasons for some of the quantitative outcomes reported above.

Generally, dispute resolution processes were held at the premises of the NCP, virtually, at embassy facilities, or at government offices. At times deciding on the location and format of the process posed a hurdle for the parties, for instance because of cost concerns of the complainants. There appears to be good and efficient coordination between the NCPs when more than one is involved in a specific instance.[63]

As evident from the quantitative results reported above, in most cases the NCP dispute resolution process was unsuccessful. In many cases, the process offered by the NCP was declined by the company.[64] In some cases, the process offered by the

---

[61] On the CSR legal framework in the Netherlands, see Enneking and Scheltema (2020), p. 529.

[62] On Dutch legal culture and structure, see Blankenburg (1994); Hertogh (2010).

[63] OECD Database for Specific Instances, Natixis and Unite Here (2016), https://mneguidelines.oecd.org/database/instances/fr0023.htm (last accessed 14 April 2024) (involving cooperation between the French and United States NCPs).

[64] OECD Database for Specific Instances, https://mneguidelines.oecd.org/database/instances/ (last accessed 14 April 2024) (Individuals & ElectraNet Pty Limited (2020); A family in central Europe, supported by an Australian national & a French Group (2020); AhTop & Airbnb (2020); Individuals & Vale S.A. (2020); Mr. Carlos Cleber Guimarães Júnior and Ms. Carla de Laci França Guimarães & Vale S.A. (2020); Lawyers for Palestinian Human Rights (LPHR) & JCB (2019); West Virginians for Sustainable Development & Rockwool International A/S (2019); Individuals from Argentina & Nokia (2019); Korean Civil Society Task Force Team & SK Engineering & Construction (2019); Group of neighbors of Villa Estadio & Minera Candelaria (Lundin Mining and Sumitomo) (2019); Individuals & Telefónica de Argentina S.A. and Telecom Argentina S.A. (2018); FNV, ITF, PSI and IndustriALL Global Union, supported by Friends of the Earth & Chevron

NCP was declined by the complainant.[65] In several cases the process failed, because the complainant breached its confidentiality or otherwise engaged in inappropriate conduct.[66] In one specific instance filed by an NGO, the Canadian NCP noted that the mediation process had been compromised by the fact that "the communities whose interests were allegedly at stake, were neither fully aware nor adequately consulted by [the NGO] on its decision to submit the [Request for Review] to the Canadian NCP".[67] Another common reason for the failure of an NCP dispute resolution process was the existence of parallel judicial proceedings in the courts.[68]

In terms of dispute resolution mechanisms, there was considerable inconsistency in NCPs' use of the labels "good offices", "mediation", and "conciliation", and a dearth of meaningful information on how each of these mechanisms was used and why. While there is no theoretical obstacle to using "good offices" as an umbrella term that includes both mediation and conciliation, NCPs have not been consistent in this practice and have not been clear regarding what "good offices" entails.

In many cases, when an NCP used what it termed as "good offices", the process involved the NCP facilitating an exchange of information between the parties and/or a dialogue or discussion with a view to the parties reaching an agreement on their own. This process therefore resembled "negotiation" more than a process that involves the NCP as a facilitator.[69] Other times good offices was undertaken by the

---

Netherlands BV and 13 other affiliated entities (Chevron et al.) (2018); Osaka Branch of Skynetwork & Emirates (2018); The Japan Cabin Crew Union & KLM Royal Dutch Airlines (2018); MAERSK Container Industry and Trade Union Number 1 of MAERSK Container Industry (2018)).

[65] OECD Database for Specific Instances, https://mneguidelines.oecd.org/database/instances/ (last accessed 14 April 2024) (Union Hidalgo Agrarian and Indigenous Sub-Community and ProDESC & EDF, EDF Renewables, and EDF Renewables Mexico (2018); Salini Impregilo S.p.A and Survival International Italia concerning activities in Ethiopia (2016); World Wide Fund for Nature International (WWF) and Survival International Charitable Trust (2016); Environmental impacts in Mozambique (2010); Mining in Guatemala (2009); Copper mining in Ecuador (2005)).

[66] OECD Database for Specific Instances, https://mneguidelines.oecd.org/database/instances/ (last accessed 14 April 2024) (Swiss-Tibetan Friendship Association, Tibetan Youth Association in Europe, Tibetan Community of Switzerland and Liechtenstein and Tibetan Women's Association Switzerland & International Olympic Committee (2021); Four trade unions & McDonalds Corporation (2020); Milieudefensie/Friends of the Earth Netherlands, WALHI/Friends of the Earth Indonesia and SDI/Friends of the Earth Liberia and ING (2019); Environmental issues relating to the construction of a harbour (2013)).

[67] OECD Database for Specific Instances, https://mneguidelines.oecd.org/database/instances/ (last accessed 14 April 2024) (Imperial Metals Corporation and the Southeast Alaskan Conservation Council (2016)).

[68] OECD Database for Specific Instances, https://mneguidelines.oecd.org/database/instances/ (last accessed 14 April 2024) (Maharashtra Association of Pesticide Poisoned Persons (MAPPP), Pesticide Action Network (PAN), Constitutional and Human Rights (ECCHR) and Pesticide Action Network Asia Pacific (PANAP) & Syngenta (2020); PUTZMEISTER Makina San ve Tic. A.Ş and Turkish Metal Union (Türk Metal) (2017); Jamaa Resources Initiatives and a United States company for conduct in Kenya (2016); Suzuki Motor Corporation, Suzuki Motor (Thailand), trade unions and NGOs (2016); Agricultural investment in Cambodia (2012); Failure to respect employee's right to representation in Malaysia (2007); Environment and worker's health issues in Brazil (2006)).

[69] The Mediation Manual defines "negotiation" as "a form of direct dialogue and exchange among stakeholders, intended to resolve disputes, produce agreement on a course of action, and craft

NCP separately with each party rather than by way of a direct dialogue between the parties. In some cases, NCPs described "good offices" as a distinct stage of the dispute resolution process, in other cases it was referred to interchangeably with "mediation" or "dialogue", while in other cases a "dialogue" was referred to as a stage within an external "mediation" process.[70] In some cases, the NCP (particularly the Netherlands NCP) reported facilitating a "dialogue" between the parties although the process seemed to be rather formal and structured and included terms of reference.[71] Indeed, the website of the Netherlands NCP refers to its dispute resolution process as "mediation".[72] The manner in which the Netherlands NCP facilitated these "dialogues" may be one explanation of its success in reaching agreements, as described above.

In some cases where NCPs have employed what they termed as "mediations", the process involved an external mediator contracted by the NCP as well as terms of reference and/or a mediation agreement.[73] Based on the quantitative results reported above, this approach seems to lead to a higher likelihood of successful resolution of grievances. In addition, the Norwegian NCP used a multi-step mediation process set out in the Mediation Manual,[74] which includes a pre-mediation assessment meeting and a stakeholder assessment.[75] However, other NCPs used the label "mediation" somewhat loosely and interchangeably with more informal "dialogue" facilitation. In other cases, the "mediation" process was conducted by the NCP itself. In some of those cases it seems that the term "mediation" was used by the NCP to mean a

---

outcomes that satisfy multiple interests. Negotiators attempt to settle their differences on their own using techniques ranging from coercion and confrontation to compromise and value creation". The Consensus Building Institute (2012), NCP Mediation Manual, https://files.nettsteder.regjeringen.no/wpuploads01/blogs.dir/263/files/2015/10/NCP_mediation_manual.pdf (last accessed 14 April 2024), p. 21.

[70] OECD Database for Specific Instances, https://mneguidelines.oecd.org/database/instances/ (last accessed 14 April 2024) (Statkraft AS and the Sami reindeer herding collective in Jijnjevaerie Sami Village (2012)).

[71] OECD Database for Specific Instances, https://mneguidelines.oecd.org/database/instances/ (last accessed 14 April 2024) (FIVAS, the Initiative to Keep Hasankeyf Alive and Hasankeyf Matters & Bresser (2017); ING Bank and NGOs concerning climate policy (2017); Gold mining in Mali (2015); Human rights breaches related to manufacturing of iron in India (2012); Oil spills in the Niger Delta (2011)).

[72] Ministry of Foreign Affairs (n.d.), Mediation, https://www.oecdguidelines.nl/notifications/mediation (last accessed 14 April 2024). Nonetheless, in order to ensure consistency these cases were coded as "good offices" rather than as "mediation" in the quantitative part of the study if only "dialogue" was referenced by the NCP.

[73] In one case, the mediation was preceded by an external "stakeholder assessment". See OECD Database for Specific Instances, https://mneguidelines.oecd.org/database/instances/ (last accessed 14 April 2024) (Statkraft AS and the Sami reindeer herding collective in Jijnjevaerie Sami Village (2012)).

[74] The Consensus Building Institute (2012), NCP Mediation Manual, https://files.nettsteder.regjeringen.no/wpuploads01/blogs.dir/263/files/2015/10/NCP_mediation_manual.pdf (last accessed 14 April 2024), p 20.

[75] OECD Database for Specific Instances, https://mneguidelines.oecd.org/database/instances/ (last accessed 14 April 2024), Fisheries and fish processing in Western Sahara (2011).

dialogue or negotiations rather than a structured mediation process.[76] But in other cases the "mediation" process conducted by the NCP was more structured and formal and included terms of reference.[77] The United States NCP, which often engaged external mediators, has defined "mediation" as a process in which "the parties are responsible for arriving at their own solution, and the process is designed to create an environment for cooperative problem-solving between the parties".[78]

When NCPs used what they termed as "conciliation", the process seemed similar to a formal type of mediation, with terms of reference and often the engagement of an external conciliator. However, conciliators appeared to be more actively involved in the process than mediators, for instance by proposing draft terms of settlement to the parties.[79] This is in line with the general understanding of conciliation as involving a more active role for the facilitator than mediation. Again, the quantitative results reported above suggest that conciliation of this kind has the potential to lead to successful resolution of grievances although it has been used in relatively few cases.

In sum, the qualitative analysis of the specific instances in the dataset reveals several deficiencies in the manner in which NCPs use dispute resolution mechanisms. First, there are no uniform definitions of "good offices", "mediation", and "conciliation", and it is not clear what precisely each mechanism entails. Second, there is no consistency in the choice of particular mechanisms, with some NCPs typically opting for informal "good offices" while others tending to prefer more

[76] OECD Database for Specific Instances, https://mneguidelines.oecd.org/database/instances/ (last accessed 14 April 2024) (Centre d'Actions pour la Vie et la Terre et al. vs. COPAGEF, SOMDIAA and SOSUCAM (2020); UNI Global Union and 4 French Trade Union federations (CFDT Fédération Communication Conseil Culture, CGT-FAPT, CGT Fédération des Sociétés d'Etudes and FO-FEC) & Teleperformance (2020); Market Forces & Mizuho Financial Group,Inc., Sumitomo Mitsui Banking Corporation and Mitsubishi UFJ (2018); Development Yes – Open Pit Mines No! Foundation & Group PZU S.A. (2018); Rabobank, Bumitama Agri Group (BGA) and the NGOs Friends of the Earth Europe and Friends of the Earth Netherlands/Milieudefensie (2014); Environmental issues relating to the construction of a harbour (2013). Nonetheless, in order to maintain consistency these cases were coded as "mediation" rather than as "good offices" in the quantitative part of this study.

[77] OECD Database for Specific Instances, https://mneguidelines.oecd.org/database/instances/ (last accessed 14 April 2024) (Four trade unions (IUF, EFFAT-IUF, SEIU, UGT) & APG Asset Management 2020); Korean Transnational Corporations Watch (KTNC Watch), PUSAKA, SKP-KAMe, and WALHI Papua & POSCO INTERNATIONAL, the National Pension Service (NPS) and the Export–Import Bank of Korea (KEXIM) (2019); Building and Wood Worker's International & LafargeHolcim (2019); Milieudefensie/Friends of the Earth Netherlands, WALHI/Friends of the Earth Indonesia and SDI/Friends of the Earth Liberia and ING (2019); Mineworkers Union & Teck-Quebrada Blanca Mining Company (2017).

[78] OECD Database for Specific Instances, https://mneguidelines.oecd.org/database/instances/ (last accessed 14 April 2024), The Coca-Cola Company and IUF regarding alleged conduct in Indonesia (2017). The United States NCP has used professional mediators from the Consensus Building Institute (CBI), a not-for-profit organization, and from the Federal Mediation and Conciliation Service, an independent United States government agency.

[79] OECD Database for Specific Instances, https://mneguidelines.oecd.org/database/instances/ (last accessed 14 April 2024) (Ali Enterprises Factory Fire Affectees Association (AEFFAA) and other associations & RINA Services S.p.A (2018); ENI S.p.A., ENI International BV, and CWA and ACA (2017)).

structured mediation and/or conciliation procedures. Finally, the use of these mechanisms is reported inconsistently across NCPs in terms of accuracy and depth. Some of these inconsistencies may be viewed as a function of the uniqueness of each specific instance. Nonetheless, having basic uniform procedures applicable to all NCPs for using, as well as reporting on the use, of each mechanism would ensure predictability, uniformity, and transparency across the NCP system.

To remedy some of the inconsistencies in the use of dispute resolution mechanisms, NCPs could adopt the definitions of "mediation", "conciliation", and "negotiation" set out in the Mediation Manual rather than using "good offices" as an ambiguous umbrella term and/or divergent and inconsistent definitions of other mechanisms.

Where mediation is used, it should also be determined whether, and if so in what form, terms of reference or a mediation agreement should be used and whether mediations are to be conducted by the NCP or by an external mediator. As already noted, such a practice seems to lead to better results in specific instances. Similarly, where conciliation is used, it should be determined whether conciliations are to be conducted by the NCP or by an external conciliator, and this process should be clearly distinguished from mediation in terms of the role of the facilitator. The role that NCPs take in parties' negotiations should be consistent, and the process should be clearly distinguished from mediation and conciliation.

It is also crucial that NCPs adopt uniform reporting practices in their statements regarding their use of dispute resolution processes. One of the hurdles to understanding what processes work and how they might be improved is the challenge of conducting effective analysis of existing practices without complete, consistent, and reliable data.

Finally, it is worth considering the potential for arbitration to be offered by external arbitrators contracted by NCPs. NCPs have traditionally been viewed as a tool primarily for "promot[ing] dialogue and offer[ing] a convenient forum to all parties to take further steps",[80] and arbitration is currently not used by NCPs.[81] Yet given the recently launched Hague Rules on Business and Human Rights Arbitration (Hague Rules),[82] arbitration could prove useful when facilitated by NCPs.[83]

Arbitration in this context may be defined as a dispute resolution process in which objective decision-makers chosen by the disputing parties apply a procedure chosen by the parties and render a binding decision.[84] Unlike good offices, mediation, and

[80] Buchholtz (2020), pp. 133, 144.

[81] In two specific instances, the United Kingdom NCP engaged an external "arbitrator and mediator" but he acted as a "conciliator-mediator" for the purpose of these specific instances, which were both successfully resolved. OECD Database for Specific Instances, https://mneguidelines.oecd.org/database/instances/ (last accessed 14 April 2024) (Dismissal of workers in Pakistan (2008); Failure to respect employees' rights in India (2007)).

[82] Centre for International Legal Cooperation (2019), Hague Rules on Business and Human Rights Arbitration, https://www.cilc.nl/cms/wp-content/uploads/2019/12/The-Hague-Rules-on-Business-and-Human-Rights-Arbitration_CILC-digital-version.pdf (last accessed 14 April 2024).

[83] See Meshel (2021), p. 101; Duggal and Rangachari (2021), p. 83; Yiannibas (2020), p. 89.

[84] Rees & Vermijs (2008), p. 3.

conciliation, arbitration typically produces an outcome that is legally binding on the parties and enforceable in domestic courts. Although there are concerns surrounding public interests and unequal playing field in the business and human rights context, the Hague Rules "aim to adapt existing international arbitration rules to the unique needs of" this field and to address these concerns[85]:

The provisions of the Rules concerning the independence, impartiality, and expertise of arbitrators promote the legitimacy of arbitration proceedings, strengthen the parties' confidence in the process, and provide them with decision-makers who are versed in business and human rights issues.[86]

Importantly, arbitration is not limited to the resolution of legal disputes. It can also be used for the resolution of factual disagreements, which are often at the core of the specific instances submitted to NCPs. Arbitration could also be combined with existing mechanisms used by NCPs, such as conciliation or mediation.[87] Moreover, all parties stand to benefit from arbitration in terms of predictability, procedural control, and finality. As the author has noted elsewhere,

> [r]ights holders stand to benefit from an accessible, neutral, and enforceable mechanism that largely eliminates the jurisdictional and domestic law hurdles they face in national courts. Businesses faced with the threat of domestic litigation, at times in states with unstable judicial institutions, may also prefer a more predictable dispute resolution process over which they can exercise some degree of procedural control.[88]

4 Conclusion

This study has shown that the OECD NCPs can serve as effective grievance mechanisms in disputes involving alleged violations of the Guidelines. While a partial or final agreement was reached by the parties within the NCP process only in 34% of specific instances examined, the rate of success increased where all of the parties participated (which occurred most frequently where "good offices" was offered) and, in particular, where an external facilitator was engaged. Therefore, more attention should be paid to devising ways in which parties might be encouraged to cooperate within the NCP dispute resolution process and NCPs should engage external facilitators more frequently, which could in itself promote party participation.

What was termed by NCPs as "mediation" was the most frequently offered dispute resolution process, but the rate at which agreements were reached was relatively low. What was termed as "good offices" was also frequently offered by NCPs, but it led to the least agreements being reached. What was termed as "conciliation" was used far less by NCPs, but an agreement was reached more frequently and most frequently in conciliations involving an external facilitator.

---

[85] Meshel (2021), p. 119.

[86] Meshel (2021), pp. 126–127.

[87] Schneider (1996).

[88] Meshel (2021), pp. 112–113.

The single variable that was consistently related to reaching an agreement in a statistically significant way was submitting specific instances to the top six NCPs, and in particular to the Netherlands NCP. The practices of the Netherlands NCP, in particular, should be examined in depth in order to identify what might set it apart from other NCPs in terms of the successful resolution of specific instances.

From a qualitative perspective, the study reveals two major deficiencies that may undermine the ability of NCPs to resolve specific instances effectively, although both deficiencies are relatively simple to rectify. First, NCPs have largely failed adopt uniform definitions of "good offices", "mediation", and "conciliation", and to apply these mechanisms consistently in specific instances. Second, NCPs have failed to adopt detailed and uniform reporting practices regarding the dispute resolution processes used in specific instances. Such reporting practices would not only ensure consistency in the use of the various mechanisms but also facilitate data collection and analysis and thereby improve the transparency of NCPs' dispute resolution processes.

References

Bağlayan B (2017) Corporations and human rights: searching for international norms for corporate conduct in domestic case law. Dissertation, University of Luxembourg.

Blankenburg E (1994) The infrastructure for avoiding civil litigation: comparing cultures of legal behavior in the Netherlands and West Germany. Law Soc Rev 28(4):789–808

Buchholtz G (2020) Social and labour standards in the OECD Guidelines enforcement mechanisms. Intern Org Law Rev 17(1):133–152

Buhmann K (2020) National contact points under OECD's guidelines for multinational enterprises: institutional diversity affecting assessments of the delivery of access to remedy. In: Enneking L et al (eds) Accountability, international business operations, and the law: providing justice for corporate human rights violations in global value chains. Routledge, Oxfordshire, pp 38–60

Davarnejad L (2011) In the shadow of soft law: the handling of corporate social responsibility disputes under the oecd guidelines for multinational enterprises. J Dispute Resol 2011(2):351–386

Duggal K, Rangachari R (2021) Business, human rights, and international arbitration: family, friend, or foe? Dispute Resol J 75(3):83–122

Enneking L, Scheltema M (2020) The Netherlands. In: Kessedjian C, Rivera HC (eds) Private international law aspects of corporate social responsibility. Springer, Cham, pp 529–553

Franciose C (2007) A critical assessment of the United States implementation of the OECD guidelines for multinational enterprises. Boston College Intern Comp Law Rev 30(1):223–236

Hertogh M (2010) The curious case of dutch legal culture: a reassessment of survey evidence. J Comp Law 5(2):146

Hill R (1998) The theoretical basis of mediation and other forms of ADR: why they work. Arbitr Int 14(2):173–184

Karin L et al (2016) Corporate accountability: the role and impact of non-judicial grievance mechanisms. Edward Elgar Publishing, Cheltenham

Khoury S, Whyte D (2019) Sidelining corporate human rights violations: the failure of the oecd's regulatory consensus. J Human Rights 18(4):363–381

Merrills JG (2005) International dispute settlement. Cambridge University Press, Cambridge

Meshel T (2021) International Arbitration: the new frontier of business and human rights dispute resolution. Dalhou Law J 44(1):101–128

Olsen B, Sørensen K (2014) Strengthening the enforcement of csr guidelines: finding a new balance between hard law and soft law. Legal Iss Econ Integ 41(1):9–35

Rees C, Vermijs D (2008) Mapping grievance mechanisms in the business and human rights arena. Corporate Social Responsibility Initiative Report No 28. John F Kennedy School of Government, Harvard University

Reif L (2007) The use of conciliation or mediation for the resolution of international commercial disputes. Canadian Bus Law J 45(1):20–48

Schneider M (1996) Combining arbitration with conciliation. In: van den Berg A (ed) International dispute resolution: towards an international arbitration culture, ICCA Congress Series, vol 8. Springer, Seoul, pp 57–100

Yiannibas K (2020) The effectiveness of international arbitration to provide remedy for business-related human rights abuses. In: Enneking L et al (eds) Accountability, international business operations, and the law: providing justice for corporate human rights violations in global value chains. Routledge, Oxfordshire, pp 89–104

The Broader Impact of the OECD Guidelines for Multinational Enterprises

Influence of the OECD Guidelines and Jurisprudence in the Legislative Process of the EU Directive on Corporate Sustainability Due Diligence

Monika Feigerlová

Abstract The EU Directive on Corporate Sustainability Due Diligence (CS3D) has established a legal obligation for large companies to conduct due diligence in their operations and value chains to prevent and address adverse impacts on human rights and the environment. The CS3D builds on and seeks to align with international due diligence standards on business and human rights, including the OECD Guidelines for Multinational Enterprises on Responsible Business Conduct. This paper examines the extent to which the OECD Guidelines played a role in the legislative process of the CS3D. By analysing the *travaux préparatoires* of the CS3D, the interactions between these two instruments will be identified. The findings may also help to understand the relevance of the OECD jurisprudence to the interpretation and implementation of the CS3D in the future, particularly in those EU Member States whose governments have adhered to the OECD Guidelines, in relation to the failure of corporate behaviour to comply with human rights and environmental due diligence.

1 Introduction

There is a clear trend towards making human rights due diligence legally binding on certain companies, moving from soft law instruments to hard law.[1] This trend is evident in legislative initiatives on mandatory corporate due diligence, where companies are legally required to conduct human rights due diligence throughout their operations and supply chains in order to assess human rights risks, investigate

"The research for this section has been supported/subsidized within the *Lumina quaeruntur* award of the Czech Academy of Sciences for the project 'Climate law' conducted at the Institute of State and Law."

M. Feigerlová (✉)
Institute of State and Law of the Czech Academy of Sciences, Centre for Climate Law and Sustainability Studies, Praha, Czech Republic
e-mail: monika.feigerlova@ilaw.cas.cz

[1] Krajewski (2023); Deva (2023); Villiers (2022); Bueno and Bright C (2020); Joseph and Kyriakakis (2023).

O. Davaanyam and M. Krajewski (eds.), *Exploring Corporate Human Rights Responsibilities in OECD Case Law*, Interdisciplinary Studies in Human Rights 14,
https://doi.org/10.1007/978-3-031-75717-4_9

human rights abuses, adopt prevention plans and report on the actions or measures they have taken. The EU has taken up the idea of establishing legally enforceable human rights obligations for certain companies in the recently adopted EU Corporate Sustainability Due Diligence Directive (CS3D).[2,3]

Despite its lengthy and complicated legislative development, the CS3D represents the most ambitious framework for mandatory corporate due diligence with the aim "to ensure that companies active in the internal market contribute to sustainable development" through human rights and environmental due diligence, including by ensuring that those affected by a failure to comply with due diligence obligations have access to justice and legal remedies.[4] The directive seeks to ensure compliance by introducing sanctions and civil liability, and to create a level playing field across EU countries. All of this has required considerable political compromise.[5]

The notion of human rights due diligence was developed within the United Nations framework and is linked to international efforts to regulate the responsibility of business enterprises for human rights abuses, as summarised in the United Nations Guiding Principles on Business and Human Rights (UNGPs), which were unanimously endorsed by the UN Human Rights Council in 2011.[6] The UNGPs recognise that corporations have a responsibility to respect human rights, stemming from "a global standard of expected conduct applicable to all businesses in all situations".[7] They set out principles for businesses to prevent and address human rights abuses. The OECD Guidelines for Multinational Enterprises on Responsible Business Conduct (OECD Guidelines)[8] complement this by extending the concept of due diligence to other areas, including corporate impact on environment, corruption, industrial relations or consumer interests. The UNGPs and the OECD Guidelines are not legally binding. However, they have established a normative framework for responsible

---

[2] Directive (EU) 2024/1760 of the European Parliament and of the Council of 13 June 2024 on corporate sustainability due diligence and amending Directive (EU) 2019/1937 and Regulation (EU) 2023/2859.

[3] The CS3D in-scope companies are a narrow category that includes both EU and non-EU companies that meet the following thresholds (i) more than 1,000 employees, and (ii) more than 450 million EUR in worldwide turnover (EU companies); or more than 450 million EUR in turnover generated in the EU (non-EU companies).

[4] Directive (EU) 2024/1760 of the European Parliament and of the Council of 13 June 2024 on corporate sustainability due diligence and amending Directive (EU) 2019/1937 and Regulation (EU) 2023/2859,

(CS3D), recital 16.

[5] Bueno et al. (2024), pp. 1–7.

[6] United Nations Human Rights Council (HRC) (2011), *Guiding Principles on Business and Human Rights: Implementing the United Nations "Protect, Respect and Remedy" Framework* (New York 2011)UN Doc. A/HRC/17/31(last accessed 31 May 2024).

[7] UN Human Rights Office of the High Commissioner (UN HROHC) (2012), *The Corporate Responsibility to Respect Human Rights: An Interpretative Guide*, UN Doc. HR/PUB/12/02, p. 13, https://www.ohchr.org/sites/default/files/Documents/publications/hr.puB.12.2_en.pdf, (last accessed 31 May 2024).

[8] Organisation for Economic Cooperation and Development (OECD) (2011), *OECD Guidelines for Multinational Enterprises*, 2011 edition. https://www.oecd.org/corporate/mne/1922428.pdf.

business conduct and have been widely adopted and implemented by companies of various sizes across different sectors and contexts. Developed over several years in consultation with business, civil society and government representatives, they call on companies to conduct human rights and environmental due diligence to proactively identify, prevent, mitigate and account for how they address the most serious human rights risks to people from their operations.[9]

The OECD Guidelines are recommendations jointly addressed by governments to multinational enterprises operating or based in countries that adhere to the Declaration on International Investment and Multinational Enterprises of 1976 (Declaration).[10] They were substantially updated in 2023[11] to reflect on recent developments and societies' priorities, including for example climate change and biodiversity, and underline the importance of environmental due diligence.[12] The update process took three years, involved many stakeholders, and ran in parallel with the negotiations on the draft CS3D. Save for Malta, all EU Member States that will be subject to the CS3D have endorsed the 2023 update of the OECD Guidelines.[13] The Commission of the European Union, which itself is a full OECD participant, was also engaged in the OECD's work on the updated guidelines.[14]

The OECD Guidelines are not directly binding on companies but are the only international guidelines for sustainability due diligence to be formally endorsed by governments. Their force comes from the political commitment of the adhering countries to take steps to ensure their implementation by multinational enterprises. At the heart of the implementation mechanisms set out in the OECD Guidelines is a network of National Contact Points (called National Contact Points for Responsible Business Conduct after the 2023 update, the NCPs) in adhering countries. The NCPs are government-appointed bodies or agencies responsible for promoting compliance with the OECD Guidelines and helping to resolve issues that arise from their implementation (known as specific instances).[15]

---

[9] Principle 17 of the UNGPs; Chapter VI of Guidelines.

[10] OECD (2023) *The Declaration form part of the Guidelines for Multinational Enterprises on Responsible Business Conduct*, OECD Publishing, Paris, p. 6.

[11] OECD (2023), *OECD Guidelines for Multinational Enterprises on Responsible Business Conduct*, OECD Publishing, Paris, version 2023. See https://www.oecd-ilibrary.org/docserver/81f92357-en.pdf?expires=1718862893&id=id&accname=guest&checksum=6A2B78D42D101BF7BBCB0AC39FEA1CBD, (last accessed 31 May 2024). The update came into force on 8 June 2023 based on the unanimous decision of the OECD Council at Ministerial Level.

[12] See e.g. Ingrams (2023); OECD Watch (2023) *What's new?: 'Targeted update' strengthens OECD Guidelines for Multinational Enterprises*, https://www.oecdwatch.org/whats-new-targeted-update-strengthens-oecd-guidelines-for-multinational-enterprises/ (last accessed 31 May 2024).

[13] 26 EU Member States adhered to the Declration on International Investment and Multinational Enterprises of 1976, as amended in 2023, of which 22 are OECD members and three (Bulgaria, Croatia and Romania) are adhering countries. https://www.oecd.org/daf/inv/investment-policy/oecddeclarationanddecisions.htm (last accessed 31 May 2024).

[14] The EU participate in the OECD Working Party on Responsible Business Conduct and the OECD Investment Committee.

[15] Article 1 of Part II of the OECD Guidelines.

In its recitals, the CS3D makes an explicit reference to the OECD Guidelines as internationally recognised frameworks that set out practical due diligence steps for companies.[16] Given the similar objectives of the two instruments, the overlapping of authors, the fact that both the CS3D and the OECD Guidelines provide for both human rights and environmental due diligence, the calls by majority EU Member States to align the CS3D with the OECD Guidelines,[17] and the divergences of the CS3D from international standards already described in literature and policy papers,[18] this contribution will analyse the extent to which the OECD Guidelines played a role in the legislative process of the CS3D and the interactions between the two instruments, which may shape the relevance of the OECD jurisprudence for the future application of the CS3D.

2 The Legislative History of the CS3D

The legislative development of the CS3D has been accompanied by more than two years of difficult negotiations, including the unexpected uncertainty surrounding its final adoption after the trialogue discussions between 2023 and 2024. The EU Council gave its final approval to the text on 24 May 2024, following the approval of the European Parliament, which voted in favour of the CS3D on 24 April 2024 by a narrow majority of its members,[19] and the agreement that was reached on 15 March 2024 between the EU Member States.[20] The drafts of the CS3D from the

[16] Directive (EU) 2024/1760 of the European Parliament and of the Council of 13 June 2024 on corporate sustainability due diligence and amending Directive (EU) 2019/1937 and Regulation (EU) 2023/2859,

(CS3D), recital 6.

[17] Ministerial Meeting on Responsible Business Conduct (OECD), Declaration on Promoting and Enabling Responsible Business Conduct in the Global Economy of 15 February 2023, OECD/LEGAL/0489, in which OECD members called for alignment between national and regional responsible business conduct initiatives and the OECD Guidelines. https://legalinstruments.oecd.org/en/instruments/OECD-LEGAL-0489 (last accessed 31 May 2024).

[18] See e.g. Bueno et al. (2024), pp. 1–7; Hogan and Reyes (2023), pp. 434–440; NCP Netherlands (2023) Analysis of the Draft Corporate Sustainability Due Diligence Directive, on the basis of the OECD Guidelines, 30 June 2023, https://www.oecdguidelines.nl/documents/publication/2023/10/5/ncp-analysis-of-draft-csddd-on-the-basis-of-oecd-guidelines (last accessed 31 May 2024); OECD Watch (2023) *Achieving Alignment: Syncing EU due diligence legislation with the updated OECD Guidelines*, June 2023, https://www.oecdwatch.org/achieving-alignment-synching-eu-due-diligence-legislation-with-the-updated-oecd-guidelines/ (last accessed 31 May 2024).

[19] European Parliament legislative resolution of 24 April 2024 on the proposal for a directive of the European Parliament and of the Council on Corporate Sustainability Due Diligence and amending Directive (EU) 2019/1937 (COM(2022)0071 – C9-0050/2022 – 2022/0051(COD)).

[20] Council of the European Union, Proposal for a Directive of the European Parliament and of the Council on Corporate Sustainability Due Diligence and amending Directive (EU) 2019/1937 - Letter to the Chair of the JURI Committee of the European Parliament, 6145/24, 15 March 2024; Council of the European Union, Interinstitutional File: 2022/0051(COD)Voting result Brussels, 27 May 2024 (OR. en)10,263/24.

different EU institutions (i.e. from the European Parliament, the EU Council and the European Commission) represented different levels of ambition regarding the scope of corporate sustainability due diligence in terms of adverse impacts covered, value chain reach, civil liability, and also the references to the OECD Guidelines and their National Contact Points.

The directive was originally proposed by the European Commission on 23 February 2022 (Commission Proposal),[21] following recommendations made by the European Parliament in a Resolution of 10 March 2021[22] and the Council Conclusions on Human Rights and Decent Work in Global Supply Chains from 1 December 2020.[23] The Commission Proposal was preceded by a public consultation carried out by the Commission between October 2020 and February 2021, as well as the Inception Impact Assessment on Sustainable Corporate Governance.[24] In addition, two studies were commissioned, one focused on human rights and environmental due diligence in the supply chain,[25] and the other on board duties and sustainable corporate governance.[26]

The European Council released its negotiating position on the Commission Proposal on 30 November 2022 (Council Approach).[27] Among others, the European Central Bank and the European Economic and Social Committee delivered its opinion on 6 June 2023, respectively 14 July 2023.[28] The European Parliament voted

[21] Proposal for a Directive of the European Parliament and of the Council on Corporate Sustainability Due Diligence and amending Directive (EU) 2019/1937 (CSDDD), COM(2022) 71 final, 23 February 2022.

[22] European Parliament resolution of 10 March 2021 with recommendations to the Commission on corporate due diligence and corporate accountability, P9_TA(2021)0073. See also European Parliament Committee on Legal Affairs, Draft report with recommendations to the Commission on corporate due diligence and corporate accountability (2020/2129(INL)) https://www.europarl.europa.eu/doceo/document/A-9-2021-0018_EN.html (last accessed 31 May 2024).

[23] European Council, Council Conclusions on Human Rights and Decent Work in Global Supply Chains, 1 December 2020, doc. 13,512/20.

[24] European Commission, Inception Impact Assessment on Sustainable Corporate Governance (2020)4,034,032, https://ec.europa.eu/info/law/better-regulation/have-your-say/initiatives/12548-Sustainable- corporate-governance (last accessed 31 May 2024).

[25] Smit et al. (2020) Study on due diligence requirements through the supply chain, https://op.europa.eu/en/publication-detail/-/publication/8ba0a8fd-4c83-11ea-b8b7- 01aa75ed71a1/language-en (last accessed 31 May 2024).

[26] EY (2020) Study on directors' duties and sustainable corporate governance, https://op.europa.eu/en/publication-detail/-/publication/e47928a2-d20b-11ea-adf7- 01aa75ed71a1/language-en (last accessed 31 May 2024).

[27] Proposal for a Directive of the European Parliament and of the Council on Corporate Sustainability Due Diligence and amending Directive (EU) 2019/1937 - General Approach, 2022/0051(COD), 30 November 2022.

[28] OJ C 2023 C 249/2, 14.7.2023, p. 3; and OJ C 2022 C 443, 22.11.2022, p. 81.

in plenary the JURI report,[29] and adopted amendments to the Commission Proposal on 1 June 2023 (EP Amendments).[30]

Subsequent "trilogue negotiations" between the European Parliament and the Council, mediated by the Commission, led to a provisional agreement on 14 December 2023 under the Spanish presidency (2023 Political Agreement).[31] This agreement was surprisingly blocked by the Council, due to concerns by some Member States about its scope and application. Normally, the official votes that follow are a formality. But after the 2023 Political Agreement, Germany, France, and Italy in particular withdrew their support. With vocal support from civil society, academics but also businesses, another round of negotiations started, resulting in a substantially amended draft on 15 March 2024 under the Belgian presidency (2024 Provisional Agreement).[32] The revised directive was narrowed down in terms of who would be covered, including in the supply chain (only direct downstream partners), and its date of entry into force was also postponed. On 24 April 2024, the Parliament adopted the text of the directive endorsed by the Council on 15 March 2024 without further amendments, following its adoption by the JURI Committee on 19 March 2024.[33]

The CS3D, which was also finally formally adopted by the Council on 24 May 2024, was published in the Official Journal on 5 July 2024 and the EU Member States have two years to transpose it into their national law.[34] The obligations for in-scope companies will be phased in over a period of three to five years from 2027.

---

[29] Report on the proposal for a directive of the European Parliament and of the Council on Corporate Sustainability Due Diligence and amending Directive (EU) 2019/1937, 23 April 2023.

[30] Amendments adopted by the European Parliament on 1 June 2023 on the proposal for a directive of the European Parliament and of the Council on Corporate Sustainability Due Diligence and amending Directive (EU) 2019/1937 (COM(2022)0071 – C9-0050/2022 – 2022/0051(COD).

[31] Council of the EU (2023) Press release Corporate sustainability due diligence: Council and Parliament strike deal to protect environment and human rights, 14 December 2023, https://www.consilium.europa.eu/en/press/press-releases/2023/12/14/corporate-sustainability-due-diligence-council-and-parliament-strike-deal-to-protect-environment-and-human-rights/ (last accessed 31 May 2024).

[32] Council of the European Union, Proposal for a DIRECTIVE OF THE EUROPEAN PARLIAMENT AND OF THE COUNCIL on Corporate Sustainability Due Diligence and amending Directive (EU) 2019/1937 - Letter to the Chair of the JURI Committee of the European Parliament, 6145/24, 15 March 2024.

[33] Council of the European Union, Draft DIRECTIVE OF THE EUROPEAN PARLIAMENT AND OF THE COUNCIL on corporate sustainability due diligence and amending Directive (EU) 2019/1937 and Regulation (EU) 2023/2859 (first reading) - Adoption of the legislative act, Interinstitutional File: 2022/0051(COD) 23 May 2024 (OR. en) 9264/1/24 REV 1; European Parliament. Press Release "Due diligence: MEPs adopt rules for firms on human rights and environment" 24 April 2024, available https://www.europarl.europa.eu/news/en/press-room/20240419IPR20585/due-diligence-meps-adopt-rules-for-firms-on-human-rights-and-environment (last accessed 31 May 2024).

[34] Directive (EU) 2024/1760 of the European Parliament and of the Council of 13 June 2024 on corporate sustainability due diligence and amending Directive (EU) 2019/1937 and Regulation (EU) 2023/2859; date of entry into force within 20 days of its publication in the Official Journal, i.e. 25 July 2024.

3 References to the OECD Guidelines in the *Travaux Préparatoires*

The 2023 update of the OECD Guidelines contains a number of innovations in response to current developments in climate change or information technology and is likely to serve as a reference point for the development of mandatory due diligence laws. The difficult legislative process of the CS3D illustrates that there are many different national perspectives on how to translate human rights and environmental due diligence from international soft law instruments into hard law and how to design liability and enforcement provisions.

It is important to remember that the OECD Guidelines have shaped the business practices of EU companies over the years, embedding due diligence processes into their operations,[35] and that almost all EU Member States have committed themselves to enhancing the application of and compliance with the OECD Guidelines. The lack of coherence and alignment on key concepts between the OECD Guidelines, as well-established international standards, and the CS3D, as legally binding and enforceable instrument, can lead to legal uncertainty and potentially conflicting views on what is expected of companies in terms of human rights and environmental due diligence in general beyond the CS3D. The existence of inconsistent expectations can also lead to fragmentation of due diligence norms and jeopardise the achievement of corporate respect for human rights and the environment.

Although the OECD Guidelines might become less relevant to companies falling within the scope of the CS3D, it is not excluded that courts may consider the OECD Guidelines and their interpretation by the NCPs when interpreting common concepts of due diligence contained in both the CS3D and the OECD Guidelines, such as the understanding of the level of involvement of a company in an adverse impact. The policy harmony would undoubtedly contribute to effective implementation of human rights and environmental due diligence by companies. The following text therefore analyses the role of the OECD Guidelines in the legislative history of the CS3D in order to better understand the intended interactions between these instruments.

Looking at the *travaux préparatoires*, the OECD Guidelines proliferate in the CS3D recitals as the authoritative standard for human rights and environmental due diligence. The recitals of the CS3D in all three drafts of the EU Institutions (i.e. the Commission Proposal, the Council Approach and the EP Amendments) refer to the OECD Guidelines,[36] with which the proposed CS3D is to be aligned, respectively is said to be in line with the EU's aim to "actively promote the global implementation

[35] Perillo (2022), p. 39.

[36] Recital 5 of the Proposal for a Directive of the European Parliament and of the Council on Corporate Sustainability Due Diligence and amending Directive (EU) 2019/1937 (CSDDD), COM(2022) 71 final, 23 February 2022, Proposal for a Directive of the European Parliament and of the Council on Corporate Sustainability Due Diligence and amending Directive (EU) 2019/1937 - General Approach, 2022/0051(COD), 30 November 2022 and Amendments adopted by the European Parliament on 1 June 2023 on the proposal for a directive of the European Parliament and of the Council on Corporate Sustainability Due Diligence and amending Directive (EU) 2019/1937 (COM(2022)0071 – C9-0050/2022 – 2022/0051(COD).

of the OECD Guidelines".[37] Further, the CS3D recitals explicitly state that the due diligence process should cover the six steps, including external communication of due diligence policies and findings, as defined in practical sense by the OECD Due Diligence Guidance for Responsible Business Conduct,[38] which are incorporated into the OECD Guidelines.[39] Likewise, the recitals explain that the CS3D relies on the definition of the high-impact sectors as outlined in existing sectoral OECD due diligence guidance.[40] In addition, the Council Proposal refers to the OECD Guidelines when pointing to the specificities of financial services and when modifying some of their obligations under the CS3D (e.g. exemptions for regulated financial undertakings to temporarily suspend or terminate the business relationship).[41]

From perusing the preparatory documents that were impulses to the Commission Proposal of 2022, it is clear that there were deeper reflections on the OECD Guidelines and the NCPs, which were left out in the Commission's final text. The European Parliament's recommendations, which introduced the idea of regulating corporate due diligence and corporate accountability, emphasised the need to create clarity, certainty and consistency in companies' practices, while noting that companies have a significant number of international due diligence instruments at their disposal, including the OECD Guidelines.[42] To this end, the national authorities of the CS3D should be encouraged to cooperate and share information with the NCPs,[43] and the Commission, in consultation with the OECD and Member States, should develop general non-binding guidelines, to be periodically updated, to assist the CS3D in harmonising standards across Member States for all companies.[44] The common understanding of due diligence requirements across sectors, company sizes

[37] Proposal for a Directive of the European Parliament and of the Council on Corporate Sustainability Due Diligence and amending Directive (EU) 2019/1937 (CSDDD), COM(2022) 71 final, 23 February 2022, p. 9 and recital 12.

[38] OECD (2018), *OECD Due Diligence Guidance on Responsible Business Conduct*, adopted 6 March 2018, OECD.

[39] Proposal for a Directive of the European Parliament and of the Council on Corporate Sustainability Due Diligence and amending Directive (EU) 2019/1937 (CSDDD), COM(2022) 71 final, 23 February 2022, recital 16.

[40] Proposal for a Directive of the European Parliament and of the Council on Corporate Sustainability Due Diligence and amending Directive (EU) 2019/1937 (CSDDD), COM(2022) 71 final, 23 February 2022, recitals 22 and 44. Sector-specific guidance is available at: https://www.oecd.org/investment/due- diligence-guidance-for-responsible- business-conduct.htm (last accessed 31 May 2024).

[41] Proposal for a Directive of the European Parliament and of the Council on Corporate Sustainability Due Diligence and amending Directive (EU) 2019/1937 - General Approach, 2022/0051(COD), 30 November 2022, Recitals 36b and 40b.

[42] European Parliament resolution of 10 March 2021 with recommendations to the Commission on corporate due diligence and corporate accountability, P9_TA(2021)0073.

[43] European Parliament resolution of 10 March 2021 with recommendations to the Commission on corporate due diligence and corporate accountability, P9_TA(2021)0073, Recital 54 of the Text of the Proposal Requested, forming Annex to the Resolution.

[44] European Parliament resolution of 10 March 2021 with recommendations to the Commission on corporate due diligence and corporate accountability, P9_TA(2021)0073, Recital 59 and Article 14 of the Text of the Proposal Requested, forming Annex to the Resolution.

and countries, in line with the OECD Guidelines, was also considered by the Council, pointing to the need for a level playing field with the same standards for all, including competitors from third countries.[45]

However, only the European Parliament extended the references to the OECD framework beyond mere recitals in the EP amendments and gave these standards the most space in its text. In addition, the Parliament stressed that any information, toolboxes or guidance for businesses to be developed by the Member States to support the implementation of the CS3D should be complementary and coherent with similar existing measures, such as the information and promotion provided by the OECD National Contact Points.[46] In particular, NCPs are considered in the context of enforcing the rights of persons affected by corporate human rights abuses and environmental damage, and in coordinating the use of corporate leverage to enable remediation and access to a grievance mechanism.

Pursuant to Article 9 para. 4b of the EP Amendments, a submission of a notification or grievance to a company shall not preclude a complainant from having access to the substantiated concerns procedure to an administrative body anticipated under the CS3D or to judicial or other non-judicial mechanisms, explicitly mentioning the OECD National Contact Points. As clarified in the recitals, under the CS3D a company should provide an effective notification and non-judicial grievance mechanisms at the operational level that is publicly available and can be used by individuals and organisations to report to the company or request redress in the event of legitimate concerns about actual or potential adverse human rights and environmental impacts in the value chain.[47] Therefore, recourse to such a complaint mechanism at company level established according to the CS3D should not prevent the complainant from turning to the NCPs under the OECD Guidelines.

Similarly, the supervisory authorities, which are to be designated by each Member State to supervise compliance with the obligations set out in the national provisions transposing the CS3D, should, according to the Parliament, recognise the role of the OECD National Contact Points, as implementing bodies under other relevant international instruments.[48] The recitals of the EP Amendments explicitly state that the Member States, when designating supervisory authorities and establishing the procedures under which they operate, should ensure coordination and complementarity

---

[45] European Council, Council Conclusions on Human Rights and Decent Work in Global Supply Chains, 1 December 2020, doc. 13,512/20, paras 22 and 23.

[46] Amendments adopted by the European Parliament on 1 June 2023 on the proposal for a directive of the European Parliament and of the Council on Corporate Sustainability Due Diligence and amending Directive (EU) 2019/1937 (COM(2022)0071 – C9-0050/2022 – 2022/0051(COD)„ Article 14 (1).

[47] Amendments adopted by the European Parliament on 1 June 2023 on the proposal for a directive of the European Parliament and of the Council on Corporate Sustainability Due Diligence and amending Directive (EU) 2019/1937 (COM(2022)0071 – C9-0050/2022 – 2022/0051(COD)„ Recital 42.

[48] Amendments adopted by the European Parliament on 1 June 2023 on the proposal for a directive of the European Parliament and of the Council on Corporate Sustainability Due Diligence and amending Directive (EU) 2019/1937 (COM(2022)0071 – C9-0050/2022 – 2022/0051(COD)„ Article 17 (8b).

with the non-judicial grievance mechanism operated by the OECD National Contact Points.[49] The Commission may, in consultation with the OECD, develop guidelines for the coordination between supervisory authorities and the OECD National Contact Points.[50]

In addition, the recitals of the EP Amendments describe the National Contact Points as bodies that play an important role in promoting corporate due diligence through their role in promoting the OECD Guidelines and acting as non-judicial grievance mechanisms.[51] They could also play the role of national single helpdesks on corporate sustainability due diligence, providing guidance to companies on how best to fulfil their due diligence obligations and on sector-specific aspects, or the activities of the NCPs should be coordinated with such single helpdesks.[52]

The European Parliament also clarified that issues of corruption and bribery, which are covered by the OECD Guidelines, should be taken into account by companies when carrying out human rights and environmental due diligence under the CS3D.[53] This clarification remained in the final text of the adopted CS3D, however, without reference to the OECD Guidelines. According to the Parliament, the OECD as such and in cooperation with the Commission and other stakeholders could play a role in assessing various industry schemes and multi-stakeholder initiatives on different aspects of human rights due diligence, in order to provide guidance to companies on the alignment and credibility of such initiatives with the CD3D, "building on the OECD's alignment assessment methodology".[54] A centralised and public digital

[49] Amendments adopted by the European Parliament on 1 June 2023 on the proposal for a directive of the European Parliament and of the Council on Corporate Sustainability Due Diligence and amending Directive (EU) 2019/1937 (COM(2022)0071 – C9-0050/2022 – 2022/0051(COD),, Recital 53.

[50] Amendments adopted by the European Parliament on 1 June 2023 on the proposal for a directive of the European Parliament and of the Council on Corporate Sustainability Due Diligence and amending Directive (EU) 2019/1937 (COM(2022)0071 – C9-0050/2022 – 2022/0051(COD),, Article 17 (8b).

[51] Amendments adopted by the European Parliament on 1 June 2023 on the proposal for a directive of the European Parliament and of the Council on Corporate Sustainability Due Diligence and amending Directive (EU) 2019/1937 (COM(2022)0071 – C9-0050/2022 – 2022/0051(COD), Recital 6.

[52] Amendments adopted by the European Parliament on 1 June 2023 on the proposal for a directive of the European Parliament and of the Council on Corporate Sustainability Due Diligence and amending Directive (EU) 2019/1937 (COM(2022)0071 – C9-0050/2022 – 2022/0051(COD), Article 14a.

[53] Amendments adopted by the European Parliament on 1 June 2023 on the proposal for a directive of the European Parliament and of the Council on Corporate Sustainability Due Diligence and amending Directive (EU) 2019/1937 (COM(2022)0071 – C9-0050/2022 – 2022/0051(COD), Recital 25d.

[54] Amendments adopted by the European Parliament on 1 June 2023 on the proposal for a directive of the European Parliament and of the Council on Corporate Sustainability Due Diligence and amending Directive (EU) 2019/1937 (COM(2022)0071 – C9-0050/2022 – 2022/0051(COD), Article 13 (1), Article 14 (4) and Recitals 37 and 46.

platform would be set up to provide such independent third-party assessments of these schemes, with the OECD expected to be one of the assessors.[55]

The 2024 Preliminary Agreement, which led to the adopted CS3D, retained references to the OECD Guidelines in the recitals, but dropped all explicit references to the OECD Guidelines or the National Contact Points in the text itself. An additional reference in a new recital 36b was added, which represents a compromise between the positions of the Parliament and the Council on including only the upstream part of the value chain of regulated financial undertakings in the due diligence obligations of the CS3D, while referring to the recognition of the specificities of financial services by the OECD Guidelines. Regulated financial undertakings are expected to consider adverse impacts and to use their leverage to influence companies, including the exercise of shareholder rights.[56]

4 OECD Guidelines in the Adopted CS3D and Related Sustainability EU Legislation

The recitals of the adopted text of the CS3D continue to reference the OECD Guidelines or so-called MNE Guidelines, including the OECD Due Diligence Guidance for Responsible Business Conduct, as internationally recognised frameworks for corporate sustainability due diligence.[57] The recitals also refer more generally to relevant international frameworks, for example when describing the integration of due diligence into company's policies and risk management systems,[58] or when using the concept of the "level of involvement of the company in an adverse impact" (i.e. causing, contributing to, or being directly linked to the adverse impact).[59] In line with the Council's approach, the CS3D also references the OECD Guidelines when referring to the specificities of financial services and when prescribing due diligence

[55] Amendments adopted by the European Parliament on 1 June 2023 on the proposal for a directive of the European Parliament and of the Council on Corporate Sustainability Due Diligence and amending Directive (EU) 2019/1937 (COM(2022)0071 – C9-0050/2022 – 2022/0051(COD), Article 14 (4) (b).

[56] Second Preliminary Agreement, Recital 36b.

[57] Directive (EU) 2024/1760 of the European Parliament and of the Council of 13 June 2024 on corporate sustainability due diligence and amending Directive (EU) 2019/1937 and Regulation (EU) 2023/2859, (CS3D), Recitals 6, 14, 20 and 62.

[58] Directive (EU) 2024/1760 of the European Parliament and of the Council of 13 June 2024 on corporate sustainability due diligence and amending Directive (EU) 2019/1937 and Regulation (EU) 2023/2859, (CS3D), Recital, 39.

[59] Directive (EU) 2024/1760 of the European Parliament and of the Council of 13 June 2024 on corporate sustainability due diligence and amending Directive (EU) 2019/1937 and Regulation (EU) 2023/2859, (CS3D), Recitals 45 and 53.

obligations for regulated financial undertakings only in relation to the upstream part of their chains of activities.[60]

With regard to the OECD National Contact Points, only a few references, which were contained in the EP Amendments, have been retained in the final text of the CS3D. Recital 59 and Article 14 (7) of the CS3D state that the use of a company-level notification or complaint mechanism established according to the CS3D should not prevent the complainant from turning to other non-judicial mechanisms, which, according to the recital, include the NCPs under the OECD Guidelines. There is no explicit mention of further co-ordination activities or of the role of the NCPs as a single helpdesk for corporate sustainability due diligence, or when new tools are proposed they are not linked to the NCPs.[61] The CS3D further provides that the Commission should issue guidance to companies or to Member State authorities, drawing on relevant international guidelines and standards as reference, and, where appropriate, in consultation with international organizations and bodies with expertise in due diligence.[62] Such an international organization can be understood also the OECD, which was explicitly mentioned in the same context in the EP Amendments.

When the CS3D is compared with other EU legislation aimed at a sustainable economy, the OECD Guidelines have become more relevant in other areas. For example, the EU taxonomy for environmentally sustainable economic activities refers to procedures that companies should put in place to ensure their alignment with the OECD Guidelines, which constitute the Minimum Safeguards, as one of four mandatory criteria for an economic activity to be considered sustainable for investment purposes.[63] In other words, companies whose economic activities are to be considered Taxonomy-aligned must, among other things, align themselves with the standards of the OECD Guidelines. Although guidance on the meaning of this criterion is limited and the practice is only emerging, a company's failure to establish a human rights due diligence process is likely to be considered as such non-compliance, and have consequences for cost of capital.[64] The Platform on Sustainable Finance also considers a company's failure to collaborate with the NCP, or the NCP's

[60] Directive (EU) 2024/1760 of the European Parliament and of the Council of 13 June 2024 on corporate sustainability due diligence and amending Directive (EU) 2019/1937 and Regulation (EU) 2023/2859, (CS3D), Recital 51.

[61] Directive (EU) 2024/1760 of the European Parliament and of the Council of 13 June 2024 on corporate sustainability due diligence and amending Directive (EU) 2019/1937 and Regulation (EU) 2023/2859, (CS3D), Recital 70.

[62] Directive (EU) 2024/1760 of the European Parliament and of the Council of 13 June 2024 on corporate sustainability due diligence and amending Directive (EU) 2019/1937 and Regulation (EU) 2023/2859, (CS3D), Recital 67 and Article 19.

[63] Article 18 of Regulation (EU) 2020/852 of the European Parliament and of the Council of 18 June 2020 on the establishment of a framework to facilitate sustainable investment, and amending Regulation (EU) 2019/2088.

[64] Achtouk-Spivak and Garden (2022), p. 635.

assessment that the company is in breach of the OECD Guidelines, to be signs of non-compliance with the Minimum Safeguards.[65]

In addition, the Corporate Sustainability Reporting Directive,[66] through the harmonised European Sustainability Reporting Standards,[67] requires companies within its scope to report on their alignment with the OECD Guidelines in a number of areas. For example, on the meaningful engagement of the company with affected stakeholders, including own workforce.[68] One of the objectives of the new reporting requirements, in terms of the level of detail required, was to ensure consistency with international instruments such as the OECD Guidelines and the OECD Due Diligence Guidance for Responsible Business Conduct.[69] Accordingly, the European Sustainability Reporting Standards shall enable companies to understand the extent to which the undertaking aligns with the OECD Guidelines.[70] In addition, it is likely that companies will mention in their sustainability reports any specific instances before National Contact Points that they have been confronted with (cases explained further below).[71]

5 Interaction Between OECD and CS3D Institutional Frameworks and the OECD Jurisprudence

The relevance of the OECD Guidelines is not negligible. As some authors have pointed out, CS3D is not "European" due diligence, but due diligence based on existing international standards.[72] Companies have been implementing the concept

[65] Platform on Sustainable Finance (2022) Final Report on Minimum Safeguards, October 2022, https://finance.ec.europa.eu/system/files/2022-10/221011-sustainable-finance-platform-finance-report-minimum-safeguards_en.pdf, (last accessed 31 May 2024), p. 5.

[66] Directive (EU) 2022/2464 of the European Parliament and of the Council of 14 December 2022 amending Regulation (EU) No 537/2014, Directive 2004/109/EC, Directive 2006/43/EC and Directive 2013/34/EU, as regards corporate sustainability reporting.

[67] Commission Delegated Regulation (EU) 2023/2772 of 31 July 2023 supplementing Directive 2013/34/EU of the European Parliament and of the Council as regards sustainability reporting standards.

[68] Commission Delegated Regulation (EU) 2023/2772 of 31 July 2023 supplementing Directive 2013/34/EU of the European Parliament and of the Council as regards sustainability reporting standards, 1 (3.4.); ESRS - S1-1 (20); ESRS - S1-17 (103).

[69] Directive (EU) 2022/2464 of the European Parliament and of the Council of 14 December 2022 amending Regulation (EU) No 537/2014, Directive 2004/109/EC, Directive 2006/43/EC and Directive 2013/34/EU, as regards corporate sustainability reporting, recital 31.

[70] Commission Delegated Regulation (EU) 2023/2772 of 31 July 2023 supplementing Directive 2013/34/EU of the European Parliament and of the Council as regards sustainability reporting standards - S1-7.

[71] Achtouk-Spivak and Garden (2022), p. 632.

[72] Shift, FAQs: on the EU Corporate Sustainability Due Diligence Directive (CS3D), April 2024. Available: https://shiftproject.org/wp-content/uploads/2024/04/CS3D-FAQ-April-3.pdf (last accessed 31 May 2024).

of due diligence based on international soft norms in their practices for many years and it is important to avoid, as far as possible, creating conflicting expectations for companies as regards international standards on sustainability due diligence. The OECD has published a number of guides and explanatory notes on due diligence across sectors that are publicly available to companies, and, through their high degree of authority, have influenced the efforts of both companies and various standard-setting bodies to manage business-related human rights and environmental risks.

In addition, since 2000, the National Contact Points have been responsible for interpreting the OECD's due diligence standards, as the specific bodies that the signatory governments of the OECD Declaration have agreed to establish. The NCPs are responsible for promoting awareness of the OECD Guidelines and helping to address issues arising from their implementation. Within the latter mandate, the NCPs provide a mediation and conciliation platform for helping to resolve complaints, referred to as specific instances. It is reported that the NCPs have collectively dealt with over 650 cases to date, covering a wide range of business impacts.[73] The NCPs operate according to certain core effectiveness criteria set out in the OECD Guidelines, but their form, structure, staffing, resources, and activities vary considerably from country to country. Some academic work shows that the successful outcome of the cases handled and the NCP's potential to provide an effective remedy depend very much on these conditions set for the individual NCP,[74] including its institutional classification within the public administration of the country concerned and its financial support.[75]

The purpose of this section is not to analyse the synchronisation between the CS3D and the OECD Guidelines in terms of the degree of alignment of the final text of the CS3D with the OECD Guidelines, but to consider how the activities of the NCPs can be coordinated with the implementing bodies of the CS3D and how the practice developed under the OECD Guidelines, on which the provisions of the CS3D are based, can support or detract from the application of the CS3D.

5.1 OECD Jurisprudence

First, the lessons learnt from the NCPs over the past decade can offer valuable insights on human rights and environmental due diligence. Based on an exemplary analysis of several final statements and recommendations issued by the NCPs, Buhmann observes that the NCP cases provide valuable sources of norms for human rights due diligence and detailed guidance on what risk-based due diligence entails.[76] The final statements are not enforceable judgments but the "jurisprudence" developed by the

---

[73] OECD, Database of specific instances. See https://mneguidelines.oecd.org/database/ (last accessed 31 May 2024).

[74] Bhatt and Türkelli (2021), p. 440.

[75] Černic (2008), p. 93–94.

[76] Buhmann (2018), p. 390.

NCPs in applying and interpreting the OECD Guidelines, with frequent references to the UNGPs, has created certain expectations and understanding of responsible business conduct on the part of companies. Building on the experience of NCPs in human rights and environmental due diligence can contribute to coherence, predictability and legal certainty for companies, as well as for victims and other stakeholders.

According to the OECD, since 2011, NCPs have addressed due diligence expectations to some extent in more than half of the cases and have addressed recommendations on how companies should conduct due diligence effectively and credibly.[77] The database of specific instances, which is publicly available on the OECD website, documents the interpretation of various aspects of corporate due diligence under the OECD Guidelines by different NCPs in the so called final statements.[78] There is no uniform format for these statements, some are more detailed than others and some contain detailed forward-looking recommendations.

For example, NCP case law has already addressed interpretations of the core definitions and conceptual issues related to corporate due diligence responsibilities, such as the concept of prioritization based on severity of adverse impacts, the use of leverage (i.e. the ability of a company to influence the behaviour of an entity causing harm), meaningful engagement with affected stakeholders in due diligence, addressing the climate change dimension of due diligence, or using industry or multi-stakeholder schemes.[79] These issues that have arisen in the application of due diligence can be built upon.

In the context of the CS3D, the sub-concepts or elements of due diligence required by the CS3D, which are accompanied by the phrase „in line with the international frameworks " in the CS3D recitals or which are considered to be substantially aligned with the risk-based approach of the OECD Guidelines, can draw in particular on relevant OECD case law. These include, for example, the concepts of prioritisation in addressing impact, leverage, integration of due diligence into company's policy, involvement with negative impacts, or meaningful stakeholder engagement.[80] Similar

---

[77] OECD (2024), *Implications for OECD National Contact Points: Background note on Regulatory Developments concerning Due Diligence for Responsible Business Conduct*, https://mneguidelines.oecd.org/implications-for-oecd-national-contact-points.pdf, p. 7.

[78] See https://mneguidelines.oecd.org/database/ (last accessed 31 May 2024). Other organisations also collect NCPs' cases and maintain unofficial databases, focusing on specific issues, such as labour (TUAC database accessible by subscription at: https://mneguidelines.tuac.org) or on complaints submitted by civil society organisations (OECD Watch database accessible at: https://www.oecdwatch.org/complaints-database/?fwp_search_complaints=climate%20change) (last accessed 5 July 2024).

[79] For example, Buhmann provides examples of NCP's final statements and references to OECD case law that are instructive in terms of general guidance on due diligence, directly linked business relationships, leverage and use of influence, meaningful stakeholder conclutation and effective stakeholder egagement, and assessment of impacts and integrating and acting upon findings. See Buhmann (2018), pp. 390–410, and the NCP cases cited therein.

[80] See recitals 39, 45, 53 and 79 of the Directive (EU) 2024/1760 of the European Parliament and of the Council of 13 June 2024 on corporate sustainability due diligence and amending Directive (EU) 2019/1937 and Regulation (EU) 2023/2859, (CS3D). For the alignment of the CS3D with the OECD Guidelines see e.g. OECD Watch (2023), *Achieving Alignment: Syncing EU due diligence legislation*

to the OECD Guidelines, the CS3D requires that due diligence be informed by meaningful engagement with stakeholders. A number of NCPs have already provided guidance on this point, and some of these statements have been analysed in academic papers.[81] For example, in the case of *Framtiden i våre hender vs Intex Resources*, the Norwegian NCP considered that a mining company operating in the Philippines, while complying with the requirements of national law, had failed to observe the OECD Guidelines by, among other things, failing to engage adequately with stakeholders and failing to consult broadly enough and obtain the consent of all affected communities (indigenous peoples affected by the project and associated infrastructure).[82] Finding appropriate ways to re-engage with affected communities or potentially affected communities, increasing the information available to them and taking their view into account is a crucial element of stakeholder engagement, as the UK NCP highlighted in the case of *IAC & WDM versus GCM Resources plc*, which involved the displacement of local people and environmental degradation that would have occurred if a coal mine project had gone ahead in Bangladesh.[83]

The jurisprudence of the NCPs is also significant beyond the OECD, as can be seen from an analysis of certain cases dealt with by the NCPs in the leading climate change database managed by the Sabin Centre for Climate Change Law.[84] In particular, cases addressing the responsibility of companies for the environmental and climate impacts of their operations are attracting the attention of climate law experts.[85] The evolution in the interpretation of the content of corporate due diligence obligations in relation to climate change under the OECD Guidelines, which occurred in the case dealt with by the Dutch NCP, was highlighted in a supporting study commissioned by the European Commission prior to the start of its work on the CS3D.[86] In a specific instance against a financial institution and its climate policy, the NCP has progressively interpreted

---

with the updated OECD Guidelines, June 2023, https://www.oecdwatch.org/achieving-alignment-synching-eu-due-diligence-legislation-with-the-updated-oecd-guidelines/ (last accessed 31 May 2024); Shift, FAQs: on the EU Corporate Sustainability Due Diligence Directive (CS3D), April 2024. Available: https://shiftproject.org/wp-content/uploads/2024/04/CS3D-FAQ-April-3.pdf, (last accessed 31 May 2024).

[81] See e.g. Buhmann (2018); Bhatt and Türkelli (2021); Achtouk-Spivak and Garden (2022).

[82] NCP Norway, *Framtiden i våre hender vs Intex Resources (Nikel project in the Philippines)*, Final Statement, 28 November 2011, https://web-archive.oecd.org/2014-01-27/206620-Norwegian%20NCP%20intex_final.pdf (last accessed 5 July 2024), p. 6–7.

[83] NCP UK,, *IAC & WDM versus GCM Resources plc (Displacement of local populations and environmental degradation in Bangladesh)*, Final Statement,, 20 November 2014, https://www.gov.uk/government/publications/iap-and-wdm-complaint-to-uk-ncp-about-gcm-resources-plc (last accessed 5 July 2024), para 81.

[84] See https://climatecasechart.com/non-us-case-category/disclosures/ (last accessed 31 May 2024).

[85] See e.g. Aristova et al. (2024); Macchi (2022); Rajavuori et al. (2023); Setzer J and Higham C (2023) Global Trends in Climate Change Litigation: 2023 Snapshot https://www.lse.ac.uk/granthaminstitute/wp-content/uploads/2023/06/Global_trends_in_climate._change_litigation_2023_snapshot.pdf, (last accessed 31 May 2024), p. 8.

[86] Smit et al. (2020) Study on due diligence requirements through the supply chain, https://op.europa.eu/en/publication-detail/-/publication/8ba0a8fd-4c83-11ea-b8b7-01aa75ed71a1/language-en (last accessed 31 May 2024), pp. 163–164.

the OECD Guidelines and clarified how companies' individual due diligence can include climate change objectives and align their indirect emissions with the goals of the Paris Agreement on climate change.[87]

As the case of *Dutch NGOs v ING Bank* was one of the first climate-related "finance emissions" complaints, challenging a financial institution's financial flows to investments and activities that are not aligned with the Paris Agreement's goals, and as such cases are expected to increase in the coming years,[88] the case deserves a brief description. In their complaint, filed in 2017, several Dutch NGOs alleged that ING, as a global financial institution, had failed to observe the OECD Guidelines by not setting targets to reduce GHG emissions. They called on ING to determine and publish its total carbon footprint, including its indirect GHG emissions from the activities and products it finances worldwide, and for the bank to set its own measurable targets to align its indirect emissions with the goals of the Paris Agreement.[89] ING argued that in 2017, there was no reliable data and method to link bank clients' emissions to the Paris Agreement's temperature target, and no international standard for measuring the carbon emissions of a bank's loan portfolios.[90]

In its final statement, the Dutch NCP, recognising the complexity of the issue, encouraged action on climate change, and suggested ways in which corporate due diligence could include climate change objectives. The NCP noted: "[t]he OECD Guidelines demand that ING, and other commercial banks, put effort into defining, where appropriate, concrete targets to manage its impact towards alignment with relevant national policies and international environmental commitments. Regarding climate change, the Paris Agreement is currently the most relevant international agreement between states, a landmark for climate chang[e]."[91] As a result of the NCP procedure, the parties reached an agreement in which ING committed to align its lending portfolio with the Paris Agreement's temperature goal of well-below 2 ºC and to set and publish interim targets.[92]

---

[87] NCP Netherlands, *Oxfam Novib, Greenpeace Netherlands, BankTrack and Friends of the Earth Netherlands (Milieudefensie) versus ING,* Final Statement, 19 April 2019, https://mneguidelines.oecd.org//database/instances/nl0029.htm (last accessed 5 July 2024).

[88] Setzer J and Higham C (2024) Global Trends in Climate Change Litigation: 2024 Snapshot, https://www.lse.ac.uk/granthaminstitute/wp-content/uploads/2024/06/Global-trends-in-climate-change-litigation-2024-snapshot.pdf (last accessed 5 July 2024), p. 39.

[89] NCP Netherlands, *Oxfam Novib, Greenpeace Netherlands, BankTrack and Friends of the Earth Netherlands (Milieudefensie) versus ING,* Final Statement, 19 April 2019, https://mneguidelines.oecd.org//database/instances/nl0029.htm (last accessed 5 July 2024), Sect. 3.

[90] NCP Netherlands, *Oxfam Novib, Greenpeace Netherlands, BankTrack and Friends of the Earth Netherlands (Milieudefensie) versus ING,* Final Statement, 19 April 2019, https://mneguidelines.oecd.org//database/instances/nl0029.htm (last accessed 5 July 2024), Sect. 3.

[91] NCP Netherlands, *Oxfam Novib, Greenpeace Netherlands, BankTrack and Friends of the Earth Netherlands (Milieudefensie) versus ING,* Final Statement, 19 April 2019, https://mneguidelines.oecd.org//database/instances/nl0029.htm (last accessed 5 July 2024), Sect. 5.4.

[92] NCP Netherlands, *Oxfam Novib, Greenpeace Netherlands, BankTrack and Friends of the Earth Netherlands (Milieudefensie) versus ING,* Final Statement, 19 April 2019, https://mneguidelines.oecd.org//database/instances/nl0029.htm (last accessed 5 July 2024), Sect. 5.4.

The *Dutch NGOs v. ING Bank* case is considered to be the first NCP climate change due diligence case,[93] primarily focusing on the setting and disclosure of emission reduction targets. Although other climate-related complaints have followed, some with contrary findings,[94] Aristova et al. note that the complaints have so far been limited in linking human rights and climate change,[95] and in asserting the climate dimension of human rights due diligence, which is strongly supported by academic work,[96] UN documents[97] and litigation.[98] Following the 2023 update of the OECD Guidelines, which reflects the increased expectations for corporate climate due diligence and whose commentary explicitly refers to the achievement of the Paris Agreement objectives by enterprises,[99] it can be exptected that cases involving climate impact of corporate activites on human rights will increase. A recent example is a specific instance in the case of the *VU Climate Change and Sustainability Law Clinic* et al. *versus One-Dyas*, filed with the Dutch NPC in 2024, in which several NGOs and associations of academics and scientists concerned with climate justice allege, *inter alia*, that the life-cycle GHG emissions caused by a project to extract fossil gas from fields in the North Sea will harm human rights and the environment and will undermine the objectives of international and European climate policy. Consequently, the petitioners seek a comprehensive assessment of the human rights impacts of the project (including the harm caused by the project's scope 3 emissions) and, on the basis of that assessment, the termination of the project.[100]

---

[93] Smit et al. (2020) Study on due diligence requirements through the supply chain, https://op.europa.eu/en/publication-detail/-/publication/8ba0a8fd-4c83-11ea-b8b7-01aa75ed71a1/language-en (last accessed 31 May 2024), p. 164.

[94] For example, in the case of *Australian Bushfire Victims and Friends of the Earth Australia v. ANZ Bank*, the Australian NCP considered a complaint brought against the Australia and New Zealand Banking Group in 2020 by an NGO and individuals affected by climate-related bushfires in Australia, alleging a lack of disclosure and that the bank's investments in fossil fuels industry fell short of the Paris Agreement targets. The NCP concluded that the bank met its obligations under the OECD Guidelines because the Guidelines were ambiguous in terms of what was expected in relation climate change, in particular the disclosure of Scope 3 emissions from the bank's corporate value chain, and recommended that this be clarified in the next revision of the Guidelines. See NCP Australia, *Australian Bushfire Victims and Friends of the Earth Australia versus ANZ Bank*, Final Statement, 15 December 2021, https://ausncp.gov.au/sites/default/files/2021-12/AusNCP_Final_Statement_Friends_of_Earth_0.pdf (last accessed 5 July 2024).

[95] Aristova et al. (2024), p. 515.

[96] See e.g. Macchi (2022).

[97] Working Group on the issue of human rights and transnational corporations and other business enterprises, *Information Note on Climate Change and the Guiding Principles on Business and Human Rights* (June 2023).

[98] See e.g. *Milieudefensie* et al. *v. Royal Dutch Shell*, The Hauge District Court C/09/571932 / HA ZA 19–379 26, Judgment May 2021; Republic of the Philippines Commission on Human Rights, *National Inquiry on Climate Change Report*, 2022.

[99] Paragraphs 76–79 of Chapter VI of the OECD Guidelines (2023 version).

[100] NCP Netherlands,, Complaint, *VU Climate Change and Sustainability Law Clinic* et al. *versus One-Dyas*, 23 January 2024, https://www.oecdwatch.org/complaint/vu-climate-change-and-sustainability-law-clinic-et-al-vs-one-dyas/ (last accessed 5 July 2024).

These developments in OECD jurisprudence are highly relevant to the application and possible future development of the CS3D. Both the Commission Proposal and the Council Approach explicitly excluded climate change from the scope of the company's due diligence obligations,[101] while the EP Amendments included climate change as a covered "adverse environmental impact". The final CS3D omits any explicit mention of climate change in the context of due diligence and appears to focus solely on the company's obligation to mitigate climate change through a climate transition plan to be developed by certain companies. However, adverse impacts on human rights and environment can also arise out of climate mitigation activities and it remains to be seen how the mandatory human rights and environmental due diligence will be operationalised.[102] The Commission is required to report regularly to the European Parliament and the Council on the implementation of the CS3D and its effectiveness in achieving its objectives, inlcuding whether the rules on climate change need to be revised.[103] Parallel developments in NCP's case law on climate-related human rights abuses and corporate climate due diligence can be an important source for such reflection and future amendments or clarifications of the CS3D.

5.2 *Institutional Mandates*

Secondly, the bodies established under the CS3D may have an impact on the activities of the NCPs, whose role was most recognised by the Parliament in the EP Amendments, which explicitly took into account the relationship between the CS3D's supervisory authorities and the NCPs, as described in the text above. NPCs' activities in informing and training companies on sustainability due diligence, and supervising companies' compliance can overlap with the roles of the CS3D supervisory authorities given that the CS3D reflects core principles and concepts of the OECD Guidelines. The final text of the CS3D does not explicitly mention the NCPs save for recital 59, which, however, does not concern their role. The interactions between the NCPs and the CS3D's authorities associated with due diligence can take different qualitative forms, which is essentially reflected in the Parliament's Amendments and

[101] Article 29 (d) of the Proposal for a Directive of the European Parliament and of the Council on Corporate Sustainability Due Diligence and amending Directive (EU) 2019/1937 (CSDDD), COM(2022) 71 final, 23 February 2022 and of the Proposal for a Directive of the European Parliament and of the Council on Corporate Sustainability Due Diligence and amending Directive (EU) 2019/1937 - General Approach, 2022/0051(COD), 30 November 2022.

[102] Feigerlová M (2024), p. 25–26.

[103] Directive (EU) 2024/1760 of the European Parliament and of the Council of 13 June 2024 on corporate sustainability due diligence and amending Directive (EU) 2019/1937 and Regulation (EU) 2023/2859,

(CS3D), recital 98, Article 36 (2) (e).

the recently issued OECD note.[104] It is derived from the various activities that both the CS3D supervisory authorities and the NCPs perform.

The first function, which can be described as informational and promotional, can be seen in relation to both the NCPs and the bodies involved in due diligence under the CS3D. The latter foresees the establishment by the Commission of a single helpdesk through which companies will be able to seek information, guidance, and assistance in fulfilling their obligations under the CS3D. The relevant national authorities in each Member State will be required to collaborate with the single helpdesk to assist in the dissemination of information and guidance.[105] According to the EP Amendments, the NCPs could directly perform the role of national single helpdesks on corporate sustainability due diligence, providing guidance to companies on how best to fulfil their due diligence obligations and on sector-specific aspects, or the activities of the NCPs should be coordinated with such single helpdesks.[106] The potential overlap between information and promotion activities under the CS3D and the OECD Guidelines is obvious, and using or coordinating with NCPs for this purpose could not only lead to cost savings and benefit from the NCP's previous experience in training, but also support coherence between the sustainability due diligence standards in each instrument. Similarly, the Parliament considered it relevant for the OECD and the NCPs to work with the Commission to develop practical general and sector-specific guidelines or guidelines on specific adverse impacts to assist businesses. The CS3D anticipates such cooperation in general terms, but without explicitly mentioning the OECD in Article 19.

The second function relates to the grievance resolution. The compliance, monitoring, and enforcement role of supervisory authorities under the CS3D differs significantly from the non-judicial, voluntary, specific instance procedures under the OECD Guidelines, the primary objective of which is to encourage companies to implement the OECD Guidelines. While the CS3D supervisory authorities will have investigative and sanctioning powers, the NCPs provide a forum for discussion where parties can choose to participate or not. Although the procedures are diametrically different, recourse to the CS3D does not preclude recourse to the NCPs as set out in Article 14 (7) of the CS3D in light of recital 59. Given that the scope of the voluntary OECD Guidelines is broader than that of the legally binding CS3D, and that their dialogue-based procedure is easily accessible (with no fees and no time limits for submissions)

---

[104] OECD (2024), *Implications for OECD National Contact Points: Background note on Regulatory Developments concerning Due Diligence for Responsible Business Conduct*, https://mneguidelines.oecd.org/implications-for-oecd-national-contact-points.pdf.

[105] Directive (EU) 2024/1760 of the European Parliament and of the Council of 13 June 2024 on corporate sustainability due diligence and amending Directive (EU) 2019/1937 and Regulation (EU) 2023/2859,

(CS3D), Article 21.

[106] Amendments adopted by the European Parliament on 1 June 2023 on the proposal for a directive of the European Parliament and of the Council on Corporate Sustainability Due Diligence and amending Directive (EU) 2019/1937 (COM(2022)0071 – C9-0050/2022 – 2022/0051(COD),, Article 14a.

it is likely that an alleged non-compliance with the CS3D will also qualify as a non-observance of the OECD Guidelines and could give rise to parallel proceedings. In other words, authorities may be confronted with the same complaint under both instruments and deal with it according to their own procedural rules. This is, however, not a new situation for the NCPs, where in the past specific instances have arisen in parallel with court proceedings on similar or related matters, and which is provided for in the OECD implementation procedures.[107] Some commentators predict that the NCP's findings in the context of a specific instance, particularly in relation to the due diligence recommendations under the OECD Guidelines, could be taken into account for the purposes of compliance with the CS3D, which in turn could lead to administrative fines or civil liability.[108]

As noted above, the interpretations of the OECD Guidelines that have emerged over the past decade may be relevant to supervisory authorities under the CS3D in assessing whether a company has complied with its due diligence obligations. However, the parallel proceedings may also raise questions about how to manage their positive and negative interactions (e.g., conflicting conclusions as the OECD Guidelines aim to encourage best practices by businesses, transfer of file information from the NCP to the CS3D supervisory authority and associated confidentiality barriers). To this end, the EP amendments provided in proposed Article 17 (8b) that the Commission, in consultation with the OECD, may develop guidelines for coordination between supervisory authorities and the NCPs.

As the final text of the CS3D does not provide for specific rules for the NCPs under the CS3D, the OECD itself, in its note of 2024, considers three possible models for how the NCPs can contribute to the mandate of national authorities under the emerging mandatory due diligence laws. Namely, from the OECD perspective the potential interactions can take the form of a partial integration, a co-operation and a co-existence.[109] The first model of integration, in which the NCPs are entrusted with the tasks set out in the mandatory due diligence laws or are integrated into the structure of the implementing authorities, would make use of the NCPs' experience in corporate due diligence, but would also require a strict separation between the enforcement and non-judicial dispute resolution functions. A more likely model of cooperation, as envisaged in the EP Amendments, may include various elements of exchange of information and experience, such as sharing the results of specific instances, or capacity building in terms of training or compliance monitoring. Close cooperation between NCPs and CS3D supervisory authorities can contribute to a more consistent approach to corporate sustainability due diligence and minimise the potential for misinterpretation of international due diligence standards.

---

[107] OECD (2023) *Commentaries on the Implementation Procedures*, C/MIN(2023)13/ADD2, 30 May 2023, para 35.

[108] Achtouk-Spivak and Garden (2022), p. 635.

[109] OECD (2024), *Implications for OECD National Contact Points: Background note on Regulatory Developments concerning Due Diligence for Responsible Business Conduct,* https://mneguidelines.oecd.org/implications-for-oecd-national-contact-points.pdf, p. 15–16.

The final text of the CS3D more or less corresponds to the last model of coexistence, which does not recognise a specific role for the NCPs and which is also the approach that generally prevails in today's mandatory due diligence legislation.[110] According to the OECD, such a model risks undermining the dispute resolution role of the NCPs, confusing potential users, and ultimately reducing the relevance of the NCPs.[111] In addition, companies may be reluctant to participate in the voluntary special instances because of the unclear implications of these procedures for the CS3D proceedings, which will result in legally binding decisions and sanctions.

6 Conclusion

The CS3D, which is the EU framework for mandatory corporate sustainability due diligence, refers in its recitals to the OECD Guidelines as the global standard for human rights and environmental due diligence and is intended to be based on the provisions of the OECD Guidelines. A perusal of the *travaux préparatoires* of the CS3D reveals that the European Parliament's documents contained the most detailed reflections on the OECD Guidelines and the OECD National Contact Points, which were largely omitted from the Commission's original proposal and the adopted CS3D.

Only the European Parliament extended the references to the OECD framework beyond mere recitals and gave these standards and the NCPs the greatest relevance in its proposed text, voted on 1 June 2023. The Parliament advocated complementarity and coherence between measures to support the implementation of the CS3D and similar existing measures provided by the NCPs. For example, the supervisory authorities designated by each Member State under the CS3D to monitor compliance with national provisions transposing the CS3D would recognise the role of the NCPs, or the European Commission would develop guidelines for such coordination in consultation with the OECD. The NCPs could even take on the role of the single national helpdesks foreseen in the CS3D to advise companies on how best to fulfil their due diligence obligations. The OECD as such could also assist in assessing various industry schemes and multi-stakeholder initiatives on different aspects of human rights due diligence in order to provide guidance to companies on the alignment and credibility of such initiatives with the CD3D.

The adopted text reflects very little from the above. The final CS3D is much sparse in referring explicitly to the OECD Guidelines and the NCPs, and any explicit references are contained only in the recitals. The use of a company-level notification or complaint mechanism established under the CS3D will not prevent the

[110] OECD (2024), *Implications for OECD National Contact Points: Background note on Regulatory Developments concerning Due Diligence for Responsible Business Conduct*, https://mneguidelines.oecd.org/implications-for-oecd-national-contact-points.pdf, p. 16.

[111] OECD (2024), *Implications for OECD National Contact Points: Background note on Regulatory Developments concerning Due Diligence for Responsible Business Conduct*, https://mneguidelines.oecd.org/implications-for-oecd-national-contact-points.pdf, p. 12.

complainant from turning to the NCP as other non-judicial mechanism. On the spectrum of possible modes of interaction between the CS3D national authorities and the NCPs as outlined by the OECD, i.e. from integration, cooperation, to coexistence, the CS3D represents the last option. The European Commission can issue guidance to companies or Member State authorities on due diligence process, which may be developed in consultation, "where appropriate", with international organisations with expertise in due diligence. The OECD is likely to be one such potential body to be approached.

Given that the OECD Guidelines have to a certain extent shaped the due diligence practices of EU enterprises over the years, and that almost all EU Member States have committed themselves to enhancing the application of and compliance with the OECD Guidelines, the policy harmony would undoubtedly contribute to the effective implementation of human rights and environmental due diligence by companies in the EU. The elements of due diligence required by the CS3D that are accompanied by the phrase "in line with the international frameworks" in the CS3D recitals or that are considered to be substantially aligned with the risk-based approach of the OECD Guidelines, such as the concepts of prioritisation in addressing impacts, involvement with negative impacts, leverage, integration of due diligence into company's policy or meaningful stakeholder engagement, can draw in particular on relevant OECD case law. Some commentators predict that the NCP's findings in the context of a specific instance, particularly in relation to the due diligence recommendations under the OECD Guidelines, could be taken into account for the purposes of compliance with the CS3D. Following the update of the Guidelines in 2023, in particular developments in OECD jurisprudence on climate-related human rights abuses and corporate climate due diligence may be an important source of reflection on the practice, interpretation and possible future changes to the CS3D.

Despite a critical assessment of the NCPs in terms of their potential to provide an effective remedy to victims, the 2023 update of the OECD Guidelines supports the continued existence of the NCPs and focuses on strengthening their procedures to ensure the visibility, effectiveness and functional equivalence of the NCPs. Against this background, the limited engagement of the CS3D with the NCPs is a missed opportunity to define a functional relationship between the CS3D national authorities and the NCPs and to support coherence, predictability and legal certainty in the interpretation and use of sustainability due diligence processes by companies. It is up to each Member State to decide which CS3D supervisory authority it will designate to meet the CS3D requirements and how it will seek potential synergies with the NCPs, drawing on their expertise in the practical application of corporate human rights and environmental due diligence, as well as examples of good practice developed in sectors or in relation to specific challenges, their training and their advisory role.

References

Achtouk-Spivak L, Garden R (2022) OECD national contact point specific instances: when 'soft law' bites? J Int Dispute Settl 13(4):608–642

Aristova E, Higham C, Higham I, Setzer J (2024) Conceptualising corporate climate change responsibilities under the OECD Guidelines for Multinational Enterprises on responsible business conduct. Intern Comp Law Quart 73(2):505–525

Bhatt K, Türkelli GE (2021) OECD national contact points as sites of effective remedy: new expressions of the role and rule of law within market globalization? Bus Human Rights J 6(3):423–448

Bueno N, Bernaz N, Holly G, Martin-Ortega O (2024) The EU directive on corporate custainability due ddligence (CSDDD): the final political compromise. Bus Human Rights J :1–7

Bueno N, Bright C (2020) Implementing human rights due diligence through corporate civil liability. Intern Comp Law Quart 69(4):89–818

Buhmann K (2018) Analysing OECD national contact point statements for guidance on human rights due diligence: method, findings and outlook. Nordic J Human Rights 36(4):390–410

Černic JL (2008) Corporate responsibility human rights: a critical analysis of the OECD guidelines for multinational enterprises. Hanse Law Rev 4(1):71–100

Deva S (2023) Mandatory human rights due diligence laws in Europe: a mirage for rightsholders? Leiden J Intern Law 36(2):389–414

Feigerlová M (2024) Moving from pledges to commitments: analysing climate transition plans in the EU proposal for a corporate sustainability due diligence directive. Carbon Climate Law Rev 18(1):17–30

Hogan BF, Reyes J (2023) Downstream human rights due diligence: informing debate through insights from business practice. Bus Human Rights J 8:434–440

Ingrams MG (2023) The 2023 update of the OECD Guidelines sets stronger standards for companies but weak expectations for governments–high and lowlights from the new text. Bus Human Rights J 8(3):427–433

Joseph S, Kyriakakis J (2023) From soft law to hard law in business and human rights and the challenge of corporate power. Leiden J Intern Law 36(2):335–361

Krajewski M (2023) Mandatory human rights due diligence laws: blurring the lines between state duty to protect and corporate responsibility to respect? Nordic J Human Rights 41(3):1–14

Macchi C (2021) The climate change dimension of business and human rights: the gradual consolidation of a concept of 'climate due diligence.' Bus Human Rights J 6(1):93–119

Perillo PS (2022) The role of the OECD guidelines for multinational enterprises and the national contact points in shaping the future of corporate accountability. Intern Comm Law Rev 24(1–2):36–56

Rajavuori M, Savaresi A, van Asselt H (2023) Mandatory due diligence laws and climate change litigation: Bridging the corporate climate accountability gap? Regul Govern 17(4):944–953

Villiers C (2022) New directions in the European union's regulatory framework for corporate reporting, due diligence and accountability: the challenge of complexity. European J Risk Regul 13(4):548–566

NCP cases

Norway National Contact Point for the OECD Guidelines, Final Statement, Framtiden i våre hender vs Intex Resources (Nikel project in the Philippines), 28 November 2011, https://web-archive.oecd.org/2014-01-27/206620-Norwegian%20NCP%20intex_final.pdf (last accessed 5 July 2024)

UK National Contact Point for the OECD Guidelines, Final Statement, IAC & WDM versus GCM Resources plc (Displacement of local populations and environmental degradation in Bangladesh), 20 November 2014, https://www.gov.uk/government/publications/iap-and-wdm-complaint-to-uk-ncp-about-gcm-resources-plc (last accessed 5 July 2024)
Netherlands National Contact Point for the OECD Guidelines, Final Statement, Oxfam Novib, Greenpeace Netherlands, BankTrack and Friends of the Earth Netherlands (Milieudefensie) versus ING, 19 April 2019, https://mneguidelines.oecd.org//database/instances/nl0029.htm (last accessed 5 July 2024)
Australian National Contact Point for the OECD Guidelines, Final Statement, Australian Bushfire Victims and Friends of the Earth Australia versus ANZ Bank, 15 December 2021, https://ausncp.gov.au/sites/default/files/2021-12/AusNCP_Final_Statement_Friends_of_Earth_0.pdf (last accessed 5 July 2024)
Netherlands National Contact Point for the OECD Guidelines, Complaint, VU Climate Change and Sustainability Law Clinic et al. versus One-Dyas, 23 January 2024, https://www.oecdwatch.org/complaint/vu-climate-change-and-sustainability-law-clinic-et-al-vs-one-dyas/ (last accessed 5 July 2024)

The manufacturer's authorised representative in the EU is Springer Nature Customer Service Centre GmbH, Europaplatz 3, 69115 Heidelberg, Germany. If you have any concerns regarding our products, please contact ProductSafety@springernature.com

Printed and bound by CPI Group (UK) Ltd, Croydon, CR0 4YY
30/09/2026
02225592-0006